UNDERSTANDING
THE BORDERLINE
MOTHER

UNDERSTANDING THE BORDERLINE MOTHER

Helping Her Children Transcend
the Intense, Unpredictable, and
Volatile Relationship

Christine Ann Lawson, Ph.D.

JASON ARONSON INC.
Northvale, New Jersey
London

First softcover printing 2002

This book was set in 12 pt. Bembo by Alabama Book Composition of Deatsville, AL.

Copyright © 2000, 2002 by Jason Aronson Inc.

10 9 8 7 6 5 4

The author gratefully acknowledges permission to reprint material from *Grimm's Tales for Young and Old* by Jakob & Wilhelm Grimm, translated by Ralph Manheim, copyright © 1977 by Ralph Manheim. Used by permission of Doubleday, a division of Random House, Inc., and the Orion Publishing Group Ltd, Victor Gollancz publisher.

Library of Congress Cataloging-in-Publication Data

Lawson, Christine Ann.
    Understanding the borderline mother / helping her children transcend the intense, unpredictable, and volatile relationship / Christine Ann Lawson.
        p.   cm.
    Includes bibliographical references and index.
    ISBN 0–7657–0288–6 (hardcover)
    ISBN 0–7657–0331–9 (softcover)
    1. Borderline personality disorder.. 2. Mothers— Mental health. 3. Maternal rejection.
    I. Title.

    RC569.5.B67 L39 2000   00–038966
    616.85'852'00852—dc21

Printed in the United States of America on acid-free paper. For information and catalog write to Jason Aronson Inc., 230 Livingston Street, Northvale, NJ 07647-1726, or visit our website: http://www.aronson.com

To the children of borderlines
and their mothers

Contents

Acknowledgments

I could not have written this book without the assistance and support of many people. John B. Scofield, M.D., is primarily responsible for inspiring me to write a book on this subject and has been an ardent advisor each step of the way. Words cannot convey my gratitude for the knowledge I have gained from Dr. Scofield.

I am deeply grateful for the expertise and patience of Candace Tremps, who spent countless hours revising the manuscript for greater clarity. Tom Mullen's unfailing optimism and guidance led me through the initial stages of organizing my ideas. His later assistance in discarding clinical jargon helped the book become readable for those who need it most—borderline mothers and their children.

My good friends, psychotherapist Deborah Bowes and Dr. Holly Cloonan, read early drafts and enthusiastically cheered me to the finish line. Colleagues such as Veronica Needler, Amy Armstrong, and Drs. Dorothy Wittenberg and Beth Dixon convinced me that such a book would be useful to clinicians as well as to patients.

The patients who granted permission to use excerpts from their treatment, their journals, and their lives are giving you, the reader, the deepest part of themselves. Their identities have been carefully concealed. Composites of patients were developed and pseudonyms were used in order to prevent recognition. I hope this book is a tribute to these remarkable people who have earned my deepest respect.

It is important to acknowledge the contribution of educators and leaders in the field of clinical social work. The general public is often surprised to learn that a growing number of clinical social workers are rigorously trained psychoanalysts. Had I not met Dr. Jason Aronson at a workshop on professional writing at the 7th Annual Conference of the National Membership Committee on Psychoanalysis in Clinical Social Work, this book might have been only a dream. The enthusiastic interest expressed by Dr. Aronson took me by surprise, and I am tremendously grateful for his belief in the importance of the subject.

Judith Cohen, the production editor, and Sigrid Asmus, a meticulous copy editor, deserve acknowledgment for their thorough review of the manuscript and for patiently responding to my many concerns.

Finally, I want to thank my husband and children, who understood my preoccupation with this subject matter and gave me the time, the space, and the computer when I needed to write. Their love sustains me, as I hope mine does for them.

Preface

The first thing we must understand in life is our mother. Recognizing her face, the sound of her voice, the meaning of her facial expressions, and the meaning of her moods is so universal, so natural and normal, and so crucial to survival that we scarcely give it a thought. In fact, we forget how much we know about her despite having powerful reactions to a certain gesture, a tone of voice, or a facial expression in someone else . . . that person, of course, often being our spouse. Understanding our mother is the first step to understanding ourselves.

This book is about mothers who suffer from Borderline Personality Disorder (BPD). BPD is defined as "a pervasive pattern of instability of interpersonal relationships, self-image, and affects, and marked impulsivity" (APA 1994, p. 650). The term *borderline* means that their emotional state can border between psychosis and neurosis, particularly when faced with abandonment or rejection. Thus, children with borderline mothers grow up in a contradictory and confusing emotional world.

This book is also about children with borderline mothers. Developmental psychologists now know that before the age of 3, children are incapable of understanding deception because they are unable to discern the difference between what they believe and what their mother believes. They also do not understand incongruence, that mother might feel one emotion while expressing another or that hostility can be masked by a smile. And yet their survival depends on the ability to understand this individual who controls their universe.

Adult children of borderline mothers enter therapy in order to understand themselves. They feel fragmented, depressed, and confused because understanding their mothers seems impossible. They bring the therapist parts of a complex puzzle, twisting and turning pieces of themselves and their mothers to see what fits, unable to connect or separate parts that once formed a whole. Without intervention the intense, unpredictable, and volatile relationship between the borderline mother and her child can have devastating consequences. Children of borderlines are not only at risk for developing BPD, but in some cases, the lives of both mother and child can be endangered.

The stories from children raised by mothers with borderline personality disorder should awaken the consciousness of all. During therapy, some young children depicted their view of their mothers in drawings; adult children shared journals, photographs, and tape recordings. Regardless of their age, these children longed to be heard and to be believed. They longed for freedom, for validation, and for escape from the emotional labyrinth of the relationship with their mothers.

Some children of borderlines experience childhood as an emotional prison camp ruled by arbitrarily hostile guards. Their feelings are captured by the words of adult survivors of concentration camps: "*We were terribly afraid that . . . people would never notice a thing, that nobody in the world would notice a thing: us, the struggle, the dead . . . that this wall was so huge that nothing, no message about us, would ever make it out*" (Krall and Edelman 1977, p. 7).

Although the emotional world of the borderline's child can be a dark and forsaken land, the purity of heart, the resilience of spirit, and the open-mindedness of children illuminate the darkness. A borderline mother who sees herself through her child's eyes can find the life-saving motivation to seek treatment. Unrestrained love can be found in the gleam in her child's eyes. Without treatment, these mothers are at risk for passing the disorder to the next generation and for missing the love they so desperately seek.

Learning to recognize the symptoms of borderline personality disorder is the first step in helping these mothers and their children. We must listen to their stories, learn from their pain, and share the responsibility for abandoning these mothers and children. As a famous survivor of Auschwitz, Primo Levi, reminds us, "Maybe each of us is Cain to some Abel, and slay him in the field without knowing it" (Todorov 1996, p. 137).

Introduction

Borderline personality disorder (BPD) is the single most common personality disorder affecting approximately six million Americans. Individuals with BPD are volatile, impulsive, self-destructive, and fearful of abandonment. Clinically, the term describes their behavior as bordering between sanity and insanity because separation and loss can trigger suicidal and psychotic reactions. Although males can develop BPD, women outnumber men two to one within clinical populations. Males with BPD may be diagnosed as antisocial due to aggressive and violent behavior, and consequently are more likely to enter the justice system rather than the mental-health system.

Children with borderline mothers begin their lives with an insecure attachment to an emotionally unstable mother. Thus, these children risk becoming impulsive, rage-filled, oppositional, aggressive, depressed, and violent. They are also at risk for developing BPD themselves. Borderline personality disorder can be passed from one generation to the next, making early recognition and intervention essential.

Identifying BPD can be difficult because the disorder includes individuals with different symptom clusters. Therapists often fail to recognize BPD when stereotypical characteristics such as depression or suicidal feelings are not present. Prior to 1980, many borderline mothers were misdiagnosed as manic depressive or schizophrenic.

Children with borderline mothers often describe their mothers as "ridiculous, unbelievable, outrageous, absurd, or foolish." Indeed, young children see these mothers as make-believe mothers who may fit one of four basic profiles: the Waif mother, the Hermit mother, the Queen mother, and the Witch mother. Some adult children of borderlines literally described their mothers in these terms.

For generations, folktales have helped children categorize and understand various kinds of people. Fairy tales and folktales capture a child's view of the grown-up world, one that adults often fail to see.[1] *Understanding the Borderline Mother* explores four profiles of BPD as perceived through the eyes of the borderline mother's child. In most cases, the child was female.

Females have greater difficulty separating their identity from their mothers', primarily because mother and daughter share the same gender. Therefore, most of the case examples discussed are mothers and daughters. Although borderline mothers obviously raise sons as well as daughters, males are less likely to enter therapy. If male children of borderline mothers develop BPD, they are more likely to be identified among prison populations. A male child who does not develop BPD is most likely the all-good child. The all-good male child tends to display narcissistic traits and, as an adult, may marry a borderline woman, re-creating his role of rescuer. Such men are often successful professionals who are highly defended against recognizing their mother's disorder.

Understanding the Borderline Mother brings readers into the emotional world of the borderline's child, where they may find themselves thinking, "I don't want to know this." For some readers, the content may be profoundly disturbing. Those who grew up with a borderline mother may need time and distance in order to fully

---

1. Unless otherwise noted I have used R. Manheim's (1977) *Grimm's Tales for Young and Old*.

digest the contents of this book. One does not eagerly look back on a dark and painful past. The willingness to look, however, allows us to see the present more clearly and to create a brighter future for our own children.

1

Make-Believe Mothers

When I used to read fairy tales, I fancied that kind of thing never happened, and now here I am in the middle of one!

—Lewis Carroll, *Alice's Adventures in Wonderland*[1]

"It's like drowning. There's a darkness within her that can suck you in and swallow you whole . . . yet it's unfathomable . . . because she's your mother."

Laura's voice sounded flat and far away. She spoke in a child's voice, as if trapped at the bottom of a well.

"There's no way out." She drew into herself and left me with her fear. I wasn't sure if I could reach her in time.

Laura's mother was no ordinary mother. Submerged in the cold darkness of despair, mothers with borderline personality disorder (BPD) struggle to keep their heads above water. They cling desperately to whoever is near and can pull their own children into the blackness. Borderline mothers are intense, unpredictable, and

---

1. Quotations in this chapter introducing topic headings are from Lewis Carroll's *Alice's Adventures in Wonderland* and *Through the Looking-Glass* (1865).

sometimes volatile. One day they may see their children as angelic; other days their rage or sarcasm can shatter their children's souls. Mothers with several children may perceive one child as all-good and another as no-good, splitting and projecting contradictory feelings about themselves onto different children.

Borderline mothers go off—over the emotional edge, falling into despair or exploding into tirades. Yet at other times they may be loving, supportive, and nurturing mothers. If researchers are correct in their estimate that approximately six million people in the United States suffer from BPD, the number of children living with borderline parents could be staggering (Santoro and Cohen 1997).

Children who grow up with borderline mothers live in a make-believe world that is neither fiction nor fantasy. *Borderland* is an emotional world where loving mothers resemble storybook characters: helpless waifs, frightened hermits, bossy queens, or vindictive witches. This whimsically dangerous world is filled with contradiction and fraught with emotional storms that defy prediction. A 7-year-old patient drew a picture of her borderline mother as a wicked witch threatening to turn her into a frog with the wave of a magic wand.

Trapped in a world that others cannot see, feel, or understand, the borderline's child feels hopelessly lost. Laura saw her mother as a self-centered queen who periodically transformed into a witch. Christina Crawford (1978), the adopted daughter of actress Joan Crawford, grew up with a mother like Laura's, and described her experience in her famous autobiography: "Each time I ran head-long into an abyss, that black hole where nothing followed logically, where fabrication and anger and turmoil ruled supreme, that place where there was no help and no peace, no escape from the juggernaut of chaos. From her throne in the eye of the hurricane, brandishing her magic wand of obsession, ruled the queen of chaos herself: Mommie dearest" (p. 174).

Because BPD was previously misdiagnosed as schizophrenia, no reliable way exists to estimate the number of adult children with BPD mothers (Kroll 1988). BPD was first identified as a formal diagnosis in the *Diagnostic and Statistical Manual of Mental Disorders* in 1980, three years after Joan Crawford's death.

Confusion, controversy, and misdiagnosis are not surprising considering the growing number of individuals who suffer from borderline personality disorder. BPD has been ascribed to personalities as diverse as Susan Smith, a vilified mother who drowned her two young sons in 1994, and the late Diana, Princess of Wales, the "caring princess" (Smith 1999, p. 194). Charlotte du Pont, the Civil War heiress to the Du Pont powder mill fortune, and Sylvia Plath, the award-winning author who committed suicide in 1963, may also have suffered from BPD. The tragedy that marked the lives of these uncommon women could well be attributed to an increasingly common disorder that is transmitted from mother to child.

Emotional intensity, impulsivity, unpredictability, and fear of abandonment are symptoms observable primarily by those who have an intimate relationship with the borderline. Casual acquaintances, co-workers, or neighbors are less likely to witness the borderline's sudden shifts in mood, self-destructive behavior, paranoid distortions, and obsessive ruminations. Like Alice in *Alice's Adventures in Wonderland*, children in Borderland are puzzled by the contradictions of their world and live on the fine line between sanity and insanity.

Although she can function extraordinarily well in other roles, mothering is the single most daunting task for the borderline female. Her fear of abandonment and her tendency to experience separation as rejection or betrayal lock the borderline mother and her children in a struggle for survival. The child is emotionally imprisoned. Children must separate to survive, but separation threatens their mother's survival. The following thoughts are common among children with borderline mothers:

1. "I never know what to expect."
2. "I don't trust her."
3. "She says it didn't happen."
4. "She makes me feel terrible."
5. "Everyone else thinks she's great."
6. "It's all or nothing."
7. "She's so negative."
8. "She flips out."
9. "Sometimes I can't stand her."
10. "She drives me crazy."

"I NEVER KNOW WHAT TO EXPECT"

> . . . they don't seem to have any rules in particular: at least, if there are, nobody attends to them—and you've no idea how confusing it is . . .

Erik Erikson (1950) explained that the first stage of psychological development in children is "trust versus basic mistrust." Erikson claimed that the infant's first developmental achievement is the ability to tolerate the mother's absence without undue anxiety "because she has become an inner certainty" (p. 219). Consistency, continuity, and sameness of experience are essential to the development of trust and security for children. Unfortunately, the hallmarks of borderline behavior are inconsistency, unpredictability, and inappropriate intensity. Because borderlines were abused, neglected, or suffered a traumatic loss as children, they are desperately afraid of abandonment. They seek emotional control over others, even threatening abandonment in order not to be abandoned themselves. Their rules and expectations are vague, nonexistent, unreasonable, rigid, or unpredictably enforced. Children with borderline mothers experience chronic anxiety because they are uncertain of their mothers' behavior.

Laura's mother was inconsistent and had difficulty maintaining structure. When Laura was a child she was forbidden from playing with some of her friends, except when her mother felt ill. When her mother was tired or sick the only rule was "don't bother me." By the time she was an adolescent, her mother gave up enforcing rules. Laura enjoyed the lack of structure when she was a teenager, but as a child she was frustrated and confused. When Laura visited her mother as an adult, her mother admonished her, asking, "Why don't you ever call me?" But when Laura telephoned, her mother sounded annoyed, answering the phone impatiently and asking, "What? What do you want?" Interactions with borderline mothers often leave the child feeling guilty and confused.

Joan Crawford, on the other hand, rigidly enforced unreasonable rules that suited her needs, rather than her children's needs. Christina explained that her mother programmed every minute of the day, allowing exactly half an hour for eating each meal and for washing the dishes. Christina lamented that her mother's moods fluctuated so dramatically, despite rigid rules, that she was never certain of how she might be treated: "I never knew whether it would be a big hug of loving affection or a verbal slap in the face" (Crawford 1978, p. 13).

Children of borderlines never know from one minute to the next how their mother feels about them. Like the game "she loves me, she loves me not," the mother's moods can suddenly change from affection to rage, creating an uncertain and insecure emotional environment. Winnicott (1962) emphasized the importance of the child's need for "the good enough mother" (p. 57) who provides enough consistency and calmness so that the child is not overwhelmed with anxiety. Without structure and predictability in their emotional world, children have no reality base upon which to build self-esteem and security.

"I DON'T TRUST HER"

"There's no use trying," she said: "one can't believe impossible things."

Trust is a major issue between borderlines and their children. Children cannot trust the borderline mother for many reasons: (1) She is manipulative. (2) She distorts the truth and may even blatantly lie. (3) She may physically harm them. (4) She is unpredictable. (5) She overreacts. (6) She is impulsive. (7) She has poor judgment. (8) She has an unreliable memory. (9) She is inconsistent. (10) She is intrusive. Like Alice who confided in the Cheshire Cat, children of borderlines may learn to trust a pet more than their own mother.

Jerome Kroll (1988), a psychiatrist specializing in the treatment of borderlines, explains that the "cognitive style seen in borderlines consists of a lack of focus or attention to the matter at hand . . . a balanced understanding of an event is impossible to achieve" (p. 32). Borderline mothers create their own reality, one that is rarely confirmed by their children or others. Regardless of how outrageous the mother's perspective may be, borderline mothers may punish their children for expressing their own views, beliefs, and feelings.

Laura questioned her mother's assertion that she was close to bankruptcy. Because Laura knew that her mother earned a substantial income, she suggested consulting a financial planner. When her mother snarled back, "You have no idea how this world works!" Laura was caught off guard and felt belittled by her mother's response. Like Alice in *Through the Looking-Glass*, Laura questioned her own view of reality. " 'Try again!' the White Queen demanded of Alice. 'Why, sometimes I've believed as many as six impossible things before breakfast!' " (Carroll 1865, p. 100).

Borderline mothers negate the child's perspective by implying that the child's perspective is wrong. Laura was rebuked for not sharing her mother's belief that they were desperately poor. Yet her mother's perceptions fluctuated with her mood. She felt demeaned by Laura's recommendation to consult a financial planner; subsequently, her mother responded by demeaning Laura. Borderline mothers feel betrayed and attacked when others do not validate their feelings and perceptions. Unfortunately, they reject, abandon, punish, or vilify those whom they perceive as disloyal, creating a terrifying dilemma for their children.

During her adolescence, the lack of trust between Laura and her mother was evident in her mother's tendency to hug and sniff her at the same time. Her mother used such covert methods in order to determine whether or not Laura might be drinking alcohol or smoking marijuana. Naturally, her mother's hugs felt insincere, and Laura resented the use of affection to mask suspicion.

Children of borderlines feel helpless when their mothers invade their privacy, manipulate them, invalidate their feelings, and distort the truth. Borderlines distort the truth because their perceptions are distorted. In one instance, a borderline mother claimed that her daughter had been sexually abused by her ex-husband. The daughter was appalled that her mother would make such a claim. The mother, however, had been sexually abused by her own father and interpreted a goodbye kiss between her daughter and ex-husband as evidence of sexual abuse.

Distortion is an unconscious way of processing information that reflects the individual's reality. Distortion misleads and aggravates family members, who may take a borderline's statement at face value before discovering the facts. Laura grew weary of her mother's overreactions and learned to disregard her mother's statements such as "something terrible just happened." Borderlines tend to catastrophize and panic easily. "Stop everything and help me NOW!" may mean they lost their car keys. "I have a terrible headache" may mean "Leave me alone." "I had a car accident" may mean a grocery cart scratched the car.

Some borderlines consciously distort the truth in order to prevent abandonment, maintain self-esteem, or avoid conflict. Others may lie to evoke sympathy, attention, and concern. From the borderline's perspective, however, lying feels essential to survival. (Although not all borderlines consciously lie, all borderlines experience perceptional distortions.) When desperation drives behavior such as lying or stealing, they feel innocent of wrongdoing and do not feel guilt or remorse. Apologies are rare, therefore, and borderlines may be confused about why others expect them to feel remorse. They believe that others would do what they did in order to survive. Their explanation is succinct, "But I *had* to!" Thus the borderline is unconcerned with the consequences of lying because she feels she had no other option.

Borderline mothers who habitually lie are especially destructive because they destroy their children's trust. Because they rarely apologize for their behavior, they lead their children to believe that the child is wrong, rather than the mother. Their survival instinct can lead to many behaviors that others consider abhorrent. When the borderline is hurt or frightened, she feels that her survival is at stake; thus, morality is temporarily suspended. Christina Crawford (1997) describes the child's predicament: "I guess it was impossible for an adult who had not been present to believe that she was the one who was lying and I was telling the truth. She was always so convincing" (p. 137).

Conflicts and disagreements may escalate into violence because borderline mothers have difficulty managing the intensity of their own emotions. Consequently, physical fights are common between some borderline mothers and their children. In such circumstances, children have had to call the police, escape their homes through windows, flee to neighbors' homes, rescue siblings, and intervene in physical fights between their parents. Some borderline mothers may physically or verbally attack their children in the middle of the night, when the children, unfortunately, are most vulnerable. In one case, a patient felt so unsafe that she slept with a steak knife under her pillow until she was 18, when she moved away from home.

"SHE SAYS IT DIDN'T HAPPEN"

Alice said nothing: she had never been so much contradicted in all her life before, and she felt that she was losing her temper.

Borderlines often forget painful experiences that their children remember vividly. Studies show that chronically intense emotions damage the part of the brain that is responsible for memory (Christianson 1992). Chronic emotional stress exposes the brain to an excess of glucocorticoids, hormones that normally help the brain cope with stress. The hippocampus, which controls memory functioning, contains a high number of glucocorticoid receptors and is therefore susceptible to damage (Schacter 1996). Because borderline mothers experienced overwhelming emotional distress as children, areas in their brain responsible for memory and emotional regulation may be damaged. Studies using magnetic resonance imaging to examine the brains of females who were abused as children found that the left hippocampus was actually smaller than those in subjects from a control group.[2] Consequently, bor-

___

2. See Schacter's (1996) reference to Putnam and colleagues' 1986 study, "The Clinical Phenomenology of Multiple Personality Disorder. Review of 100 Recent Cases," *Journal of Clinical Psychiatry* 47:285–293.

derline mothers may not remember experiences recalled by their children. A vicious cycle results as children with borderline mothers are immersed in an emotionally intense environment that, if unmitigated, may also damage *their* cognitive functioning.

Because the borderline mother is unable to remember intensely emotional events, she is unable to learn from experience. She may repeat destructive behaviors without recalling previous consequences. Laura and her sister remembered many episodes when their mother was set off by some trivial incident such as a misplaced item of clothing. When confronted years later with her behavior, their mother denied ever having lost control and stated, "How dare you say I did such things after all I've done for you!" Therapists report that borderline mothers are often unable to confirm their children's traumatic memories.

It is impossible to learn from experience if the experience is not remembered. Thus, borderlines become trapped in repetitive, self-destructive behaviors. They may spend more money than they have, have sex without protecting themselves, drink too much, smoke too much, or eat too much. Although they feel terrible later, they may repeat the behavior because they do not remember the consequences. Their behavior alarms family members and can endanger their children.

Some adult children recall riding in cars when their mother was driving drunk, or having utilities disconnected as the result of the borderline's impulse spending. Some recall literally saving their mother's life. One night Laura noticed the smell of burning carpet and extinguished a cigarette her mother had dropped while smoking in bed. Unfortunately, her mother continued to smoke in bed after the near tragedy.

When borderlines abuse drugs or alcohol, they can become psychotic. Christina Crawford (1978) described many episodes of her mother's horrific night raids. Psychotic behavior, however, is not limited to rage. Equally terrifying is the borderline mother who dissociates, withdraws into despair, self-mutilates, or attempts suicide. Fear and despair can also trigger what are called psychotic breaks. One patient recalled disturbing memories of his mother locking herself in the bathroom and threatening to kill herself as the patient, at age 7, tried to calm her down. Other patients report mothers who threatened to run away and mothers who actually left home. Psychosis can occur when *any* emotion becomes unmanageable.

Studies indicate that people who were exposed to chronic stress in childhood have higher levels of somatostatin, a stress-related hormone and neurotransmitter, in their spinal fluid (Heit et al. 1999). Severe stress in childhood appears to have long-term effects on the brain and immune system. Children of borderlines are at risk, therefore, for a variety of physical and emotional disorders as adults. They may also be prone to stress-related physical symptoms such as colitis or migraine headaches.

Christina Crawford (1978) once visited a psychiatrist who asked her if she knew what might be causing her headaches. Christina stated simply, "Yes. I hate my mother" (p. 219). Adrenaline causes the blood vessels in the brain to constrict and forces blood to the muscles as a necessary preparation for the fight-or-flight response. Following the stressful interaction, the blood vessels dilate, causing the pain of a migraine headache. Kandel and Sudderth (2000) explain that some researchers believe that "a migraine is actually a dysfunction of the nervous system and an unstable threshold in the brain. When internal or external stressors increase, this threshold is exceeded, and a migraine headache is produced. It's sort of like one part of your body says 'don't step over this line,' but you do anyway" (p. 15).

For children with borderline mothers, migraines prevent the child from acting on unbearable feelings of rage: the child is paralyzed with pain. The unpredictable behavior of the borderline mother can trigger adrenaline surges, yet children cannot respond with a fight-or-flight response without suffering negative repercussions.[3] Consequently, many adult children of borderlines develop headaches after visiting with their mothers or talking to them on the telephone.

Kandel and Sudderth (2000) explain that "researchers have found that the speed of blood flow in the middle cerebral artery decreases during a migraine attack. Somehow, your brain turns on the 'yellow light' and the blood flow slows down" (p. 14). Many children with borderline mothers function with a brain continually flashing caution.

"SHE MAKES ME FEEL TERRIBLE"

"It might end you know," said Alice to herself, "in my going out altogether, like a candle."

Fear of abandonment is the most common symptom of BPD and is shared by all borderlines. Many researchers and clinicians observe that borderlines fear "falling into the abyss" when faced with rejection or abandonment. The feeling is sometimes described as survival anxiety. The borderline feels numb, disconnected, and unreal. Thus, borderlines invest enormous effort in preventing

---

3. Otto Kernberg (1985) states that "bringing together extremely opposite loving and hateful images of the self and of significant others would trigger unbearable anxiety and guilt because of the implicit danger to the good internal and external object relations; therefore there is an active defensive separation of such contradictory self- and object-images; in other words, primitive dissociation or splitting becomes a major defensive operation" (p. 165).

abandonment, and family members may feel suffocated, intimidated, and controlled.

Borderlines may display dramatic or hysterical behavior such as gasping and crying, sending surges of adrenaline through family members, and triggering the startle response. Overreactions to illness and accidents, and dramatic displays of rage or withdrawal leave family members feeling sucked in and emotionally depleted. The borderline's children can feel trapped and suffocated, as if their own lives might be extinguished by their mother's neediness.

Just as a 2-year-old clings to the parent when faced with separation, borderlines have difficulty letting go, saying good-bye, hanging up the phone, ending conversations, and may become suicidal when relationships end. The other person feels held back, dragged down, or pulled under, in response to the borderline's message: "Don't leave me." Borderlines can self-destruct as a result of their fear of abandonment and often use emotional blackmail to control others. Understandably, children of borderlines struggle to manage feelings of shame, guilt, anxiety, and rage.

Shame

When a child disagrees with the borderline mother or does not satisfy her needs or wishes, the borderline will attempt to shame, punish, degrade, or vilify the child. In a starkly candid interview, Joan Crawford revealed her draconian philosophy of disciplining 8-year-old Christina: "It is not easy to discipline her, but I am forced to, when she insists on doing things her own way. *I find punishing her by hurting her dignity is very effective*" (Thomas 1978, p. 168, emphasis added). Borderline mothers may use denigration as a method of discipline without being aware of its destructiveness. Those who use it intentionally are severely disturbed but are not likely to seek treatment because they believe in their sovereign right to discipline their children as they see fit. In their view, they are doing their job as a parent. They believe that a child must be hurt in order to learn appropriate behavior because that is what they were taught as children. Only mothers who are unable to remember the pain of their own denigration are likely to denigrate their children.

Shame extinguishes the sense of entitlement to one's existence and can trigger self-destructive fantasies in children. Mary Todd Lincoln's stepmother referred to her as a limb of Satan. One of Mrs. Lincoln's biographers explained, "to be shamed and humiliated is to feel a disgrace to the whole self " (Baker 1987, p. 30). Unfortunately, borderline mothers project their own shame onto others.

Anxiety

Children of borderlines grow up in fear—the fear that mother will hurt herself or them. Either way, their survival could be at stake. My patient, Laura, was unable to leave home without experiencing separation anxiety, the fear that something terrible might happen to her mother or herself. Some days she left the house screaming, "I hope you die!" But by the time she got to school, she felt sick to her stomach. Children of borderlines become preoccupied with reading their mother's mood in order to ward off a possible crisis or to prevent being attacked. Their emotional energy is invested in contradictory positions: fighting with their mother as well as protecting her. They may have difficulty concentrating on anything else.

Borderlines experience separation anxiety in part because disturbing memories of previously abusive and denigrating experiences are most likely to surface when the borderline is alone. Laura's mother told her that memories of being molested by her own father flashed through her mind at night. Sometimes she thought she heard his footsteps outside her bedroom door. The sounds and images made her feel crazy. Laura's mother begged her not to go out and sometimes feigned illness to keep her from leaving. Laura hated to leave her mother alone, yet was desperate to get away from her.

Although children of borderlines grow up afraid, they learn not to show their fear and seem oblivious to painful or dangerous situations. They may refuse to cry and learn to shut down when hurt or upset. An adolescent patient explained, "After awhile you become immune . . . you don't feel anything anymore."

The ability to conceal their feelings is adaptive for children in Borderland, because some borderline mothers use fear to control their children. Christina Crawford recalled the horror of being locked in the linen closet with the lights off because her mother knew that Christina was afraid of the dark (Crawford 1978). Borderline mothers may threaten to call the police, cut off financial support, threaten physical harm, or take away loved objects. Both Laura and Christina had loved objects destroyed as punishment. Christina was forced to give away her own Christmas presents. Laura's mother smashed and broke her favorite record albums. Such children learn to hide what they love. When parents use fear to control their children, they shatter the sacred bond of trust.

Guilt

When Laura was 3 years old her mother told her that "God punishes bad little girls." Being "good" meant not disagreeing with her mother. As an adult, her mother punished her by refusing to return phone calls, answer letters, or respond to e-mail. She would cut her off until Laura's guilt and anxiety built to an intolerable level. Only then would her mother respond. Laura felt completely emotionally invaded, as if her mother could read her mind. From the time she was a young child, her mother used fear and guilt to control her. Her mother was unable to respect Laura's need for privacy and lacked appropriate boundaries. She listened in on phone conversations and later used the information to humiliate Laura.

Children of borderlines may suffer from separation guilt. Christina Crawford felt that her mother expected not only complete devotion, but wanted to *become* her (Crawford 1978). Although Christina felt compassion for her mother, she was torn with guilt for wanting a life of her own. Borderlines view separateness as betrayal and test loyalty with comments such as, "If you love me you will do this . . ." or, "You would never do this if you really loved me." Children must constantly prove their love by providing total devotion at the expense of their own needs.

Young children naturally fear the withdrawal of their mother's love. When borderlines feel betrayed they may cut off communication, support, and resources. Adult children may be cut out of their mother's will. Photographs may be removed or destroyed, and family members may be forbidden to mention the name of the offending individual. When enraged, the borderline mother may declare, "I have no children," indicating her desire to wipe them out of her mind, a terrifying emotional experience for a child.

Borderlines are extraordinarily sensitive to criticism and expect allegiance from their children. Because the borderline often turns to her children as allies, her children have no choice but to side with her even if they must turn against their own father. They know the price they will pay if they do not support her and they fear her annihilating rage.

Rage

"Sometimes I feel like killing her" are words that reflect the rage within some children of borderlines. When a psychiatrist asked serial killer Edmund Kemper why he murdered his mother, Kemper stated, "I couldn't handle the hate" (Cheney 1976, p. 132). Female children are less likely to attack their mother physically, although their anger is no less intense. Christina Crawford (1978) expressed the child's murderous rage: "In that moment I hated her so much I wanted to kill her . . . It didn't even *matter* to me that I'd have to spend the rest of my life in jail" (p. 173) The borderline's children can become extraordinarily frustrated because no one understands that they are drowning emotionally. No one sees beneath the surface of their mother's façade that she is pulling her own children into her darkness. Some children fear that in order to live, their mother must die.

"EVERYONE ELSE THINKS SHE'S GREAT"

> "I know they're talking nonsense," Alice thought to herself, "and it's foolish to cry about it." So she brushed away her tears and went on, as cheerfully as she could.

In her book, *Cognitive-Behavioral Treatment of the Borderline Patient*, Marsha Linehan (1993b) describes the façade of normalcy that borderlines present to others, particularly in work settings where they feel confident and in control. Linehan explains that the borderline's apparent competency leads others to assume that she is equally capable of coping in other roles. When co-workers hear the borderline mother complain about her children they assume that the children are troubled, rather than the mother. Unfortunately, for their children, this means that their private experience is unlikely to be validated by others.

Laura's friends could not understand why her mother drove her crazy. They never witnessed her mother's attacks because Laura avoided having her friends stay for an extended period of time. When Laura told them about her mother's dark side they said, "But your mother seems so nice!" Laura's sister was the only person who validated her experience. One time when Laura's boyfriend was at her house, her mother "flipped out just because she thought my skirt was too short." Laura was embarrassed but also relieved that someone other than her sister had witnessed the attack.

In social situations the borderline mother can be engaging, gracious, and endearing. Christina Crawford (1978) was particularly annoyed with the façade her mother presented when entertaining. Christina summarized the child's feelings regarding the dichotomy of the private versus public persona of the borderline mother: "I just wanted to scream that it was all a fake" (p. 80). Remarkably, Christina's account of her experience continues to be challenged. In his biography entitled *Joan Crawford: The Last Word*, Fred Lawrence Guiles (1995) contends that "One of the chief flaws in Christina's memoir is a distortion of known facts in Joan's life, or, sometimes, a questionable interpretation of those facts" (p. 158). Guiles fails to consider the possibility that the distortion of facts might have originated with Joan Crawford. Emotional manipulation and the tendency to distort facts epitomize borderline behavior.

Widespread ignorance regarding BPD perpetuates the hopelessness that children with borderline parents experience. They feel abandoned by society at large whenever their reality is discounted. Carl Jung (in Stein 1995) once said, "we need more understanding of human nature, because the only real danger that exists is man himself. . . . His psyche should be studied, because we are the origin of all coming evil" (p. 1). The borderline's children are haunted by a darkness within their mothers that others may fail to recognize until it is too late.

"IT'S ALL OR NOTHING"

. . . once she remembered trying to box her own ears for having cheated herself in a game of croquet she was playing against herself, for this curious child was very fond of pretending to be two people.

The borderline's emotional thermostat consists of two settings: on and off. There is no middle ground. Melissa Thornton (1998), a borderline who wrote about her own experience, explains that "[borderlines] split things into simple, polemic pairs of good or bad, sadness or joy, black or white. Unable to grasp that something might be both good and bad, a person with BPD can only see the ends of the spectrum" (p. 16). Thus, the borderline's inability to experience more than one perspective at a time conveys only one side of the story and one part of the picture.

Children see themselves as reflected in the mirror of their parents' eyes. Therefore, children of borderlines may develop two contrasting perceptions of themselves. The resulting confusion, guilt, and shame may be manifested in self-destructive tendencies such as banging their heads against walls, hitting, or cutting themselves. Believing in her child's basic goodness is only possible if the mother believes in her own goodness. Unfortunately, some borderlines have an inner conviction of being evil.[4]

Like most children of borderlines, Christina Crawford and Laura

---

4. J. Gunderson (1984) explains that "the conviction of being evil and nihilistic beliefs are two extremes that the borderline patient achieves when the usual defenses of action and substitute objects are not available" (p. 37).

were confused about their identity. Hopelessness and despair can consume the borderline's child. Laura was not yet in high school when she wrote in her journal: "I'm losing my mind—oh god—I know how it feels to be buried alive."

"SHE'S SO NEGATIVE"

"You don't know much," said the Duchess; "and that's a fact."

Alice did not at all like the tone of this remark, and thought it would be as well to introduce some other subject of conversation.

Borderlines have negative thoughts because they have negative feelings about themselves and others. Memory difficulties, difficulty focusing attention, confused and disorganized thinking, the inability to reason logically, morbid introspection, and intrusively negative thoughts are common (Kroll 1988). Children are subjected to deflating comments that increase despair or destroy their enthusiasm as some borderline mothers assume that the worst possible thing will happen in any given situation.

Laura avoided talking to her mother about her problems or worries. She knew that her mother would tell her either that she was "too sensitive and worried too much," or say something that made her feel worse. When children bring concerns to the attention of the borderline parent, they receive a response that either increases their distress or entirely dismisses their concern. A child who is worried about not passing to the next grade might be told, "and then you won't be with your friends your age, you'll be behind forever, why didn't you study harder this year?" The borderline absorbs and intensifies the child's fear, "and then this and this could happen," and is unable to reassure and comfort the child.

Glickauf-Hughes and Mehlman (1998) report that daughters of borderline mothers "all reported painful memories of turning to their mother for comfort and feeling worse afterwards" (p. 297).

When Laura was 12, she proudly announced that she was invited to accompany a friend on vacation. Her mother responded desperately, "Oh no! Now we've got to get you some new clothes and I don't have any money!" Laura's excitement was replaced by anxiety. Borderlines can deflate the child's enthusiasm by emphasizing negative outcomes. A patient recalled dismay at her mother's reaction to the announcement of her longed-for pregnancy. Her mother's response was, "Oh no! Not now!" and insinuated that some horrible mistake had been made.

When Christina Crawford (1978) won a part as a guest star on a television program, she telephoned her mother to share the exciting news. Her mother, however, hung up on her in the middle of their conversation. Bewildered, Christina broke into tears wondering what had gone wrong. Later she learned that her mother was intensely jealous of her career. Shortly thereafter Christina became convinced that her mother could never allow her to enjoy her own success.

Emotionally stable parents share their children's joy and quiet their fear. But caretaking roles are reversed for children of borderlines whose mothers are chronically upset. Children repress their fear in order to calm their mother. Situations that should frighten children may not because they have learned not to feel. A dramatic (and hopefully rare) example occurs when children rescue the borderline mother from suicide attempts.

Borderlines are ambivalent about their existence but do not necessarily want to kill themselves. Their fear of living, however, may be stronger than their fear of death, placing them at risk for harming themselves. Acts of self-mutilation, such as cutting, burning, or hitting oneself do not represent a death wish and should not be confused with suicidal behavior. Self-mutilation is disturbing to family members, who may feel manipulated by such behavior. The borderline, however, may be expressing self-hatred, not necessarily searching for sympathy or attention. Occasionally, some borderlines may inadvertently succeed in committing suicide.

Suicidal behavior is a conscious and immediate attempt to end one's life. Threats of suicide and suicidal gestures are so commonly associated with BPD that in their absence the diagnosis may be overlooked. Professionals and family members often fail to identify BPD when suicidality, self-destructive behavior, or depression are not present. *Many borderlines do not engage in self-mutilation or suicidal behavior.*

Joan Crawford apparently never attempted suicide although her self-destruction was insidious, both through her alcoholism and her refusal to seek psychiatric treatment. Laura's mother, however, overdosed twice, exacerbating Laura's separation anxiety and guilt. She was 8 years old the first time she saved her mother's life. Borderline mothers who threaten or attempt suicide keep their children emotionally trapped, and their children may suffer from extreme anxiety even as adults.

"SHE FLIPS OUT"

"We're all mad here. I'm mad. You're mad."
"How do you know I'm mad?" said Alice.
"You must be," said the Cat, "or you wouldn't have come here."

When borderlines are faced with stressful situations, such as the end of a relationship, the death of a loved one, the loss of a job, rejection, or abandonment, they may become paranoid and lose touch with reality. If they abuse alcohol or drugs, their behavior can be life-threatening to themselves or others. They may feel disconnected from their body and their memory may be impaired. They may lose track of time, lose awareness of their surroundings, and become disoriented. Some borderlines talk out loud when alone, or mutter to themselves in the presence of others. They may stare blankly, carrying on a conversation while preoccupied with the chaos of their internal state.

Anyone who witnesses a psychotic episode will remember it, unless that person is a child who has witnessed it too many times. Children may repress their feelings and memories of such experiences. The mother's appearance reveals the change in her mental state. The pupils of the eyes enlarge, giving the individual a shark-like look, and indicating the potential for attack or detachment from reality. If the underlying feeling is rage, the child may feel threatened. If the underlying feeling is fear, the child may panic. Psychotic episodes are traumatic because the emotions that are evoked are overwhelming. If they are frequent, the child may numb out (dissociate), and seem oblivious to their occurrence. Depending on their frequency, the child may believe such experiences are normal.

There were times when Laura felt herself disappearing down a black hole, sinking into her mother. She dreaded the evenings when her mother drank too much and flipped out. Psychotic episodes are intensely disturbing, and Laura didn't like to talk about them. An alien seemed to emerge from her mother, muttering senselessly, tearfully, unable to recognize her own child. Laura tried to stay calm by thinking about something normal, like school or her favorite television program. But memories of "the alien" would haunt her for the rest of her life. Being alone with a psychotic parent is terrifying for children of any age.

The night before Laura left to spend the summer with her father, her mother crawled into her bed, crying. She had read a letter from Laura's father in which he told Laura how much he missed her. Laura's mother accused them of plotting against her, and was certain that Laura planned to move in with him. Laura was appalled that her mother was threatened by the innocuous letter. When Laura mentioned the incident several years later, her mother had no memory of it.

Ordinary mothers sleep at night; borderline mothers do not. Borderlines dread being alone with their own thoughts; thus, intrusive, obsessive thoughts may keep them awake at night. Noise from the radio, television, or late-night telephone calls may distract them from their anxiety and provide a sense of security. Alcohol or drug abuse increases their agitation and worsens anxiety.

Although not all borderline mothers awaken their children in the middle of the night, Christina Crawford's (1978) description of her mother's "night raids" were among the most remembered excerpts from her famous book. Her description of a psychotic episode captures the child's terror: "As the moon lit up part of her face I could see that look in her eyes again. It was a haunted, excited look . . ." (p. 57).

The still of the night is broken by the stirrings of the borderline's ruminations. One patient recalled her mother entering her bedroom and rummaging through her belongings looking for evidence of drugs. Another patient's mother awakened her father on a regular basis, rebuking him for being able to sleep when she was so upset.

"SOMETIMES I CAN'T STAND HER"

> The Queen turned crimson with fury, and after glaring at her
> for a moment like a wild beast, began screaming, "Off with
> her head! Off with . . ."

Some children of borderlines secretly wish that their mother would die, not because they hate her, but because living with her seems impossible. As an adult, Laura was still drawn into the turmoil of her mother's life. Her mother was the only person on the face of the earth who could stir up her murderous rage. Yet she was terrified that her mother would someday kill herself. Linehan (1993b) states, "The desire to be dead among borderline individuals is often reasonable, in that it is based on lives that are currently unbearable" (p. 125). Laura grew weary of her mother's rampages, mood swings, depressive episodes, and her own conflicting feelings.

Laura explained that her mother "went on tirades." Something could set her off and she would whirl around the house like a cyclone. The warning signal was "the look." The look was a piercing, threatening glare that meant "I could kill you." When Laura was a child, her mother actually said it, with no awareness of the power of her words.

Children of borderlines and survivors of hurricanes have much in common. Survival is dependent on finding a safe place, staying low, and not being fooled by the eye of the storm. When her mother found a dirty dish in Laura's bedroom or wasn't able to find her car keys, it triggered the same storm. Laura knew better than to say anything or to get in her way. Her mother calmed down to catch her breath and would start in all over again, repeating the same sentence, such as, "You make me sick" (a belief that Laura had already internalized). Laura could not remember the whole speech because she had learned to shut out the sound of her mother's voice. When Laura was young the tirades terrified her, but as she grew older, she became immune to them.

Children are confused by how quickly anger is forgotten. "Now" is all that matters to borderlines. Laura's mother could spank and scold her one minute and hug her the next. One time she threatened to get rid of her, packed her suitcase, and later the same day told her that she couldn't live without her. Contradiction breeds confusion and children may feel set up, manipulated, and provoked. Their frustration is often expressed in the words "I just can't stand my mother."

Although borderlines fear losing what they love, their rage frequently results in destroying what others love. They tend to hurt others in ways that replicate how they themselves were hurt. Borderlines may destroy what is good and loved by their children because they are intensely jealous of the loved object. They cannot give others what they do not have.[5] When enraged, some divorced borderlines may deprive their children of contact with their father either to punish him or the children.

The most tragic scenario is that of the Medean Mother who, like Medea in Greek mythology, defies the basic laws of nature by physically sacrificing her own children in response to abandonment by a husband or boyfriend. The Medean Mother's fear of abandonment endangers her child's life.

"SHE DRIVES ME CRAZY"

> Alice had got so much into the way of expecting nothing but out-of-the-way things to happen, that it seemed quite dull and stupid for life to go in the common way.

Children with borderline mothers adjust to the chaos of their lives by learning to expect the unexpected. They associate love with fear and kindness with danger. Craziness becomes normal, and life without chaos may seem boring. They may grow up without

---

5. Alice Miller (1985) writes, "Parents who have never known love, who on coming into the world met with coldness, indifference, and blindness and whose entire childhood and youth were spent in this atmosphere, are unable to bestow love—indeed, how can they, since they have no idea of what love is and can be?" (p. 2).

recognizing healthy love. In one well-known definition, "Love is patient and kind; love is not jealous or boastful; it is not arrogant or rude; it is not irritable or resentful; it does not rejoice at wrong, but rejoices in right. Love bears all things, believes all things, hopes all things, endures all things" (1 Corinthians 13: 4–7).

Although borderline mothers may love their children as much as other mothers, their deficits in cognitive functioning and emotional regulation create behaviors that undo their love. Borderline mothers have difficulty loving their children patiently and consistently. Their love does not endure misunderstandings or disagreements. They can be jealous, rude, irritable, resentful, arrogant, and unforgiving. Healthy love is based on trust and is the essence of emotional security. Their children, therefore, may grow up without knowing the meaning of healthy love.

Things never get back to normal for children with borderline mothers. As Linehan (1993b) explains, "Over time, children and caregivers shape and reinforce extreme . . . behaviors in each other" (p. 58). Children of borderlines may tune out by dissociating and disconnecting from their environment. They cannot feel embarrassed, humiliated, ridiculed, or hurt if they are no longer in their own bodies. Unfortunately, the sensation of depersonalization or dissociation makes them feel crazy.

Borderline mothers may subtly imply or blatantly accuse their children of being crazy, with statements like "There is something wrong with your head," or "You are out of your mind," or "You're crazy!" They project their own disorganized thinking onto their children, and eventually their children may give up the battle to maintain their sanity. Christina Crawford (1997) describes the child's descent into madness: "You just ease into being crazy . . . it doesn't happen overnight. . . . You get tired of the constant battle with no victories. You become exhausted hoping for the cease fire. . . . You lose your grip on the world slowly and drift into the chasm of your own hopelessness" (p. 181).

Laura suffered from depersonalization for a twelve-month period during middle school. She told no one about her feelings of unreality and suffered silently, having mastered the ability to pretend that everything was fine. She was living a fairy tale, pretending to be happy in a make-believe world. She had become Alice:

> "You know very well you're not real."
> "I *am* real!" said Alice, and began to cry.
> "You won't make yourself a bit realler by crying," Tweedledee remarked: "there's nothing to cry about."

Children of borderlines have been down the rabbit hole. They have heard the Queen of Hearts order everyone beheaded. They have attended the mad tea party and argued with the Duchess for the right to think their own thoughts. They grow weary of feeling big one minute and small the next.[6]

---

6. Two years after publishing *Alice's Adventures in Wonderland*, "Lewis Carroll" (Charles Dodgson) told a friend that the story was about "malice," which is why so many children of borderlines do not enjoy reading it. They live it. For a thorough analysis of Carroll's hidden anagrams, see Richard Wallace's (1990) *The Agony of Lewis Carroll*. Wallace states: "Analyzing the works of Charles Dodgson as others have done leads one in many directions because he built a complex web of real meaning within a structure of nonsense" (p. 19).

2

The Darkness Within

Alice had not a moment to think about stopping herself before she found herself falling down what seemed to be a very deep well.

—*Alice's Adventures in Wonderland*

"I want you to listen to something. I need to know what you think." Amanda pulled a small tape recorder out of her purse.

"Mother called yesterday and I taped our conversation. I feel so confused after I talk to her, I don't know what to think. . . ."

The twisted, fragmented conversation was difficult to follow. Her mother's train of thought frequently derailed with incomplete sentences trailing off into tangents. The borderline's stream of thought can rush or ramble like a river, bending and twisting, flowing endlessly through the same gorge and over the same stones. On the tape Amanda sounded uninterested and annoyed, as if her mother was talking nonsense.

Without indicating whom she had in mind, her mother abruptly asked, "What *was* that girl's name?" When Amanda inquired, "What girl?" her mother snapped back, "You know *exactly* who I'm talking about! Don't play that game with me!" Amanda tolerated conversations with her mother by shutting down, with-drawing into herself. Shutting down, closing up, and "going in" are instinctual, life-saving responses to threatening conditions. The borderline's tendency to blow hot and cold and suddenly lash out can catch her children off guard. Tidal waves emerge without warning, sweeping children away by gale-force rage. Naturally, borderline mothers may accuse their children of not listening, and telephone conversations frequently end abruptly with one party hanging up on the other.

Amanda envied her friends who enjoyed close, positive relation-ships with their mothers. Cristin Clark (in Ellis 1999) describes her relationship with an "ideal" mother in *Blessings of a Mother's Love*: "The greatest gift my mother has given me is the belief that I can accomplish anything I pursue. Her words of encouragement have helped me through the most difficult times in my life. She is my biggest supporter and my best friend. Her belief in me is my inspiration to try new things. . . . Her unconditional love is truly a blessing" (p. 28).

Few mothers are ideal mothers. All mothers have personality defects. The borderline mother's fear of abandonment, however, may consistently interfere with her child's need to separate. In Amanda's case, simply expressing her own thoughts could threaten her mother and trigger hostility. By replaying their taped conver-sation, Amanda was able to hear her mother's disordered mind. For the first time in her life, she considered the possibility that she was not to blame for her mother's unhappiness, and the oppressive veil of guilt began to lift.

Although no two borderline mothers are the same, clusters of symptoms reflect varying levels of functioning (see Table 2–1).

A personality disorder is a pattern of abnormal thoughts and behavior that impairs relationships with others. Personality disorders cut across all social classes, educational levels, and professions. Individuals with borderline personality disorder have different combinations of

TABLE 2–1.
VARIATIONS IN MATERNAL FUNCTIONING

The Ideal Mother	The Borderline Mother
1. Comforts her child	1. Confuses her child
2. Apologizes for inappropriate behavior	2. Does not apologize or remember inappropriate behavior
3. Takes care of herself	3. Expects to be taken care of
4. Encourages independence in her children	4. Punishes or discourages independence
5. Is proud of her children's accomplishments	5. Envies, ignores, or demeans her children's accomplishments
6. Builds her children's self-esteem	6. Destroys, denigrates, or undermines self-esteem
7. Responds to her children's changing needs	7. Expects children to respond to her needs
8. Calms and comforts her children	8. Frightens and upsets her children
9. Disciplines with logical and natural consequences	9. Disciplines inconsistently or punitively
10. Expects that her children will be loved by others	10. Feels left out, jealous or resentful if the child is loved by someone else
11. Never threatens abandonment	11. Uses threats of abandonment (or actual abandonment) to punish the child
12. Believes in her children's basic goodness	12. Does not believe in her children's basic goodness
13. Trusts her children	13. Does not trust her children

symptoms, complicating identification of the disorder. Thus, any five out of the following nine criteria are used to determine the existence of BPD (summarized from the APA 1994):

1. Frantic efforts to avoid real or imagined abandonment
2. A pattern of unstable and intense relationships
3. Unstable self-image or sense of self
4. Impulsiveness, and behavior that could be self-destructive (spending, sex, substance abuse, reckless driving, binge eating)
5. Suicidal gestures, threats, or self-mutilating behavior (hitting, cutting, burning oneself)
6. Intense moodiness, rapid mood changes
7. Feelings of emptiness
8. Inappropriate, intense anger
9. Stress-induced paranoid thoughts or dissociative symptoms (loses touch with reality)

Many borderlines do not self-mutilate or threaten suicide. Some borderlines never abuse drugs because they have a fear of taking medication. Not all borderlines express anger toward others; some direct anger only at themselves. *As individuals, borderlines have their own unique combination of symptoms and vary in their level of functioning.*

CHARACTER PROFILES
OF BORDERLINE MOTHERS

Although all borderlines experience fear, helplessness, emptiness, and anger, one of these emotional states may dominate the personality. As with the ingredients in a recipe, the main ingredient or emotional state determines the texture, or feel, of the individual. The dominant emotional state shapes the person's character and may reflect the most pervasive and unmanageable feeling experienced in childhood. Four types of borderline mothers are described from a child's perspective and are discussed in greater detail in subsequent chapters of this book. *Borderline mothers may exhibit characteristics of more than one character type, as traits of one type may be found in another.*

James Masterson (1988), an internationally renowned expert on borderline patients, compares their stories to the two classic folk-tales *Snow White and the Seven Dwarfs* and *Cinderella.* Although borderline mothers can be enchanting, their children stand as helpless witnesses to the darkness within. The angst of borderline mothers is pain born from their own childhood. Their children, consequently, live a never-ending story of pity mixed with fear. The four types of borderline mothers are the Waif, the Hermit, the Queen, and the Witch. These categories are designed merely to aid identification of the disorder and are not mutually exclusive.

The Waif Mother

The darkness within the borderline Waif is helplessness. Her inner experience is victimization, and her behavior evokes sympathy and caretaking from others. Like Cinderella, the Waif can be misleading as she can appear to have it together for a short time. Internally, she feels like an impostor, and even if invited to the ball, feels unworthy. The Waif, like Cinderella, was a victim of childhood abuse or neglect, was treated as inferior, or was emotionally denigrated. The Waif's emotional message to her children is: *Life is too hard.*

The Hermit Mother

The darkness within the borderline Hermit is fear. Her behavior evokes anxiety and protection from others. Like Snow White, the Hermit feels like a frightened child hiding from the world. The Hermit fears letting anyone in because she was hurt by someone she trusted.

She is vigilant about watching for danger and may be superstitious. The Hermit's emotional message to her children is: *Life is too dangerous.*

The Queen Mother

The darkness within the borderline Queen is emptiness. Her inner experience is deprivation and her behavior evokes compliance. She is demanding and flamboyant and may intimidate others. The Queen feels entitled to exploit others and can be vindictive and greedy. The Queen's emotional message to her children is: *Life is "all about me."*

The Witch Mother

The darkness within the borderline Witch is annihilating rage. Her inner experience is the conviction of being evil, and her behavior evokes submission. The Witch can hide in any of the other three profiles as a temporary ego-state. She is filled with self-hatred and may single out one child as the target of her rage. The Witch's emotional message to her children is: *Life is war.*

The Medean Mother is the most pathological (and rarest) type of Witch.

Recognizing individuals with borderline personality disorder is difficult because:

1. Borderlines seem normal to casual acquaintances.
2. Borderlines have unique symptom clusters.
3. Borderlines are different with different people, including their own children.
4. Borderlines have different external or public personalities.
5. Borderlines function well in structured environments and in specific roles.

Joan Crawford exhibited traits of a borderline Queen. Borderline Queens seem strong, determined, confident, and can be
intimidating. Despite her royal position, Princess Diana exhibited
traits of a borderline Waif, whose underlying feelings of helplessness
evoked sympathy and concern. She admitted, "I am much closer to
people at the bottom than to people at the top" (Smith 1999, p. 9).
Like Cinderella, the glass slipper fit Diana beautifully, but she
would never be comfortable wearing it. Biographer Sally Bedell
Smith explains: "The fairy tale, it was clear, had gone horribly
wrong. The royal love match turned out to be a sad tale of adultery,
mental illness, betrayal, mistrust, and revenge" (p. 14).

Apparent Normality

In 1942, Helene Deutsch wrote an article that led to the discovery
of BPD. Her description of "as-if" personalities identifies the
borderline's ability to behave as if she is normal in order to
compensate for an inadequate sense of self. Deutsch observed that
"the first impression these people make is of complete normality . . . It is like the performance of an actor who is technically
well trained but who lacks the necessary spark to make his imper-
sonations true to life" (p. 303). Behind their apparent competence
and public persona lie deeply troubled souls.

Thornton (1998) states: "borderlines function quite well in some
types of careers and situations. Where there is structure, they excel.
This is one reason it takes them a long time to recognize a problem,
unless someone notes their more dangerous behavior . . ." (p.
22). Gunderson (1984) explains that borderlines are compulsively
social because their sense of self depends on their relationships with
others. Smith (1999) writes, "one measure of [Princess] Diana's
insecurity was her habit of carrying as many as four mobile phones

in her pocketbook and . . . spending nearly every free minute of the day on the telephone" (p. 279).

Borderlines are often popular among those who do not know them well. In high school, Laura's mother was a member of the National Honor Society and Student Council. A biographer (Guiles 1995) stated that Joan Crawford "was forever worried about her image, about how she was perceived by others" (p. 75). She was, indeed, convincing to those who did not experience her dark side. Her personal secretary once said, "she was a star from the beginning. You would always notice her right away . . . I never saw her really be cruel to anybody, except some of the maids that she used to get angry with" (p. 87). Similarly, even those closest to Princess Diana seemed not to recognize her inner turmoil: "it was Diana's dazzling public persona that lulled even her friends and family into disbelieving that anything could be seriously wrong with her—a common fate of the borderline" (Smith 1999, p. 12).

Different Relationships with Different Children

Borderline mothers have difficulty allowing their children to grow up. The dependency of a newborn can be intensely satisfying to the borderline mother, but as the child becomes increasingly independent, conflict erupts. According to Daniel Stern (1985), the infant develops an "emergent self" during the first two months of life, and gradually learns to recognize the difference between self and mother (p. 75). The relationship between a borderline mother and her child may change dramatically when the child is approximately 2 years old, begins to speak, and expresses a separate will. The mother's anxiety intensifies because the child is no longer totally dependent and cannot be completely controlled. When the borderline mother recognizes the child's separateness, separation anxiety is triggered and different parts of her personality are split off and projected onto the child.

Christina Crawford and her brother had a different relationship with their mother than their younger sisters. Guiles writes: "To an observer, the situation ranged from one extreme to the other—the younger children rarely strayed far from Joan's side, while Christina and Christopher seemed locked in a never-ending struggle to escape their mother's tyranny, whether real or imagined" (1995, p. 144).

Adult children of borderlines may experience conflict with siblings who have different perceptions of the same mother. One patient lamented that her brother accused her of neglecting their elderly mother. The patient had been abused by her mother and minimized contact to reduce the possibility of conflict. Her brother, however, was the designated all-good child, and shared his mother's negative perceptions of his sister. Thus, conflicts are common among siblings who have different relationships with the same borderline mother.

Children who are perceived as all-good are typically loyal and protective of their mother. No-good children, such as Christina Crawford and her brother, may be cut off, ostracized, and estranged. After her mother's death, Christina (Crawford 1988) learned that she and her brother had been cut out of her mother's will and that her younger sister had been given significantly less money than her twin. Loyalty is richly rewarded whereas the price of betrayal is symbolic beheading—the child is completely cut off.

The consequences of betrayal so frighten children that they may have difficulty speaking about their mother. Upon entering therapy, adult children of borderlines are initially reluctant to discuss their childhood experiences. Several patients developed psychosomatic symptoms such as feeling a lump in their throat or experienced panic attacks following sessions during which they discussed their mother. Disclosing negative feelings is painful and is often accompanied by disclaimers such as, "I feel guilty saying this but . . ." or "most of the time it really wasn't that bad . . ."

The issue of betrayal is critical to understanding the dynamics between borderline mothers and their children. The borderline's sensitivity to betrayal results in paranoid accusations, annihilating rage, and abandonment of the offending party. Because borderline mothers can misperceive a child's normal need to separate as betrayal, children learn to deny, disavow, or repress their feelings in order to survive. All-good children may stay merged and unable to separate from mother. No-good children may distance themselves completely, although they are more likely to continue a conflicted relationship. It is rare for even adult children to abandon their mother, regardless of how many times their mother has abandoned them.

HOW BPD DEVELOPS: THE ORIGIN OF DARKNESS

Every borderline mother has a dark place in her heart. In the Waif, it is a sad and lonely place. In the Hermit, it is a frightening place. In the Queen, it is an empty space. In the Witch, it is a place that is black with hate. A 6-year-old child of a borderline mother once mourned, "Mommy only loves me with part of her heart." It is true that the borderline mother cannot love with all of her heart. Part of her heart was broken when *she* was a child.

Therapists find that borderline patients have had one or more of the following experiences:

1. Inadequate emotional support following parental abandonment through death or divorce;
2. Parental abuse, emotional neglect, or chronic denigration;
3. Being the no-good child of a borderline mother.

Given these factors, however, it is impossible to predict who will develop BPD because experience, by itself, does not cause a personality disorder. The experiences mentioned above place children at risk for BPD, but other factors can increase or decrease the chances of developing serious personality disturbance.

Children can be exposed to a variety of traumatic experiences and yet develop healthy personalities given certain circumstances. Studies indicate that the single most important factor affecting resiliency in children is the conviction of being loved (Werner 1988). The effects of parental abandonment, abuse, and neglect can be mitigated if children have access to a relationship with a loving adult such as a teacher, a minister, a neighbor, or a relative who is empathically attuned to the child's feelings.

One way of understanding how BPD develops in the aftermath of a given trauma is to consider the degree to which the child's emotional needs were met. When feelings regarding traumatic experiences are not worked through, emotional growth is stunted. Balint (1968) proposed that personality is influenced not only by traumatic events but by the degree of psychological support received from significant others. Therefore, parents must allow the child to express intense emotion in order to prevent repression of the feelings. *Very often, the traumatic experience is never discussed, let alone worked through.*

The loss of a parent through death or divorce is traumatic for children. Understandably, parents can be devastated by these experiences as well. Typically, children repress their own sadness, anger, and guilt in order to support their parents. If the child's feelings are not expressed, unexpressed grief can form an underground volcano. Parents who are emotionally preoccupied, overworked, and struggling to survive may not recognize the child's distress until minor events trigger cataclysmic reactions.

All children have the following emotional needs:

1. *To be held* (to be enveloped by safe, loving arms)
2. *To be mirrored* (to see a positive reflection of themselves in their parents' eyes)
3. *To be soothed* (to be comforted, reassured, and protected)
4. *To be given* some *control* (to elicit predictable responses to expressed needs).

Therapists have the opportunity to study the effects of trauma retrospectively. With hindsight, it seems clear that the degree to which a child's emotional needs were met following a traumatic experience determines whether or not serious personality problems develop. Understanding the borderline's inner experience, therefore, requires understanding her early experience and the feelings that were repressed.

Bowlby (1973) hypothesized that separation anxiety, grief and mourning, and defense are necessary and normal parts of attachment. He explained that anxious attachment patterns develop as a result of early abandonment, and that early experiences of loss through death, divorce, or emotional neglect trigger a fear of abandonment. As an adult, the borderline mother's behavior reflects the degree to which her emotional needs were unmet as a child and the way in which caregivers responded to her. For example, children whose parents divorce often are told, "You'll be all right, don't cry. You're a big girl. Just because Daddy is leaving doesn't mean that he doesn't love you. You'll still get to see him." Children are told how to feel instead of being allowed to express their own feelings. Healthier responses include, "You have a right to be upset about what has happened. You will have many different feelings that I want you to tell me about. Please, please, please come to me anytime and tell me how you feel. I will always take time to listen, to hold you, and let you scream and cry and tell me how you feel. It's normal to be upset when something upsetting happens in life." Unbearable pain that is expressed and acknowledged becomes bearable. But borderlines received no such responses in their childhood. Therefore, they are stuck in the past, trying to elicit what they needed as a child—validation of their unbearable pain.

Like a broken record, the borderline's behavior seems compulsively driven, with the aim of eliciting what she lacked as a child. The Waif needed to be held, the Hermit needed to be soothed, the Queen needed to be mirrored, and the Witch needed control. Although no child's emotional needs can be met perfectly, the degree to which these needs are met significantly influences personality development.

Joan Crawford's father abandoned her mother before Joan was born. She once stated, "Due to an incident in my childhood, I didn't dare trust anyone" (Thomas 1978, p. 78). Princess Diana was abandoned by her mother at age 6 and once told a friend, "I will always remember [my mother] packing her evening dresses into the car and saying, 'Darling, I'll come back.' I sat on the steps waiting for her to return but she never did" (Smith 1999, p. 19). Apparently, Princess Diana sat by herself, alone in her sorrow. A child who is left alone following abandonment yearns for someone to notice her so that she might be held and comforted. How tragic that the whole world would one day know the pain of losing an elegant mother who left in a car and never returned.

Biographical information regarding Joan Crawford's childhood suggests that following her father's abandonment her mother was consumed with issues of survival. Joan Crawford's success as an actress resulted from raw determination not to re-experience the pain of her childhood deprivation. Unmet needs for mirroring consumed her and she never again allowed herself to need anyone who might reject her.

Linehan (1993b) suggests that the key factor that leads to the development of BPD is an "emotionally invalidating environment." She states:

An invalidating environment is one in which communication of private experiences is met by erratic, inappropriate, and extreme responses. In other words, the expression of private experiences is not validated; instead it is often punished, and/or trivialized . . . Invalidation has two primary characteristics. First, it tells the individual that she is wrong in both her description and her analyses of her own experiences, particularly in her views of what is causing her own emotions, beliefs and actions. Second, it attributes her experiences to socially unacceptable characteristics or personality traits. . . . [pp. 49–51]

When a child's feelings are not expressed or validated following loss or trauma, grief is never worked through. The child feels emotionally orphaned and represses the pain of the loss. Unfortunately, abandonment followed by invalidation of the child's feelings is a recipe for disaster.

In the absence of an emotionally attuned caregiver, children who experience chronic denigration are at risk for developing BPD. Physical, sexual, and emotional abuse are inherently denigrating. Other denigrating experiences can include being teased, ridiculed, humiliated, embarrassed, and harassed. Children who experience denigration and live in an invalidating environment are destined to develop serious personality problems. Chronic denigration can destroy even an emotionally healthy adult's self-esteem. Denigration of a child can destroy the soul before self-esteem has a chance to develop.

Linehan (1993b) explains that invalidating environments do not allow the expression of painful or negative emotions. Invalidating families teach children that pretending to be happy is more important than being happy, and that talking about how you really feel only makes things worse. Unfortunately, the kind of invalidating interactions described by Linehan are typical of many borderline mothers. The no-good child who is the target of the mother's rage therefore is at risk for developing BPD. No-good children are unable to break free from their mothers' negative projections. Tragically, death may become an appealing escape. An adolescent patient who was the no-good child of a borderline mother wrote:

> What does she want from me? How can I fulfill her dreams and make her happy? Just tell me. I'm dying to do it . . . *dying*. I'll be her perfect daughter. I'll be her perfect everything. I'm just dying to. I know she doesn't want me around. I can just disappear. Please believe me. I'll be quiet. I'll be good. She won't even know I'm here. She won't even know that I'm dying. She won't even know that I'm really already just dead.

Unjustly accused, the no-good child is sentenced without trial, held without bond, and may feel imprisoned for life.

Therapists sometimes warn family members not to depend on the person with BPD to validate their self-worth, yet young children have no choice. They can and will do anything to hold onto the good mother (the loving, caring person) who unpredictably turns into the Witch mother (the terrifying, raging beast). As they mature, the conflicts created by their need to separate often intensify.

Children of borderlines may wish they had a different mother as much as borderline mothers wish they themselves could be different. Many borderlines seek treatment when they realize how destructive their behavior is to their children.

> [A borderline mother reported that her daughter's first sentence was "Is mommy okay?" The mother explained,] "When I even pretend to cry, her eyes well up with tears . . . When I am happy and beginning to pull out of the black pit, she grows and changes at lightning speed, as if to make up for the time she lost trying to cope within my shadow. I am determined to get through this horror so I

can be a real mommy, not a burden to her." [Mason and Kreger 1998, p. 182]

Children raised by borderlines may spend their childhood balanced on the edge of disaster and may suffer from anxiety for the rest of their lives.

Although BPD can develop from a variety of circumstances, being raised by a borderline mother places children at risk for developing BPD. Borderline mothers may invalidate their children's emotional experience, denigrate the no-good child, parentify the all-good child, and emotionally or physically abandon their children. Early intervention with borderline mothers and their children is essential in preventing the spread of this devastating disorder.

BRAIN FUNCTIONING AND BPD

Brain development after birth involves a process of wiring and rewiring the connections among neurons. Early experiences shape the pattern of wiring and cause the number of synapses (the connections between nerve cells) to increase or decrease by as much as 25 percent (Turner and Greenough 1985). Studies (Heit et al. 1999) of the long-term effects of stress on the brain indicate that, "early stress can produce different kinds of neurological change with different consequences" (p. 5). Therefore, borderlines such as the Waif, whose early childhood experiences created overwhelming sadness, may be more depressed than fearful. Borderlines such as the Hermit, whose early experiences created fear, become hyperperceptive of danger. Le Doux (1996) states that, "Unconscious fear memories established through the amygdala appear to be indelibly burned into the brain. They are probably with us for life" (p. 252). Although emotional regulation is a problem for all borderlines, the specific emotion that dominates an individual personality seems to vary.

Stone (in Cauwels 1992) explains that "when a borderline feels stressed and threatened, the habit memory system easily bypasses the cognitive and frontal lobe influence . . . She is like a soldier in a jungle, shooting first and then asking questions" (p. 219).[1] Aiming at her own child, however, has tragic consequences. Once the shot is fired, the child's trust is shattered.

BPD, like Post-Traumatic Stress Disorder (PTSD), may be the natural consequence of the brain's response to emotional stress. The impaired judgment and impulsivity of the borderline may be linked with deficits in the functioning of the amygdala, the part of the brain responsible for the fight-or-flight response (Schacter 1996). Thus, the mind of the borderline malfunctions like a traffic light stuck on red or green. She may stop and go at the wrong times, unable to rely on the information relayed by her brain. Malfunctioning signals in traffic or in the brain can cause confusion, injury, or death if the individual is unaware that the signal is faulty. Helping the borderline mother, therefore, requires cooperation among neuroscientists, psychiatrists, and clinicians.

One borderline patient, a 50-year-old daughter of a borderline mother, sought medical treatment to discern the cause of her cognitive difficulties. She reported that no psychotropic medication improved her mood or cognitive functioning. After seeing numerous specialists and receiving conflicting opinions, the patient was admitted to a well-known medical center. None

---

1. Cauwels refers to Michael H. Stone's discussion during the symposium on "Borderline Personality: Impulse Spectrum Disorder" at the 143rd annual meeting of the American Psychiatric Association, New York, May 16, 1990 in her 1992 book *Imbroglio: Rising to the Challenges of Borderline Personality Disorder.*

of the physicians questioned the patient regarding exposure to chronic stress during childhood. Apparently, they were unaware of the research linking cognitive and emotional difficulties with PTSD and childhood abuse. The patient, however, discovered a dramatic improvement in functioning when taking steroids for bronchitis months later. Amazed and delighted, she announced, "Now I know how normal people feel." Her cognitive problems and depression returned, however, when the treatment regime ended. Understanding the brain chemistry of BPD may require an interdisciplinary approach, providing an exciting frontier for collaboration between clinicians and researchers.

TREATING THE BORDERLINE MOTHER

Although most researchers maintain that borderlines cannot be cured, they agree that they can learn to control their behavior and significantly improve the quality of their lives. Some studies (Gunderson 1984) suggest that a minimum of four years of therapy three to four times a week is needed, and that the typical duration is between six and ten years. Successfully treated borderline patients are better able to control their behavior, anticipate consequences, and reduce self-destructive tendencies. Behavioral change is possible, thus significantly increasing the quality of relationships with others. *Borderlines, however, need access to long-term treatment.*

Psychotherapy for the adult borderline is a lifelong need and provides structure, insight, and management rather than cure. Loss, separation, or stress can trigger a crisis that brings the borderline into (or back to) treatment. Borderlines may learn to control their behavior, but the underlying feelings of helplessness, emptiness, fear, and rage appear to be immutable. Realistic expectations regarding treatment, therefore, are essential. The borderline must learn to compensate for damage to the hippocampus, the part of the brain responsible for memory functioning, and the amygdala, the part of the brain that controls the fight-or-flight response. Borderlines, like individuals with other kinds of disabilities, can learn to compensate for memory difficulties and to mitigate emotional reactions.

Knowing the proper diagnosis is the first step to treatment. Some therapists are reluctant to inform the patient or family of the diagnosis of BPD. Yet growth cannot occur without understanding. Patients with BPD have a right to the truth just as much as patients who suffer from other incurable, life-threatening conditions, especially since over 10 percent of individuals with BPD commit suicide (Cauwels 1992). Just as the diabetic must learn to manage sugar intake and output, the individual with BPD must learn to manage emotional input and output. Psychotherapy, combined with antianxiety and antidepressant medications, can significantly enhance the borderline's quality of life. In her book *The Talking Cure* (1997) Susan Vaughan explains how long-term therapy reroutes the brain's neurons and creates permanent changes in self-perception. Medication does not replace the need for a therapeutic relationship.

Linehan (1993b) developed a treatment approach for borderlines called "Dialectical Behavior Therapy." Her approach uses validation to reward the patient for behavioral change. Validation is the antidote for denigration and is the glue that repairs a fragmented self. When faced with rejection, failure, or abandonment, a healthy individual feels disappointment and sadness without experiencing disintegration of the self. Healthy individuals can withstand rejection and failure because they have had enough previous validation to maintain self-esteem.

Understanding that borderlines' traumatic childhood experiences altered their brain chemistry legitimizes their suffering and validates their internal experience. However, they must learn how to compensate for deficits in cognitive and emotional functioning.

It is ironic that the silence surrounding BPD re-creates the early experience of pretending that nothing is wrong. Like most clinicians, Linehan acknowledges the difficulty of treating borderlines. She explains that change is slow and frustrating, and warns therapists and family members to be prepared for a rocky road. Although the road is long and hard, the journey is well worth taking.

Masterson (1988) stresses the importance of early intervention for children of borderlines who may exhibit borderline symptoms during adolescence. His studies offer encouraging findings regarding the long-term outcome of borderline adolescents, most of whom have borderline mothers.

The behavior of the borderline mother can be as frightening to her as it is to her children. The vicious cycle of self-hatred is reinforced every time she behaves destructively. The good mother within the borderline would never dream of hurting her children. But when the Witch emerges, anything is possible. As Masterson (1980) explains: "[the borderline] is drowning in his struggle: he is floundering in this stormy sea, unable to swim, he cries out for help as he is about to go down for the third and perhaps last time . . . [Treatment] is as much a true rescue operation as the action of the lifeguard who dashes into the water with a life preserver" (p. 49). The earlier treatment begins, the greater likelihood of success. If left untreated, the borderline mother and her child can drown together.

3

The Waif Mother

The poor girl retired to her dismal kitchen, and could not help weeping as she sat there, thinking over her sisters' cruelty.

—Ashputtle [Cinderella]

"I'm so alone. Doomed to a life in solitary. The silence is deafening. I rail against the darkness but yet there it is. And now there's the void staring me in the face . . . the yawning mouth of the abyss . . . the unending sense of loneliness and failure. I could not have possibly belonged to such a fine, upstanding family—not me."

Her journal entry could have been Cinderella's.

"I hate being so lonely. What is wrong with me? What is this feeling of desperation? Is it really God's will that I suffer, bereft of any male companionship?"

The despairing words were written in "A Woman's Notebook." Angela left the journals for me to read, to help me understand her.

"It's hard when you're alone, not to feel annihilated. Oh my lonely, aging body—loving so futilely, so lonesomely—this empty shell trying to love again. God—what indignities the flesh/soul/spirit endures. I won't be destroyed! I must somehow hold my breaking heart together so it can go on beating."

The depth of her despair was frightening.

"I'm trying so hard to mend the broken pieces that I'm grabbing anything that looks like it might hold the glue."

The words looked as if they were sliding off the page, going over the edge. She recorded how much alcohol she drank each night; her handwriting reflected the level of intoxication. Angela was a borderline Waif.

The helplessness and hopelessness of the borderline Waif distinguish her from other borderlines. She feels cast adrift, lost in the sea of her own despair. She is a delicate creature, easily injured, with sharp edges concealed beneath her fragile exterior. When Angela is shattered, her words can feel like shards of glass. Angela struggled to understand herself, her life, and her loneliness.

The Waif is frequently victimized and evokes sympathy and concern from others. Although she can be socially engaging, she can quickly turn on those she needs, leaving friends and family members perplexed. The Waif projects her feelings of helplessness and victimization onto others. Discarded friends frequently ask themselves, "What did *I* do to deserve *this*?"

Angela was a divorced mother who alternately indulged and neglected her children. Bouts of depression periodically consumed her, leaving her children feeling abandoned. The vicious cycle of depression and withdrawal reinforced feelings of failure and hopelessness. Angela felt undeserving of her children's love.

All borderlines sense that they could drown in their own feelings and struggle to survive. The Waif grabs onto anything that might support her and keep her afloat. Traumatized by childhood abuse, abandonment, or neglect, she conceals her rage by sadness. When she is mishandled, her rage can take others by surprise.

Following her mother's death, Angela lived with her aunt and uncle, where she felt like an unwelcome guest. When she was 12, her uncle sexually molested her. Feelings of helplessness overwhelmed her, and fantasy became her escape. Books took her to fictional worlds where she discovered other lonely people like herself, heroes and heroines, and happy endings. Like many Waifs, Angela created a secret fantasy life that she rarely revealed to others. Fantasy is safer than reality for the borderline Waif.

The loneliness, depression, and despair of the Waif know no economic or historical boundaries. Charlotte du Pont, wife of an heir to the massive Du Pont armament and powder mill fortune of the 1800s, exhibited the traits of a borderline Waif (Mosley 1980). Although the nature of her mental illness was not understood during her lifetime, her behavior revealed the telltale symptoms of BPD. On March 6, 1861, she wrote her aunt a letter that is striking in its similarity to Angela's journal entries: "You know I have always disliked excessively to be alone, and now Fanny, my cousin so soon going to leave me, I will be entirely alone . . . this is very hard for me to bear, as I am very dependent upon company" (Mosley 1980, p. 52).

Charlotte du Pont's suffering is palpable in her letter to another family member: "I suppose I was born in darkness so thick that no lights could penetrate—so I have groped and stumbled in a slough of despond from which there is no extrication. May others be more fortunate" (p. 71). A relative described Charlotte as a "butterfly with a sting" (p. 55). She could be temperamental, flirtatious, venomous, bored, agitated, and seriously depressed. She provoked arguments with her husband and became violent, flinging vases, tearing down curtains, scratching, kicking and biting, after which she collapsed into a "stupor" (p. 55).

Charlotte du Pont was the mother of five children. Like Angela, she was an indulgent and loving mother, but frequently withdrew into depression. Eventually, Charlotte was sent to a Philadelphia asylum. After discharge, she returned home briefly, only to leave for a European trip. Upon returning to America, Charlotte discovered that a governess had physically abused her children during her absence. After promptly dismissing the governess, Charlotte collapsed, sobbing uncontrollably with grief and remorse. Her husband took her back to the asylum, "moaning and shrieking like the lost soul she was" (p. 73) where she died on August 19, 1877.

Of the many tragic aspects of Charlotte du Pont's life, none is more poignant than her utter despair over having failed to protect her children. Unable to care for herself, rejected by a powerful family, and grieving from familial losses in the Civil War, Charlotte died from her own brokenness. Her sense of personal failure, victimization, and rejection ultimately consumed her.

THE WAIF'S DOMINANT EMOTIONAL STATE: HELPLESSNESS

> [Cinderella] obeyed, but she wept, for she too would have liked to go dancing . . .
>
> — Cinderella

Like a butterfly caught in strong winds, the Waif feels powerless to choose direction or focus. In social situations she flits about, never connecting in depth. She can be inappropriately open, enticing others by too much self-disclosure, and then walking away with an air of indifference. She may fish for compliments and then reject them, seek attention and then hide, complain miserably and then refuse help.

The Waif leaves others feeling helpless. Unconsciously, she needs to stay helpless in order to feel safe. A patient once exclaimed, *"I can't allow myself to need your help and be in control at the same time."* This painfully honest disclosure captures the Waif's basic conflict.

The paradox of the Waif is that by accepting help she loses control. The Waif is a help-rejecting victim and helplessness is a defense against closeness and loss. A biographer (Smith 1999) remarked of Princess Diana: "One problem in offering Diana help was her combination of fragility and defensiveness. She wanted to be soothed, yet invariably rejected efforts to comfort her—especially when they came from Charles. Her silences, which often signaled reproach, were especially difficult to read, as they arose from Diana's inability to articulate what was troubling her" (p. 120).

Time after time, family members throw life preservers to the Waif and are bewildered when she throws them back. Standing on shore, those who love her wonder, "Does she *want* to drown?" The daughter of a borderline Waif wrote, "Sadness pummels me into silence. I just don't know what to say to her anymore. She is my mother. Of course I love her. I'm just so, so tired of trying to save her. I can barely save myself."

Joan Lachkar (1992) explains that borderlines who feel undeserving are prone to withdraw into isolation. The Waif is so prone to depression and withdrawal that others may find her undependable and at times exhausting. During these periods of solitary confinement she may self-mutilate or abuse substances. However, her self-destructiveness is hidden. If she self-mutilates, her scars are not likely to show. If she abuses alcohol, sex, drugs, or food, the behavior signifies resignation rather than the need for attention. When she wants to attract attention, she becomes hysterical.

The Waif seems unable to think through the consequences of her decisions. She sees herself as an incompetent failure, and is overly dependent on the approval of others. She misinterprets innocuous comments as criticism and rejects those who are critical before they reject her.

Rejection and abandonment trigger rage and depression. Although her rage may be directed at her children or partner, the Waif blames herself for her misfortune. She feels marked, doomed, struck with interminable bad luck, and is susceptible to breakdown. Because she has no underlying foundation of self-worth, she cannot tolerate minor mistakes, inconsequential failures, or mild disappointments. As Masterson (1988) explains, "Unlike a healthy man or woman who says, 'Well, this is one of those situations at which I'm not very good,' the false self [the borderline] says, 'You are totally helpless and good for nothing' " (p. 70).

The Waif's rich fantasy life leads her to read more into relationships with men than may exist. Therefore, she sets herself up for disappointment. Angela married her ex-husband when she was 18 in order to escape the loneliness of her life. Having survived victimization as a child, she believed it was safer to "take what you can get," never expecting to really be loved. In relationships, she gave too much too soon. The Waif allows herself to be exploited by men due to her desperate need to be loved. She may be unable to resist men who pay attention to her, regardless of their availability or appropriateness. Her vulnerability makes her an easy target for victimization. She may be openly or subtly seductive, or misread male attention. The borderline Waif is a hopeless romantic. Those who love her feel frustrated, annoyed, and occasionally, outraged by her behavior.

THE WAIF'S INNER EXPERIENCE: VICTIMIZATION

. . . she had to do all the work, getting up before daybreak, carrying water, lighting fires, cooking and washing. In addition, the sisters did everything they could to plague her.

—Cinderella

Like Cinderella, the Waif learned that submissive behavior was the most adaptive response to an oppressive environment. She survived her childhood by resigning herself to a hopeless situation, and her sense of security became paradoxically tied to resignation.

As an adult, the Waif resigns herself to the worst possible outcome before *it occurs.* In some cases, she increases her chances of victimization. In others, her reactions can throw others off guard. A man with a gun approached a patient as she was leaving a store, promising not to shoot her if she followed him to his car. She spitefully replied, "Look . . . if you're going to shoot me, just do it here. I'm not going anywhere with you." Her response startled the man, who expected her to comply out of fear. Instead, the gunman became frightened and fled from the store.

In another situation, a patient broke up a fight between two men by stepping in between them. She said, "Excuse me. Would either one of you like for me to call the police?" One of the bewildered men looked at her and said, "Lady, you must be crazy!" Because the Waif has unreliable fear responses and feels compelled to rescue others, she can easily become a victim. She sees herself as a loser who has nothing to lose.

The Waif has difficulty taking care of herself and her belongings; therefore, she is easily exploited. She feels incompetent, even though her intellectual capacity may be far above average. Because she relinquishes control too easily, she may die a victim's death.

The Waif's fragile demeanor evokes caretaking behavior from others. Friends and family members fear for her physical survival, and may extend vast amounts of financial and emotional support. They grow annoyed with her inability to protect herself from repeated exploitation, mishaps, and preventable illness. Her children can feel suffocated by her inability to take care of herself.

Like many Waifs, Angela never learned to nourish herself emotionally, and suffered from an eating disorder. Bingeing and purging reflected her shame and ambivalence about gratification. She simply could not take in or tolerate good feelings. She had to reject what she needed in order to protect herself from disappointment. She could not lose what she did not have.

For the Waif, having less feels safer than having more, as opposed to the borderline Hermit who hoards and the Queen who grabs. The Waif picks at crumbs, never expecting her own piece of cake, and will adamantly refuse it if offered. Although she rarely asks for what she wants, she is resentful when her needs are not met.

The Waif's vulnerability is apparent in her tentative demeanor. She has difficulty articulating her needs, is unnecessarily apologetic, and easily embarrassed. Because she does not trust others, she may identify more with children than with adults, with abandoned and neglected animals, or with victims of crime, disaster, or illness. Although she feels powerless to save herself, she feels compelled to save others.

CHARACTERISTICS OF THE WAIF MOTHER

Is too passive and permissive

The Waif is a passive, permissive mother who cannot see how her feelings of helplessness handicap her children. One Waif mother purchased a keg of beer for her daughter's fifteenth birthday party and allowed her to drive the car without a permit or license. The daughter refused to help out around the house, flunked out of school, and lived off the mother's meager income. Although resentful, the Waif mother was unable to recognize how she enabled her daughter's behavior.

The Waif's children may resent their mother's passivity or they may exploit it. Angela's daughter felt sorry for her mother and took over much of the housework. Her son, however, resented his mother's irresponsible behavior and was sometimes verbally abusive. Angela tolerated his behavior because she expected to be mistreated.

The Waif's children may question her judgment because she tolerates abuse. They may become overprotective because she is so easily victimized, choosing careers in helping professions such as medicine, social work, psychology, or psychiatry. As Ferenczi (1933) said, "A mother complaining of her constant miseries can create a nurse for life out of her child" (p. 166). Some adult children emotionally and financially support their Waif mothers.

The Waif's children can become victims themselves. The Waif's poor judgment may expose her children to dangerous situations, placing them at risk for neglect and for sexual or physical abuse by unreliable caregivers. Car accidents or household accidents can occur during periods of emotional withdrawal. The safety of the Waif's children, therefore, may depend on their ability to take care of themselves.

Invalidates her own competence, tends to be underemployed

The Waif does not see herself as competent regardless of her level of education, intelligence, or employment. She sees herself as a failure, a belief that can become self-fulfilling. Her tendency to invalidate her own competency has a negative impact on young children who do not have the ability to distinguish reality from their mother's distorted beliefs. The Waif's low self-esteem pervades all areas of her life, creating feelings of failure as a parent, a partner, and an employee. She is much brighter and more capable than she perceives herself to be and is often underemployed.

Waifs are drawn to helping professions because they identify with those who are mistreated, disadvantaged, or oppressed. They tend to be dedicated employees who work long hours and are generally underpaid. They often feel trapped in their jobs and may be exploited by the corporations or companies for which they work.

The Waif's children may internalize the message of not being good enough and may underestimate their own competency. Although Angela's daughter, Sara, had hoped to become a physician, Angela made no arrangements to finance her education. Sara worked part-time in a nursing home during high school and eventually attended nursing school. The Waif's underemployment can reduce financial resources and limit educational opportunities.

Suffers from chronic or recurrent illnesses, makes frequent medical visits, or completely neglects her health

Parentified children feel responsible for their parent's well-being and repress their own emotional needs. Other children may resent their mother's dependency. Sara was chronically anxious about her mother's physical complaints, whereas David was cynical and resentful. As adults, the Waif's children may become either emotionally detached or consumed with worry.

Charlotte du Pont's eldest daughter, Anna, was frequently assigned the role of caretaker for her four younger siblings. Charlotte's husband had a fatal aneurysm when he learned that his wife had died, leaving Anna and her siblings suddenly orphaned. Rather than be adopted by various family members, the children armed themselves with weapons and refused to be removed from their home. Anna was 17 when her parents died and insisted that she was capable of caring for the younger siblings. She did, in fact, prove to be a competent surrogate mother. Their biographer states: "The unhappy circumstances in which they had been raised had knitted them together into a unit bound by mutual suffering and adversity" (Mosley 1980, p. 80). The Waif's children learn how to care for themselves because their mother is overwhelmed by life.

Uses drugs, alcohol, money, food, and/or sex to self-soothe

The Waif may cope with feelings of helplessness by abusing drugs, alcohol, food, money, and/or sex. She is susceptible to addictive behavior because of her chronic need to reduce anxiety. Her all-or-nothing thinking results in widely fluctuating behavior that confuses her children.

Angela's children were concerned about her poor judgment and disapproved of her seductiveness with men. When men took advantage of her either financially or sexually, her adolescent son could barely contain his resentment. When relationships ended, Angela plunged into deep depressions and struggled with suicidal feelings. Usually, it was Sara, her 12-year-old daughter, who worried the most at those times. David was angry and hurt that his mother "would try to kill herself over some 'jerk' and not even think about us, her own children."

Some borderline Waifs may be unconsciously seductive, while others may avoid any interactions with males that could be misinterpreted as sexual. Charlotte du Pont was described as flirtatious and seductive "until they discovered that Charlotte could suddenly change her mood. First petulant, then accusing, and finally almost viperish, she would round on them, a burst of high color flooding her cheeks and a bright flashing in her dark eyes, and accuse them of 'going too far' and 'wanting to make a fool out of [her husband]'" (Mosley 1980, p. 49).

Angela's journal entries indicated that she developed an addiction to alcohol as well as to prescription drugs. Sara resented her mother's substance abuse and was strongly opposed to the use of alcohol and drugs among her peers. David, however, abused both alcohol and drugs and was arrested for possession of marijuana. Thus, Angela's chemical dependency had a profound but contradictory impact on her children.

Some Waif mothers may spend more money on their children than on themselves. Angela was chronically in debt and limited her therapy sessions to twice a month in order to provide her children with designer clothes. Some Waif mothers cannot bear to see their children do without and may risk their own financial well-being to assure that their children are not deprived. They may impulsively indulge their children without considering the long-term consequences, failing to set aside money for their children's college education.

The Waif cannot allow herself the hope of being loved. She feels defective and worthless, expecting to be loved only superficially, if at all. The single, divorced Waif mother may seek sexual relationships with men in the attempt to self-soothe. With each new man Angela met and dated, she defended herself against expected disappointment: *"Is it really then good to be alive? I can see, oh but a little yet, but I can see a possibility that there is yet a life that is worth dying for—I may not ever experience it, but it glimmers, it glistens, it yet exists."*

The Waif may be aware of her neediness, her desperation for love, but she is unable to contain her anxiety, which eventually drives others away. She gives herself completely and then finds herself alone, abandoned. Angela wrote, *"Sometimes death does seem an acceptable alternative to the endless pain from what has become an almost boring repetition of situations."* The Waif's attempts to self-soothe through compulsive use of alcohol, drugs, money, food, or sex lead to increased guilt and depression.

Abandonment triggers suicidal feelings and desperate acts that can endanger the Waif and her children

When faced with rejection or abandonment the Waif experiences deep depression, which can include suicidal feelings or self-mutilation. The Waif may self-mutilate as punishment or to escape emotional pain. She may literally beat up on herself, cut herself, hit her head against the wall, or pull out her own hair. Abandonment can also trigger an overdose of alcohol or medication, or other impulsive behavior. Some Waifs may seek escape by driving at high speeds. Tragically, some children witness or rescue Waif mothers from life-threatening situations.

The Waif's fear of abandonment distorts her perceptions of interactions with others, and she frequently misinterprets interactions as rejection. Angela's journal entry below illustrates the extreme sensitivity to abandonment and the sudden plunge into despair: *"He said he would call and he didn't. He didn't actually say that he would call today but I took it (was hoping) that's what he meant. You must face the darkness again, unafraid and ready to do battle with it. It is coming/has come."*

Those who do not understand the intensity of the Waif's feelings may accuse her of being melodramatic—an error that could be fatal. Like many borderlines, Angela did not understand why relationships were so difficult for her: *"My relationships are like balls I was supposed to outfield. They'd rarely come my way and when they did I'd be so excited I'd grab too soon or overrun or misjudge or otherwise try to scramble for it only to have it slip through my fingers at best and at worst to have it hurt badly because I didn't have enough practice to know how to catch it."*

Abandonment can trigger suicidal feelings in the Waif. Angela's words describe the feeling clearly: *"Oh God, there's no one . . . no one . . . and my death would be mourned by no one."* The Waif's tendency to "forget" her children, to discount their love for her, is evident in Angela's writing. She became convinced that she was a burden to them and believed that her children would be relieved if she died.

The Waif's children may fear for their mother's survival, as well as their own. Shortly after Angela's husband announced his intention to divorce her, she loaded her two young children into the car and threatened to drive off a bridge. Although they were preschoolers at the time, David and Sara recalled vivid memories of the experience. Adult children of Waifs suffer from intense anxiety if their mothers were prone to such acts of desperation. It is important to remember, however, that not all Waifs self-mutilate or experience suicidal tendencies. Nevertheless, rejection or abandonment can trigger impulsive behavior that is unintentionally life threatening and can scare their children to death.

Is alternately indulgent and negligent with her children

The Waif feels undeserving of her children's love and is therefore indulgent and protective. Yet she is powerless to protect them from the pain that lives in her own heart. Some Waif mothers have been known to relinquish custody of their children to their ex-husbands because they did not feel like good-enough mothers. From their perspective, this is the ultimate act of self-sacrifice. From their child's perspective, it is abandonment.

Like all borderlines, the Waif is driven by her need to avoid abandonment. Thus, in her relationships with her children she is likely to secure their attachment through unlimited gratification. Whereas other types of borderline mothers can be controlling and rigid in their interactions with their children, the Waif relinquishes too much control and indulges them. As adults, her children may have difficulty interacting with authority figures, accepting "no" for an answer, or doing their fair share of work. Children who assumed the role of caregiver, however, may become compulsively self-sufficient.

Attachment researchers (West and Sheldon-Keller 1994) claim that the majority of mothers who had unhappy attachment experiences "do not break the cycle of passing on the effects of unhappy attachment experiences to their own children" (p. 51). The Waif's pattern of attachment to her children is marked by her fear of losing them. She may develop an anxious enmeshment with them, which in turn can impair her children's ability to form healthy relationships as adults. Charlotte du Pont's son, Alfred, was described as sad and moody, "driven into silence, and into himself, by the awful tension around the house" (Mosley 1980, p. 88). What the Waif's children need, of course, is a mother who takes care of herself as well as her children.

Is more likely to deprive rather than indulge herself

Although Kernberg (1985) explains that deprivation may be a defense against the fear of suffering, for the Waif, deprivation is a defense against the fear of hope. Hope hurts because it leads to disappointment. Angela explained, *"You cannot hope and then hope to survive, because you may not survive the hope or the dashing of it."*

The Waif is a Spartan, a minimalist who does not feel deserving of what she needs. Her inability to experience pleasure or gratification can annoy her children. Adult children may invite the Waif mother on vacation, buy her new clothes, or take her out to dinner, only to discover that she refuses the offer or is unable to enjoy the experience. Eventually, her children may stop giving her invitations or gifts. Nothing they do makes her happy.

Gunderson (1984) observes that borderlines frequently see themselves as victimized and mistreated. The Waif, in particular, revictimizes herself through deprivation and self-sacrificing behavior. Angela describes this sense of being trapped by her own self-defeating behavior: *"The strong bird of my soul rises occasionally to flap wildly, beating his wings fiercely inside his cage until they are broken and bruised and bloody, then sinks back in his cage until he has the energy to try to fly again."*

Linehan (1993a) explains that borderlines "often find it difficult to believe that they deserve anything other than punishment and pain" (p. 74). Angela's words are reminiscent of Charlotte du Pont's in a letter to her aunt: "I suppose I am justly cursed" (Mosley 1980, p. 57). The Waif feels cursed, destined for bad luck, misfortune, and suffering. She believes that she deserves to suffer.

Uses fantasy to escape reality and longs for a fairy-tale life

The Waif typically has a rich fantasy life. Her tragic, recurrent experiences of victimization leave her longing for a magical escape, for a fairy-tale ending to her misery. Her fantasy life is locked in her heart or in a private journal. Although she dreams of marrying Prince Charming, she chooses men who are emotionally unavailable. Her children may become cynical or they may share her sadness about her despair. An entry in Angela's journal reads: *"I wonder if I have a soul-mate. Such a delicious thought—that we all have a mental twin. My good angel . . . my prince, my knight. Will you love me enough to accept all of me? The good, the bad."*

The Waif's use of fantasy provides an escape from her desolate world. Louise Kaplan (1978) explains, "exalted when they imagine they are completely filled up and perfectly held . . . they feel humiliated and worthless when they fall from grace. They idealize those whom they can coerce into becoming the all-giving, perfectly holding partner who will sustain their image of self-perfection" (p. 42). Unfortunately, idealization quickly turns to disillusionment because real people are imperfect and disappointment must be tolerated.

Gives away, loses, or destroys good things— good things don't last

Because the Waif does not feel entitled to gratification, she may give to others what she herself needs. Waifs have an uncanny unconscious ability to destroy or lose valuable possessions. Pervasive helplessness leads to carelessness, which reinforces the Waif's belief that she does not deserve good things. She may forget to lock her car, lose her car keys, misplace her purse, misuse and break appliances, and inadvertently leave what she needs behind. Therapists may notice that used tissues often mark the Waif's trail of tears.

Trying to give the Waif hope can feel hopeless. Charlotte du Pont's aunt once sent her a religious book, trying to provide a source of hope. Charlotte wrote to her aunt: "Do not think me ungrateful, it would be sheer hypocrisy for me to read the words of Jesus when I have not entered a church or opened a Bible for 10 months and never intend to again . . . I suppose I am justly cursed but then it is hard to have nothing to care for and nothing to look forward to however I am pretty well accustomed to it" (Mosley 1980, p. 57). The Waif suffers from an inability to hope because she does not expect good things to last.

Waif mothers may also give things of value away because they believe others can better care for them. Angela understood why she did not expect good things to last. The brief happiness in her childhood was suddenly gone, and she blamed herself for her misery. Sadness felt safer than anger, and she resigned herself to a life of self-denial.

Charlotte du Pont's rages wreaked havoc on her personal belongings. The stupor that followed her outbursts was most likely a dissociative state in which she experienced intense self-hatred, guilt, and shame. Her behavior depicts the Waif's hopelessness. She gives up on herself.

*Suffers crying spells, depression, and panic attacks more
frequently than rage*

The borderline Waif is like a butterfly with a sting because she is as
delicate and vulnerable as she is biting and harsh. Her unhappiness
is evident to those who are close to her. Crying spells are easily
triggered by movies, articles, memories, casual conversation, or her
own thoughts. Tears flow frequently and easily, coming and going
without warning. Depression is her reliable companion. Panic
attacks and waves of anxiety may be triggered by social situations
but most likely occur when competency must be proven. Although
she may perform well in structured situations, the Waif battles
constant anxiety.

Because she blames herself for her problems, the Waif's anger is
likely to erupt less frequently than her sadness and anxiety. She is
more likely to become anxious, paranoid, and suspicious than to
become aggressive with others. Her partner is more likely than her
children to experience outbursts of rage. The Waif's children may
become immune to her tears, and to her ups and downs in
relationships. They may either minimize or discount her suffering
or feel manipulated by her mood swings.

Loss or abandonment can trigger psychotic reactions. Abandonment or rejection by her partner arouses rage in the Waif, as she
seeks to annihilate the one who failed to love her perfectly.
Psychosis in a Waif may involve paranoid thoughts, irrational fears
of persecution, and a terrifying sense of aloneness. Although the
Waif may experience psychotic rage, fear can also trigger the break
with reality. When Charlotte du Pont's previously hostile mother-
in-law offered to assist with the care of her children, Charlotte
reacted with unbridled rage and then sank into depression. Charlotte may have interpreted her mother-in-law's offer as a suggestion
that she was a failure as a mother. Her reaction nevertheless

illustrates the Waif's extreme vulnerability to criticism and suscep-
tibility to psychotic episodes.

Angela captures the essence of a psychotic break in this journal
entry:

> *Have I gone through the fire and this is what's left on the other side? A
> nothingness, a barren, still, calm plain of nothingness. Nothing is good.
> Nothing is bad, because all is nothing. I think except for my writing that I
> am or maybe partially experiencing a mild catatonia, a decompensation of
> self. I am not unhappy. How can you be unhappy when you do not feel? A
> pleasant state, actually, except I feel I cannot get out of bed.*

The Waif's depression engulfs her and threatens her very existence.
Charlotte du Pont was swept away from her own children by her
despair. Her biographer explained: "It was not so much that she
neglected her children—she often had periods when she was
passionately devoted to them—but *sometimes she forgot their existence*" (Mosley 1980, p. 70, emphasis added).

THE WAIF MOTHER'S MOTTO:
LIFE IS TOO HARD

Life *is* hard, but the Waif communicates the message to her children
that life is *overwhelmingly* hard, that it is hopeless to try to achieve
goals. The Waif tolerates life rather than enjoying it, and her
children may thus adopt her hopelessness and feelings of inadequacy. They may feel shackled to their mother by separation
anxiety or guilt. Compulsive self-sufficiency or unhealthy dependency may characterize their adult relationships.

Because the Waif's life is hard, her children's lives can be
difficult. Adult children may assume responsibility for financial
crises, medical bills, physical care, or housing. Not knowing how

much help is appropriate or how frequently they should visit, the Waif's adult children may grow weary with guilt and worry. Loyalty conflicts can arise as adult children marry and have families of their own. Resentment may grow with time.

Messages from the Waif Mother

- "You'd be better off without me."
- "I don't deserve your love."
- "Don't need me because I can't help you."
- "You are more deserving than I am."
- "Nobody cares about me."
- "My life is so much worse than yours."
- "You are so lucky."
- "Let me do that for you."
- "I feel used."

The Waif identifies with other victims for whom life is hard. She may take in foster children or her children's friends, and may choose disadvantaged others as partners. Although the Waif's compassion for others is genuine, her children are ambivalent about it. On one hand, they may be proud to have had a mother who is socially concerned and generous. On the other hand, they may resent what they had to give up.

The Waif's adult children struggle with entitlement issues, feeling either overly entitled or not entitled at all. Magical thinking and a sense of omnipotence can develop in the all-good child who assumes responsibility for the Waif's welfare. An adult child recalled purchasing a new dress on the same day her mother was injured in a car accident. The daughter associated the act of self-gratification with her mother's accident and returned the dress to the store. Self-denial relieved anxiety because expressing her own needs felt dangerous as a child. The daughter of the Waif had become the Waif.

Blinded by her own helplessness, the Waif is unable to see the path of destruction she leaves behind or the road ahead that could lead her to safety. She can be difficult to treat and may shop for a therapist who offers sympathy rather than growth. Angela dropped out of treatment whenever she met a new partner. She held on to her fantasy of being rescued by an idealized partner, and was frightened by the hope that therapy offered. The Waif may terminate treatment just as she begins to feel better. Like a butterfly, she must be gently held in an open hand. Her therapist and children must feel free to let her go.

4

The Hermit Mother

But all day Snow White was alone, and the kindly dwarfs warned her, saying, "Watch out for your stepmother. She'll soon find out you're here. Don't let anyone in."

—*Snow White and the Seven Dwarfs*

"I want to feel walled-in, safe from the predators and their advances to which I have so foolishly succumbed. Flights of fancy take one back to Sandeffingham and a moat-enclosed castle. No one must be allowed in."

Cynthia was an English teacher who was hesitant about coming to therapy. She shut me out with silence, retreating into the blackness that threatened to consume her. Without reading her journals, I could not have known the depth of her fear. Unlike the Waif, whose vulnerability is evident in her flighty, fragile demeanor, the borderline Hermit has a hard external shell that is difficult to penetrate. The servile Waif relinquishes control too easily, whereas the Hermit is terrified of not having control. She can seem self-sufficient, confident, even driven, but her impenetrable exterior is woven with fear, terror laced with hostility. An excerpt from Cynthia's journal illustrates her fear of life:

"My poem is the life I would have lived,
But I would rather write, than suffer it
(apologies to D. Thoreau)"

Cynthia aspired to become an author but was paralyzed by her fear of rejection. Borderlines who have a gift for writing describe the intensity of their emotional experience in excruciating detail. Sylvia Plath (in Stevenson 1989) captured the essence of the Hermit's inner experience: "The only thing to love is Fear itself" (p. 143). The Hermit trusts fear more than anyone or anything. Fear keeps her alive; without it, she feels numb, dead.

Plath committed suicide in 1963 when she was only 30 years old. Many years earlier she wrote in her journal: "it is so much safer *not* to feel, *not* to let the world touch one" (Hughes and McCullough 1982, p. 63). Tragically, few people know of the Hermit's suffering. Fear prevents her from being seen and from getting help. She keeps herself locked in and locked up. She may dread being photographed and may literally cut herself out of pictures. She avoids groups, hides in the background, and is guarded with others. Only her children and closest confidantes are aware of the severity of her unyielding distrust, insecurity, anxiety, rage, and paranoia.

Borderline Hermits are often writers, artists, scholars, behind-the-scenes characters who are driven and destroyed by fear. Plath wrote, "Desperate, intense: why do I find groups impossible? Do I even want them?" (Hughes and McCullough 1982, p. 188). The Hermit is driven to excel and may be outstanding in her field but is sadly incapable of enjoying her success. If given a choice, however, she may not work at all.

The Hermit is a perfectionist, a worrier, and like most borderlines, an insomniac. Plath wrote, "the dark time, the night time is worst now" (Hughes and McCullough 1982, p. 97). Cynthia's anxieties kept her awake at night. She ruminated about the safety of her husband and children, about her job and her health. She held her husband and children to unrealistically high standards and criticized her daughter relentlessly about her grades, her appearance, and her friends. Cynthia's husband retreated from the frequent conflicts that erupted between his wife and his children.

The borderline Hermit seeks solitude but paradoxically longs to belong. In social settings the Waif can be inappropriately self-disclosing and too talkative, whereas the Hermit is closed, private, and rarely flirtatious. She can be abrupt but is rarely loud, dramatic, or showy like the borderline Queen. The Hermit prefers to live and die within the confines of her shell. Exposure feels deadly.

THE HERMIT'S DOMINANT EMOTIONAL STATE: FEAR

The poor child was all alone in the great forest. She was so afraid . . .

—*Snow White and the Seven Dwarfs*

Like Snow White, the Hermit is extraordinarily vigilant because she felt robbed or violated as a child. Sylvia Plath's father died when she was just 8 years old. She wrote, "I felt cheated: I wasn't loved, but all the signs said I was loved . . ." (Hughes and McCullough 1982, p. 268). Hermit mothers exhibit paranoid tendencies and typically experienced an early threat to their psychic survival. Needing reassurance but unable to accept it, the Hermit lives in fear of domination as well as desertion. Closeness is as threatening as abandonment.

The Hermit may be superstitious and suspicious of anything that threatens her control. Extraordinarily perceptive, she may believe that she is psychic. However, innumerable phobias obstruct her ability to relax, socialize, or enjoy life. Hermit mothers suffer from persistent fantasies of harm coming to themselves or others, and tend to attribute hostile intentions to others.

Hermits may seem strong to those who do not know them well because, unlike other types of borderlines, they can tolerate being alone. Solitude feels safer than being with others but does not alleviate anxiety. Cynthia had a generalized fear of authority figures and of groups with power such as the government. Persecution fears reflected her childhood experience with her own mother, who relentlessly violated her privacy. Cynthia described a tumultuous childhood in which she frequently screamed at her mother, "Leave me alone!"

Hermits want to be left alone, not abandoned, just not bothered. As an adult, Cynthia was unable to tolerate closeness with others because she feared emotional engulfment. Although she could have benefited from antianxiety medication, Cynthia was too fearful to use it. She felt safer living in fear, believing that medication would interfere with her ability to perceive danger. Her family begged her to try medication, but she adamantly refused, accusing them of "trying to dope her up and stick her in a nut house."

Like all Hermits, Cynthia expected conspiracy, betrayal, and disaster. She accused others, including her husband and children, of not caring about her. She looked for hidden meanings in greeting cards, gifts, invitations, and innocuous comments. The Hermit ruminates over questions such as, "What did they mean by that?" She forms alliances based on conspiracy theories and may spread anxiety like a plague throughout her family. The Hermit's relationships fluctuate between "It's you and me against the world" and "It's you against me." She sees conspiracy everywhere.

Managing her internal state consumes the Hermit's emotional energy and makes interacting with others feel overwhelming. Hermits dislike entertaining and avoid houseguests. Cynthia disapproved of her children's friends and rarely allowed them to visit.

Sylvia Plath was evidently horrified by her realization that she was not interested in other people (Hughes and McCullough 1982).

Ruminating over irrelevant details can seriously impair functioning in social situations. Illogical rules, rituals, and magical thinking fail to protect the Hermit from adversity and may, in fact, jeopardize her well-being. Cynthia could not leave her house without checking and rechecking that the doors and windows were locked. Leaving home was a major ordeal and the intensity of her anxiety annoyed her children.

The Hermit's hypervigilance regarding her children's health can leave them without a baseline of normality from which to assess their own well-being. Cynthia's son underreacted to pain as a consequence of his mother's overreaction to every sneeze and sniffle. When injured playing soccer, he avoided telling his mother and minimized his pain. After seeing a doctor several days later, he was surprised to learn that he had broken his foot. The Hermit's children may learn to ignore signals of pain from their own bodies.

The Hermit conceals her distrust, negativity, and low tolerance for frustration by presenting a façade in social interactions. She seeks refuge from the theatrics of life where relationships feel staged. In the social world, she must perform an act merely to survive. Sylvia Plath claimed that socializing required a betrayal of the self (Hughes and McCullough 1982). A friend described Sylvia as: "first the bright and smiling mask that she presented to everyone, and then, through that the determined, insistent, obsessive, impatient person who snapped if things did not go her way, and [who] flew into sudden rages" (Stevenson 1989, p. xiv).

Gerald Adler (1985) explains that borderlines constantly seek out others to provide a sense of self, to "keep separation anxiety relatively in check—to avoid annihilation panic" (p. 82). Unlike other types of borderlines who seek social interaction, the Hermit defines her tenuous self through her work, her interests or hobbies, in a single relationship with an idealized partner, or by writing in a journal.

Cynthia's success as a teacher was obvious to those who knew her, yet her confidence could be shaken by the slightest mistake. Publishing her outstanding stories felt far too dangerous; consequently, she protected herself from the possibility of rejection by refusing to submit them. Plath had a great fear of failing academically and intellectually, calling it "the worst blow to security" (Hughes and McCullough 1982, p. 86). The Hermit seeks validation through her work and is, therefore, extremely conscientious about her performance. Criticism or rejection annihilates the self: "Otherwise there is no i because i am what other people interpret me as being and am nothing if there were no people" (p. 72).

Although the Hermit's behavior seems unnecessarily dramatic and at times ridiculous, her feeling of persecution is genuine. She has no internal mechanism for calming and soothing herself, as her own mother may have functioned both as persecutor and protector. She can find no safe place inside or outside of herself. Her greatest torment, however, may be that no one understands. She feels alone in the world, lost in herself and her own terrifying thoughts. No one believes her. No wonder she panics.

THE INNER EXPERIENCE: PERSECUTION

You've got to be careful and not let anyone in when we're away.

—*Snow White*

The darkness within the borderline Hermit is fear. She suffers from acute persecutory anxiety, and spends her life warding off a nameless internal predator. She may be convinced that whole groups of people are dangerous or evil, particularly those who do not share her interests or values. Plath once said, "I am . . . in love only with myself" (Hughes and McCullough 1982, p. 34).

Hermits expect to lose what they need; consequently, they are possessive and controlling. In his poem "Apprehensions" (Hughes 1998, p. 140), Ted Hughes, Sylvia Plath's husband, described Sylvia's possessiveness. Plath wrote, "if anyone ever disarranged my things I'd feel as though I had been raped intellectually" (Stevenson 1989, p. 80). Indeed, when a friend penciled some passages in a book she had borrowed from Plath, "she brought down the wrath of the avenging angel" (p. 80).

Family members often mistake the Hermit's possessiveness as selfishness, rather than understanding that the Hermit feels violated when others move or borrow personal objects. Finding and protecting her own space, her own place, and her own things is a way of protecting herself. Cynthia depicted the Hermit's fear that others will take what is hers: *"This is mine. This is mine. This is mine. The monkey's hard, sharp nails scraping the floor to pick up and greedily hoard for herself what you cannot give her or what you do give her but could take away."* Because the Hermit is afraid of losing herself, she jealously guards her personal belongings.

The Hermit mother cannot tolerate being exposed. Sylvia Plath's husband stated, "I never saw her show her real self to anybody" (Hughes and McCullough 1982, p. xiv). What cannot be seen cannot be lost or taken. Cynthia wrote to her journal, *"only you know me."*

Like many Hermits, both Sylvia and Cynthia punished those they loved by shutting them out. When Hermits are angry, they confront family members with a wall of cold, stony silence or unbridled wrath. According to a friend, Plath had a "way of generating a climate of guilt where none whatsoever was justified" (Stevenson 1998, p. 327). Plath acknowledged, "I suppose I'll always be overvulnerable, slightly paranoid" (Hughes and McCullough 1982, p. 152).

Although the Hermit fears being engulfed by others, she engulfs her family members with her fear and desperation. When they try to separate, even momentarily, the Hermit can become enraged. Plath wrote: "I am superstitious about separations from Ted, even for an hour. I think I must live in his heat and presence, for his smells and words—as if all my senses fed involuntarily on him, and deprived for more than a few hours, I languish, wither, die to the world . . ." (Hughes and McCullough p. 221).

Cynthia rarely acknowledged the murderous rage that could well up within her. Plath, on the other hand, described it vividly, "I have a violence in me that is hot as death-blood" (p. 236). The hostility of the Hermit may take the form of biting sarcasm, belligerence, unreasonable demands, temper tantrums, pouting, or stony silence. Accusations of betrayal, neglect, or abandonment may follow minor misunderstandings.

The Hermit rarely acknowledges mistakes or apologizes for inappropriate behavior. The survival instinct prevails when the self is endangered. For the Hermit, it is a case of self-defense and she sees herself as innocent of wrongdoing.

The misery of the Hermit's life is that solitude is not enjoyed and vigilance never ends. Although she dreads being seen by others, the last thing she wants to see is herself. Very few Hermit mothers can tolerate being seen by a therapist.

CHARACTERISTICS OF THE HERMIT MOTHER

Is possessive and overcontrolling

The Hermit mother's overcontrolling and possessive parenting style can paralyze her children. Smothered by the intense, symbiotic relationship, children may feel frozen with fear or driven toward danger by defiant resentment. Hermit mothers often over-protect the all-good child and denigrate the no-good child. The no-good child may be constantly harassed by the mother's negative, paranoid projections. Relentless criticism of the no-good child's appearance, friends, school performance, and personal habits are projections of the Hermit's own shame and disgrace. The Hermit may cling desperately to the all-good child, seeking allegiance and alliance in the denigration of her husband or the no-good child. The all-good child may feel guilt-ridden and torn due to the Hermit's expectation of total loyalty.

Because the child's need for autonomy is experienced as betrayal, the Hermit's children may feel trapped by her fear. Her adult children may experience physical symptoms related to anxiety. Patients who grew up with Hermit mothers frequently report attacks of colitis or nausea, bouts of illness, headaches, muscle tension, or general malaise. Memories of childhood trauma are repressed and pain is expressed in their bodies. Adult children of Hermits may suffer from panic attacks, claustrophobia, or agoraphobia without recognizing the source of their fear—the early experience of feeling trapped by their mothers.

Avoids groups and is reclusive

Hermits, by definition, are introverts whereas borderline Waifs and Queens are extroverts. Plath wrote, "I talk to myself and look at the dark trees, blessedly neutral. So much easier than facing people, than having to look happy, invulnerable, clever" (Hughes and McCullough 1989, p. 101). Unfortunately, the Hermit mother pulls her children into her protective shell where she raises them in darkness, believing she is protecting them from danger that only she perceives. The naturally curious child, however, wants to explore the world and therefore threatens the mother's security. The

Hermit mother may thwart the child's strivings toward independence, socialization, and autonomy.

The Hermit believes she is helping her children by secluding them from a dangerous world. Adolescents, who long for freedom and independence, may resist and resent being overprotected. Some adult children of Hermit mothers report that they delayed obtaining their driver's license because of their mother's anxiety. A driver's license represents an enormous leap toward independence, and provides the ability to get away. Naturally, the Hermit's anxiety is more intense when her children become adolescents.

Fears rejection more than abandonment

Abandonment may be more tolerable than rejection for the Hermit because of her ability to tolerate aloneness. Rejection is devastating because it represents failure. Fear of rejection was the major obstacle in Cynthia's life. She was ashamed and afraid of her need for approval. Her fictional stories represented parts of herself, like "Emily the Spider," who was ridiculed for wearing four pairs of glasses. Although the fear of rejection kept Cynthia from submitting her stories for publication, Sylvia Plath was obsessed with being published. Art is an expression of the Hermit's inner experience and rejection can trigger emotional disintegration. Professional success offers comfort as well as a deeply needed source of pride. Sylvia Plath wrote thirty poems the month after her husband left her. The last poem she wrote prior to committing suicide was about the death of a woman who wore the proud "smile of accomplishment" (Stevenson 1998, p. 298). The title of the poem reveals her awareness of how close she was to the "Edge."

The borderline Hermit's fear of rejection makes her difficult to help. Treating the Hermit can be agonizing because of the risk of premature termination and suicide. For the Hermit, suicide may feel like victory rather than defeat, the last act of free will. She must have control of her death as well as her life, and may leave treatment just as she begins to trust her therapist. Trust is dangerous.

Regrettably, suicidal Hermits are likely to succeed in killing themselves. They have no desire to reveal their intentions to others, and therefore do not threaten suicide. They fear the loss of control that accompanies hospitalization. Without intervention, the tale of the Hermit mother may not end with happily-ever-after.

Ruminates excessively

Daniel Paul (1987) explains that feelings can be so overwhelming for borderlines that "they have difficulty containing affect" (p. 149). In Sylvia Plath's case, her journal entries, poetry, and short stories depict her flood of emotions: "I am drowning in negativism, self-hate, doubt, madness—and even I am not strong enough to deny the routine, the rote, to simplify. No, I go plodding on, afraid that the blank hell in back of my eyes will break through . . ." (Hughes and McCullough 1982, p. 60). The Hermit fears the darkness within her perhaps more than she fears life itself.

The Hermit's ruminations reflect the toxicity of her own thoughts. She searches for something she is afraid to find—the source of her torment, the cause of her pain. She is sick with worry and full of adrenaline. Cynthia complained that her children and husband ignored her constant warnings. Her children groaned and sighed, "It's always something." They teased her about "the panic of the day" that could be triggered by a harmless comment from a colleague and could set her off for a week. "They're trying to get rid of me!" she argued. But her husband's reassurance was met with hostility: "You never believe me. Just wait and see!"

The Hermit castigates herself mercilessly for minor or invented infractions. Her inner chaos may be evident in a home cluttered with stacks of old newspapers, magazines, and unfinished projects. Her anxiety is too diffuse to be managed, and she therefore may focus on one inconsequential object that becomes the target of her shame. Cynthia was embarrassed when an uncle stopped in unexpectedly because she had left a dirty hairbrush in the bathroom. Her husband laughed when she told him how ashamed she felt, and asked, "Do you really think he even noticed? Out of all the mess around here, why do you care about a hairbrush?" The dirty hairbrush represented the shame she felt compelled to hide.

Tragically, the Hermit cannot be appeased, calmed, or reassured. She is convinced that no one else understands the seriousness of her concerns. The Hermit suffers from basic distrust, and is destined to feel alone.

Is intensely jealous

Because the Hermit suffers from basic mistrust and intense jealousy, she may be unable to sustain long-term relationships. A friend of Plath's initially admired her but "later . . . was amazed when Sylvia defended her possessions with a rapacity that, in the end, injured their friendship" (Stevenson 1989, p. 64). Cynthia alienated colleagues by her unwillingness to share information regarding resources, by not attending social functions, and by segregating herself. She guarded her lesson plans as though they contained classified information. Her coldness was interpreted as snobbishness and some colleagues resented her, not realizing that they intimidated her.

Both Cynthia and Sylvia were intensely jealous of their husbands' relationships with other females. Plath's friend Dido Merwin wrote, "even the suggestion of Ted's going anywhere with anyone automatically triggered abreactions great or small, which went double if the 'anyone' was a woman" (Hughes and Mc-Cullough 1982, p. 328). Biographer Anne Stevenson (1989) states, "there is evidence that outsiders found Sylvia difficult to know, perverse in her habit of keeping her husband to herself, sometimes unreasonable to the point of rudeness in her dealings with friends and family" (p. 176).

Cynthia accused her husband of infidelity despite having no evidence to support her belief. She accused him of not finding her attractive, of rejecting her sexually, and of preferring younger women. On one occasion she threw a pan at him and later accused him of walking out on her, refusing to acknowledge the possibility that leaving was an act of self-protection rather than abandonment.

The Hermit's jealousy can lead to destructive and vindictive behavior. When Plath's husband was late returning from lunch with a female BBC producer, her paranoia led her to believe that, "a person she had never met, would make the first, inevitable breach in her perfect marriage" (Hughes and McCullough 1982, p. 206). The event is described in Hughes's (1998) poem "The Minotaur." While Hughes was meeting on business, Plath became hysterical and destroyed his manuscripts, as well as his favorite book, *The Complete Works of Shakespeare*, in a vicious display of unbridled rage, irrational jealousy, and paranoia. Hughes later confided in a friend that the incident was a turning point in their marriage. Biographer Stevenson (1989) states, "Yet nothing had happened to harm her marriage other than her upsurge of jealousy" (p. 245).

Is acutely perceptive

The acuity of the Hermit's senses results from her intense fear. Because she lives in a state of alarm, she notices things that others miss. Cynthia had a generalized fear of taking in, of being contaminated, and developed rituals to ward off danger. Family members teased her about decontaminating her dishes and eating utensils. She ate only at restaurants where plastic, disposable utensils were used and where she could see the food being prepared. When a local restaurant temporarily closed after several customers became ill with hepatitis, Cynthia's belief in her rituals intensified. Paranoid thoughts are exacerbated whenever they are reinforced by reality.

The Hermit's vigilance may be a consequence of post-traumatic stress disorder (PTSD). Due to childhood trauma that left her with fear, the Hermit's mind seems to be wired to misperceive danger. She may be suspicious of the psychiatric profession and refuse to seek help. A friend explained that of all the characteristics of Sylvia Plath's personality, the saddest of all was that she saw help as a threat, something to be avoided.

May be superstitious

Superstitious beliefs include magical thinking or the use of rituals to reduce fear and anxiety. A friend of Plath's made a sculpture of her head "which the superstitious Sylvia, like a savage guarding her soul, was in terror of throwing away . . ." (Stevenson 1989, p. 105). Objects representing the self carry special significance for borderlines because their self is unstable and prone to disintegration. Plath and her husband eventually hid the clay head in a willow tree where it could not be found or disturbed.

Cynthia's family viewed her rituals as harmless annoyances but resented her perception of bad omens. Vacations had been canceled or rescheduled on numerous occasions because Cynthia had a bad feeling about the trip. She insisted that her husband retract an offer on a new home after she learned that the previous owner had died suddenly of a heart attack. She was certain that the house was marked with bad luck.

Hermits may have lucky numbers (Plath's was forty-nine), magic colors with special powers, or symbols that hold special meaning. Many borderlines use the heart symbol instead of writing the word "heart" in letters and journals, perhaps to bring good luck or ward off bad luck. Hughes (1998) describes Plath's habit of painting little hearts on personal belongings in his poem "Totem." The use of magic numbers and symbols reduces anxiety by giving the Hermit a sense of control over her environment.

Overreacts to pain and illness

Although all borderlines are prone to hysterical reactions when stressed, the Hermit feels particularly threatened by illness. She is intolerant of discomfort, inconvenience, and pain. She may moan and groan, scream and cry primarily out of fear, not pain. When frightened, she becomes hostile. Her exaggerated responses confuse those who care for her.

In his poem "Fever," Ted Hughes (1998) questioned whether or not his wife was crying wolf in her bout with food poisoning. The Hermit may react with equal hysteria to stubbing a toe and breaking a bone. Because she may overreact to physical pain and illness, family members may be unable to distinguish minor injuries from major emergencies.

Overreaction to pain or illness is a consequence of the Hermit's inability to soothe or comfort herself. When she feels vulnerable, she is incapable of containing anxiety. Responding with ridicule or minimizing her complaints merely increases her anxiety. Cynthia's son ignored her physical complaints. Her daughter, however, felt compelled to take care of her. The all-good child often comforts the Hermit, serving the role of the parentified child.

Uses food, alcohol, and sex to self-soothe

The Hermit may use food, alcohol, or sex to reduce anxiety. She is less likely than the Queen to self-soothe by spending money as she is not inclined to attract attention to herself. Although she may have expensive tastes, prefer gourmet meals, fine china, or high-quality items, spending money is not generally gratifying because it threatens her security. The Hermit is most likely to abuse food, alcohol, or sex when feeling rejected.

The absence of the borderline's partner triggers the Hermit's need for self-soothing. At those times the Hermit may develop paranoid thoughts and feelings of desperation, and may use any available coping mechanism to reduce her anxiety. Sylvia Plath wrote in her journal, "let me not be desperate and throw away my honor for want of solace; let me not hide in drinking and lacerating myself on strange men . . ." (Hughes and McCullough 1982, p. 125). Before marrying her husband, Cynthia had many casual sexual relationships. A journal entry read, *"I feel dead, flat. Instead of being horrified and ashamed at my throwing myself at another man last night I feel (thankfully I guess) a strange void."*

Gunderson (1984) describes levels of functioning that correspond to the status of the borderline's primary relationship. If the person to whom she is most attached is perceived as supportive, the borderline is generally mildly depressed and angry with herself. When she perceives her partner as frustrating, the borderline is angry, manipulative, and devaluing. When the partner is absent, the borderline becomes panicky, impulsive, and possibly psychotic.

Evokes guilt and anxiety in others

The Hermit mother often uses guilt to control others. After separating from her husband, Sylvia Plath asked to stay with a male companion. Her friend politely explained why, in his small community, it would be inappropriate for her to stay with him. He later recalled that her reaction made him feel guilty, leaving him thinking that he had been mean (Stevenson 1989). Other friends recalled Plath's tendency to corner people and leave them feeling afraid to act on their true feelings. Plath's friend Dido Merwin stated, "Any firsthand evidence of the effect Sylvia had on people must reveal something about that flawed psyche that made her not so much her own worst, as her only, enemy—a vessel of wrath 'fitted to destruction'" (Stevenson 1989, p. 346).

The Hermit unconsciously projects her anxiety in a variety of ways. Borderlines who have suicidal tendencies evoke powerful feelings of guilt and fear in family members, as well as in therapists. Sorting out the factors leading to suicide is not easy. Some Hermit mothers never attempt or threaten suicide because their fear of dying is as intense as their fear of living. Others may grow weary of feeling constantly threatened and may decide that dying, paradoxically, is the ultimate act of protecting oneself from the dangers of living. The borderline Hermit is her own worst enemy and is the single greatest threat to her survival.

THE HERMIT MOTHER'S MOTTO:
LIFE IS TOO DANGEROUS

Life *can* be dangerous but the Hermit mother teaches her children that life is *overwhelmingly* dangerous. The Hermit's fears are projected onto her children and introjected, taken in as real to the child. Consequently, her children may become accustomed to high levels of anxiety, feeling normal only when they feel anxious. In some cases, the Hermit's children may intentionally seek out dangerous experiences in rebellious defiance of her negative messages. Others may protect her, sensing her vulnerability and fear, and thus suffer from acute separation anxiety and guilt.

The Hermit's emotional message that life is too dangerous can undermine the child's self-confidence. The child may be deprived of important opportunities to explore the world, to make mistakes, and to learn from experience. Recognizing risks in any given situation is essential for survival. However, the Hermit's children may be unable to discern appropriate from neurotic anxiety. An anxious child has difficulty concentrating in school, sleeping at night, forming relationships, and achieving developmental goals. The Hermit's children learn to be afraid without understanding what it is they fear.

Overwhelming or pervasive anxiety can immobilize both the Hermit and her child. The Hermit mother may home-school her children because of irrational fears, prevent her children from participating in extracurricular activities, or keep them out of school whenever they have the slightest cold or cough. Children may receive the message that they do not have the ability to cope with life.

Messages from the Hermit Mother

- "Something terrible just happened!"
- "You're going to get hurt!"
- "Look out!"
- "You've done it now!"
- "Don't tell anybody."
- "They're out to get us!"
- "Keep your doors locked."
- "What's the matter with you?"
- "Act like everything's fine."
- "Don't let them in."

In *Searching for Memory: The Brain, The Mind, and The Past*, Daniel Schacter (1996) explains that the amygdala triggers secretion of norepinephrine, which makes the senses more alert, but leaves the individual feeling edgy. The borderline Hermit is always on edge. She hears noises that others do not hear, is overly sensitive to smells, and is acutely perceptive of her environment. She never feels safe. Like "Emily the Spider," in her short story, Cynthia's favorite place to hide was her basement. The warmth from her iron, the sound of the washing machine, and the absence of daylight gave her a sense of security.

The Hermit's adult children may become the focus of her social life. Her few friends are typically individuals who are also anxious and insecure. Holidays can be particularly difficult for her and her family because of the need for increased socialization. Thus, children of Hermits often find holidays disappointing and depressing.

The Hermit mother may raise Waif daughters, women who relinquish control too easily, and angry, aggressive sons who expect to be attacked. Sadly, few Hermits have the courage to seek treatment. Those who do, however, are likely to stop when they begin to trust the therapist. They seem to catch themselves with their guard down after revealing some part of themselves that felt too shameful. Their shame is initially apparent in their avoidance of eye contact, then later, in their total withdrawal from treatment.

The Hermit mother's fear is truly incomprehensible to others. She spins an invisible web that protects her against intruders but can paralyze her children. Tragically, she may live and die in the sticky strands she weaves.

5

The Queen Mother

"Get to your places!" shouted the Queen in a voice of thunder, and people began running about in all directions, tumbling up against each other.

—*Alice's Adventures in Wonderland*

"I can be a bitch. I'm terribly impatient . . . I admit it." Lindsey kicked off her shoes and pulled her legs around her like a tigress. "You don't mind if I get comfortable, do you?"

I didn't mind. But the more comfortable she looked, the more uncomfortable I felt. Finding a time that suited Lindsey's schedule had been difficult. It hadn't occurred to me, initially, that I had agreed to meet at a time that was inconvenient for me. A flicker of resentment set off an alarm. Lindsey expected special treatment.

Ernest Wolf (1988) explains that "mirror-hungry" personalities are compelled to "display themselves to evoke the attention of others, who through their admiring responses will perhaps counteract the experience of worthlessness" (p. 73). People notice the Queen. Conspicuous in her demand for attention through her appearance, her tone of voice, her behavior, and her relationships, the borderline Queen is driven by feelings of emptiness.

Borderline Queens seek special treatment because they felt emotionally deprived as children. An only child of wealthy parents who divorced when she was 7 years old, Lindsey longed for attention. Instead of taking time to console her, her parents sent her to summer camp and later to boarding school. Lindsey soon discovered that temper tantrums elicited the attention she sought. Consequently, she learned how to win special treatment through persistence and intimidation. She warned me about her bitchiness in order to manipulate me as well. But if I allowed her to exploit me, I, too, would resent her. The relationship between patient and therapist inevitably re-creates the earlier emotional experience between parent and child. As I listened to Lindsey, another famous Queen came to mind: Mary Todd Lincoln.

She was called the "Republican Queen," the controversial first lady who meddled in presidential affairs and spent extraordinary sums of money redecorating the White House during the Civil War. "There were intervals, however, when Mary was almost her brave, normal, high-spirited self and a stranger meeting her would see no trace of an unbalanced mentality. At other times, with her brain on fire with pain, she was submerged in gloom and her heart was filled with bitterness against the sad fate which had overtaken her" (Helm 1928, p. 268).

Biographer Marion Mills Miller (in Helm 1928) summarized the life of Mary Todd Lincoln:

> *Lady of Lincoln*
> *They wreathed her head*
> *With thorns when living*
> *With nettles though dead* [title page]

Robert, her only surviving son, once confided to his wife, "The simple truth, which I cannot tell to anyone not personally interested, is that my mother is on one subject not mentally responsible"

(p. 267). Even Abraham Lincoln was quoted as saying, "The caprices of Mrs. Lincoln, I am satisfied, are the result of *partial insanity*" (Simmons 1970, p. 146, emphasis added).

"Partial insanity"—a straightforward definition of borderline personality disorder provided by a president renowned for his honesty. Mary Todd Lincoln was a prototypical borderline Queen. "[Mary] was a possessive wife who liked to wait upon her husband and interfered with household management . . . The White House domestic staff at times deplored her. She was so unpredictable that one White House aide saw fit to write, 'The Hell-cat is getting more Hell-cattical day by day'" (p. 98)

William O. Stoddard (in Simmons 1970), a member of the White House staff during the Lincoln years described the first lady in ambivalent terms. "It was not easy at first to understand why a lady who could be one day so kindly, so considerate, so generous, so thoughtful and so hopeful, could upon another day appear so unreasonable, so irritable, so despondent . . . and so prone to see the dark, the wrong side of men and women and events" (p. 98).

The borderline Queen experiences what therapists call "oral greediness." The desperate hunger of the borderline Queen is akin to the behavior of an infant who has gone too long between feedings. Starved, frustrated, and beyond the ability to calm or soothe herself, she grabs, flails, and wails until at last the nipple is planted securely and perhaps too deeply in her mouth. She coughs, gags, chokes, and spits, eyeing the elusive breast like a wolf guarding her food. Similarly, the Queen holds on to what is hers, taking more than she can use, in case it might be taken away prematurely.

Lindsey requested a reduced fee for treatment, explaining that she was overextended on her credit cards. A large diamond on her left hand and designer clothes belied her claim of financial distress. Not long before her first appointment she had taken an extravagant cruise to the Caribbean. Although Lindsey appeared to be wealthy, genuine feelings of deprivation distorted her perspective, and, like the starving infant at the breast, she grabbed for as much as she could get. Getting what she wanted, however, would never fill her up.

Adler (1985) explains that the borderline's "feelings of abandonment are often based on real experiences of parents or parent surrogates not caring for or abandoning them" (p. 213). In Mary Todd Lincoln's case, her mother died in childbirth when Mary was only 7 years old. Her father remarried, producing nine additional children. In the midst of so many others competing for her father's attention, she won his interest by discussing politics, a subject he regarded highly, and she frequently spoke of wanting to live in the White House. Although she fulfilled her ambition of becoming first lady, her dreams of happiness never materialized. She spent her last years in mourning and died in despair.

Lachkar (1992) believes that borderlines lack the memory of being special. The borderline Queen lacks the experience of *feeling* special and suffers from feelings of complete emptiness, angry yearning, and insatiable longing. She feels entitled to invade the boundaries of others and take what she needs. She can be intrusive, loud, impatient, and flamboyant. She is easily frustrated, often bursting into rages that can terrify her children. She can be disingenuous and may lie in order to get what she wants.

Lindsey complained that her ex-husband had left her almost penniless and that she was forced to live a lifestyle beneath her comfort level. When her children were young, Lindsey told them she could not afford to send them to camp. Although her ex-husband had provided the money, she flew into a rage when he asked why they did not attend, and he did not pursue the issue. Giving in to the Queen is easier than resisting.

Those who dare to confront the Queen may be treated as infidels and, as such, may be banished for their disloyalty. Mary Lincoln's niece observed her tendency to ostracize those who confronted her: "Her sisters and other relatives who voiced to Mary their indignant protests, entreating her to curb her excitement and eccentricity, only incurred her anger and had become estranged from her" (Helm 1928, p. 265).

THE QUEEN'S DOMINANT EMOTIONAL STATE: EMPTINESS

"The Queen! The Queen!" and the three gardeners instantly threw themselves flat upon their faces.

Alice's Adventures in Wonderland

Like the Queen of Hearts in *Alice's Adventures in Wonderland*, the borderline Queen treats people as if they were cards to be shuffled, arranged, and stacked so that she can win. Borderline Queens exploit others without remorse. They are competitive and envious, longing for wealth, glamour, attention, fame, or admiration. Preoccupied with themselves, they seem self-centered, greedy, and bossy. Those who cannot be used to their advantage are discarded like jokers from a deck.

The darkness within the borderline Queen is emptiness. Emptiness and loneliness are distinctly different emotional experiences. Whereas loneliness results from loss and evokes sadness, emptiness results from deprivation and triggers anger. However, not all Queens experienced loss in early childhood. The common denominator among borderline Queens is emotional deprivation. As children, they felt robbed; consequently, they feel entitled to take what they need.

Lindsey began shoplifting as an adolescent and continued to steal small, inexpensive items such as lipstick, shampoo, and greeting cards—things she could easily afford but resented having to purchase. She viewed the loss to the store as inconsequential compared to the inconvenience of paying for the items.

A low tolerance for frustration and a lack of patience leaves the Queen vulnerable to destructive and impulsive behavior. She may abuse drugs, alcohol, food, or sex or may engage in reckless spending or driving. Mrs. Lincoln's impulsive spending, especially during wartime, triggered resentment among the public. Mrs. Lincoln was said to have "developed an almost psychopathic passion to possess richer gowns, to outdress . . . [the Washington aristocracy]" (Simmons 1970, p. 86). When she exceeded the congressional appropriation for refurbishing the White House, Lincoln remarked: "It can never have my approval. I'll pay it out of my own pocket first. It would stink in the nostrils of the American people to have it said that the President of the United States had approved a bill over-running an appropriation of $20,000 for flub dubs for this damned old house, when the soldiers cannot have blankets" (p. 117). Mrs. Lincoln's lavish spending won more criticism than admiration from her husband as well as from the public.

A baseline emotional state of emptiness and anger can create a variety of psychosomatic symptoms. Mrs. Lincoln's migraines are well documented. She suffered an attack the day she arrived in Washington, in 1847. "The boys were tired and irritable, which was hard on their mother, who was suffering from one of the sick headaches that troubled her" (p. 38). Queens may experience migraines, muscle spasms, ulcers, colitis, fibromyalgia, and immune-related disorders triggered by anger and tension.

THE QUEEN'S INNER EXPERIENCE: DEPRIVATION AND ENVY

The Queen had only one way of settling all difficulties, great or small. "Off with his head!" she said without even looking round.

—*Alice's Adventures in Wonderland*

The Queen feels starved and deprived; thus, she seeks gratification and control. She initially impresses people favorably in social situations, her charm and wit masking her underlying deprivation and demand for attention. But sometimes her envy veers out of control.

> [Mrs. Lincoln] demanded what she wanted, sometimes from other wardrobes and once off a friend's head. When Willian's of Pennsylvania Avenue, Washington's best-known milliner, could not match a lavender ribbon for her bonnet strings and she spied the unusual strings on an acquaintance's hat, with a queen's mandate she insisted Mrs. Taft surrender her strings in return for others (though of a slightly darker color) freely installed by Willian himself. According to her daughter, Mrs. Taft was "amazed and provoked" but eventually surrendered. [Baker 1987, p. 195]

The Queen devalues those who do not provide gratification or special treatment. Mrs. Lincoln was known for her stinginess, demanding prices far beneath the market rate for goods and services. After her husband's assassination, her fear of impoverishment intensified. At one point, she tried to raise money by auctioning off her wardrobe at outrageous prices, drawing public ridicule and embarrassing her son, Robert.

Like Mrs. Lincoln, Lindsey also used guilt to manipulate others. She fabricated stories of hardship in order to elicit sympathy, misrepresented facts in order to win attention, and often destroyed the trust of friends. Mrs. Lincoln once wrote to a friend who had changed her mind about visiting: "You must keep your word . . . I feel I must have you with me. I have set my heart on having you with me. *If you love me* give me a favorable answer" (Baker 1987, p. 151, emphasis added).

Deprivation impairs moral judgment. Consequently, the Queen can be vindictive without feeling guilty. Mrs. Lincoln severed relationships with most of her sisters and cousins. Joan Crawford severed relationships with many people, including her own daughter and mother. After ending relationships with men, Crawford literally cut them out of her life by removing their faces from photographs. The borderline Queen readily discards those who are perceived as useless, unworthy, or unfaithful.

The Queen relates to others with superficiality and an air of detachment. She may perceive others, including her children, as a threat to her own survival unless they relinquish their needs for hers. Queen mothers compete with their children for time, attention, love, and money. Superficial interest and a lack of attunement to the child's emotional needs are typical of Queen mothers.

CHARACTERISTICS OF THE QUEEN MOTHER

Is preoccupied with the need to be mirrored

Attention is sustenance to a Queen mother. She is preoccupied with her self-image and the image of her children. In order to win her admiration and love, her children must reflect her interests, values, tastes, and preferences. The Queen expects her children to dress the part, to reflect *her* importance. Following the Civil War, Mary Lincoln frequently purchased extravagant clothing for her granddaughter during her trips to Europe. Her son and daughter-in-law considered some of the outfits inappropriately lavish. However, some Queen mothers resent spending money on their children. Lindsey bought sale clothing for her children. She had an eye for bargains and avoided paying full price for their wardrobe. Subtle resentment about her children's needs was evident in Lindsey's habit of paying full price for her own designer clothing.

The dominating Queen insists on receiving undivided attention.

In her work with borderline children, Elisabeth Geleerd (1958) observed their tendency to withdraw into angry sulking or to become aggressive when not receiving attention. Queen mothers also may sulk or become enraged when not receiving adequate mirroring. One patient recalled memories of her mother lashing out whenever the patient received attention from her father, leaving the patient feeling guilty. Queen mothers are unable to provide adequate mirroring for their children because of their own need for attention. Consequently, the Queen's children mirror their mother.

Seeks attention, fame, or prominence

All young children need to bask in the glow of their parents' admiration. The caregiver's adulation of the young toddler as she sets out to explore the world is crucial to healthy emotional development. As a child, the borderline Queen was given inauthentic responses, shamed, or ignored when she tried to elicit this crucial response. Thus, as an adult, the Queen still seeks those needed responses, like "I see you!" and "Yes, how wonderful you are!" and "Look at you!" Uncertainty about her self-worth leads to an overreliance on external validation.

Lindsey measured her self-worth by the value of her car, her home, and her personal possessions. She needed to look wealthy in order to feel valuable, and admitted that she married for money rather than for love. She wanted the biggest and the best of everything and was intensely competitive with others. Attempting to evoke envy in others, she spoke openly about her expensive vacations and the price of her possessions.

The borderline Queen is extravagant, compensating for feelings of worthlessness with displays of wealth and success. Robert Todd Lincoln wrote to his wife: "You could hardly believe it possible, but my mother protests to me that she is in actual want and nothing I can do or say will convince her to the contrary" (Helm 1928, p. 267). Soon after arriving at the White House, Mrs. Lincoln purchased eighty-four pairs of kid gloves and found herself holding off creditors. In the three months prior to her husband's assassination, she spent $3,200 on jewelry. Mary Todd Lincoln's compulsive shopping grew worse with time.

Demands total loyalty, discards those who betray her

The borderline Queen is quick to shift her affection from one person to another, depending on the degree of compliance and admiration that she receives. Baker (1987) noted that "most of Mary's acquaintances either loved or hated her . . ." (p. 292). Her meddling with presidential affairs was motivated by her need to repay those who had shown her special favor. She recommended men for official positions who would use their power to her advantage: "She promoted the claims of men who were not relatives . . . and she did so for the same reason that men did: to gain an advantage for herself" (p. 204). Baker lamented that "Rather than forget, she harbored grudges, collected injustices, and rehearsed her anger . . . Mary Lincoln demanded loyal service from her friends" (p. 151).

The Queen mother's children can feel used and manipulated, falling in and out of favor like trump cards. Mrs. Lincoln cut off communication with her only surviving son, Robert, after he had her arrested and institutionalized. Her public and private behavior had become so out of hand that Robert became concerned for her safety. Shortly after she had wandered the halls of a hotel half-dressed and accused him of trying to murder her, he began commitment proceedings. After the ensuing infamous trial, Mrs.

Lincoln terminated relationships with friends and relatives who had supported Robert's decision.

Although contemporary readers may view Mrs. Lincoln's outrage as justified, Robert's actions must be understood within the context of the times. For most of the nineteenth century, women were not allowed to vote or to enter into contracts. Therefore, the closest male relative was responsible for their welfare. The only treatment available for mental disorders during this time was institutionalization. Therefore, Robert selected Bellevue Place in Batavia, Illinois, a private and atypical asylum of the 1800s. The philosophy of treatment prevented the use of restraints and provided all possible comforts (Neely and McMurtry 1986) Despite the fact that borderline mothers rarely view their behavior as abnormal, adult children who coerce their mothers into treatment should expect retaliation.

Although few women possess the power available to a first lady, all Queens can be vindictive when enraged, emotionally bribing and blackmailing others. Mrs. Lincoln once threatened to embarrass Robert by exposing his history of poor investments in retaliation for his decision to have her institutionalized. Lindsey had a tumultuous relationship with both of her children. When she discovered that her daughter was using drugs, she kicked her out of the house, put away all photographs of her, changed the locks on the door, and told her that she was no longer her daughter. Lindsey felt entitled to disowning her daughter because she felt disgraced and betrayed. Loyalty is not a choice for children of Queen mothers.

Children are "on display"

The Queen mother uses her children to gain attention, recognition, or admiration, and children must mirror her interests. Instead of being encouraged to discover their own talents, the Queen's children live in her shadow. Queen mothers may overestimate their children's ability and encourage them to participate in potentially dangerous or humiliating experiences.

Mrs. Lincoln frequently encouraged her children to perform for guests when she entertained friends in her home. Simmons (1970) explains that "Bob, and later the other children, were brought in to dance, recite poetry and—according to one unappreciative guest 'to show off generally'" (p. 64). Christina Crawford (1978) described her humiliation as a child when her mother paraded her in front of the media, overdressed her for parties, and created a façade of grandeur and happiness. Mrs. Lincoln's daughter-in-law was "frightened" by the lavish clothing sent to her daughter (Neely and McMurtry 1986, p. 151). Robert's wife was horrified, not only at the expense, but also at the attention such clothing might draw to her daughter.

More than anything, Lindsey expected her son to make money and her daughter to marry it. Her daughter, however, chose down-to-earth friends who were neither wealthy nor popular. Skirmishes regarding her daughter's choice of friends, her clothing, and her hairstyle frequently erupted into full-blown battles. Children with Queen mothers must fight a royal battle in order to win their autonomy.

Hysterical reactions terrify or confuse her children

The dramatic and sometimes hysterical behavior of the Queen mother can terrify her children. Baker (1987) described Mrs. Lincoln as having an "anxious attachment" to her children (p. 124). When young Robert ate lime from the Lincolns' privy, his mother became hysterical. Rather than call for help, she screamed, "Bobby will die, Bobby will die, Bobby will die" (p. 124). Consumed by unbridled fear, she was unable to reassure her son or offer appropriate treatment.

Lindsey recognized her tendency to panic over details that later seemed inconsequential. Without being aware of the fear she created in her children, she frequently made statements while opening bills such as, "We're going broke," "We're going to have to sell this house!" The Queen's children learn to discount her hysteria, but have no way of discovering the truth.

As she aged, Mrs. Lincoln grew increasingly paranoid and suffered from numerous physical problems. Her son, Robert, had lived in continual apprehension regarding his mother's health and behavior. After visiting her in 1882, one year before her death, he expressed his belief that "some part of her trouble is imaginary" (Baker 1987, p. 365). Distinguishing actual physical distress from emotional overreaction is difficult for children with Queen mothers.

Is intrusive and violates boundaries

The borderline Queen rarely accepts "no" for an answer, and often violates the boundaries of others. Richard Moskovitz (1996) describes borderline characteristics that typify the Queen: "[you] feel entitled to special treatment and live outside the rules made for others. You may feel entitled to take whatever you wish and have everything good for yourself" (pp. 14–15). At 13, Mary Todd rode her new pony to the home of the famous statesman Henry Clay and demanded that he come outside to see it. When his servant answered the door and explained that Mr. Clay was in the middle of an important political meeting, Mary insisted on seeing him. Henry Clay not only submitted to her demands but also invited her to stay for dinner. Mary was "not at all abashed at rushing into dinner without a previous invitation" (Helm 1928, p. 3). Mrs.

Lincoln's intrusiveness was not always appreciated, however. Neely and McMurtry (1986) noted that Robert Lincoln's wife experienced her mother-in-law as being, "so possessive that her affectionate embrace almost crushed [her]" (p. 149).

Conflicts frequently erupted between Lindsey and her daughter over boundaries and privacy issues. Lindsey felt entitled to listen to her daughter's telephone conversations and to search her room, book bag, purse, and car. She read her daughter's personal notes, questioned her daughter's friends about their activities, and even tried to control her daughter's weight. Despite the fact that her daughter was only five pounds above the average weight for her age, Lindsey enrolled her in a weight-loss clinic.

The borderline Queen can be unrelenting in her intrusiveness. After Mrs. Lincoln complained about the competence of General of the Army Ulysses S. Grant, the President told her, "Suppose that we give you command of the army. No doubt you would do much better than any general that has been tried" (Simmons 1970, p. 120). Respecting boundaries is difficult for the borderline Queen.

Believes rules do not apply to her

Kernberg (1985) states that antisocial behavior is common among borderlines. Lying, stealing, parasitism, exploitativeness, and bribery are especially common in borderline Queens. They hide their debt, their assets, and sometimes their purchases. Lindsey had a closet filled with expensive evening gowns that had never been worn. Shopping and hoarding was an obsession. As Gunderson (1984) explains: "To stave off the panic associated with the absence of a primary object, borderline patients frequently will impulsively engage in behaviors that numb the panic and *establish contact with and control over some new object*" (p. 88, emphasis added).

The Queen has an irrepressible need to acquire and control

self-objects. Family members and personal belongings are jealously guarded. The act of acquiring and controlling what is hers provides temporary relief from feelings of emptiness. Robert Todd Lincoln feared that his mother would destroy herself financially, and hired Pinkerton agents to report on her shopping sprees. He explained, "I am thoroughly convinced in my own mind that my mother would permanently ruin herself in a comparatively short time if allowed to do so" (Neely and McMurtry 1986, p. 88).

The greedy, grasping behavior of the Queen can embarrass her children. Her disregard for rules and her perception of herself as special can be frightening. After his father's assassination, Robert was deeply embarrassed by his mother's behavior, and particularly by her attempt to solicit a pension from Congress. He referred to his mother's begging letters, which she wrote to various congressmen pleading a case of impoverishment. Yet following her death in 1882, Robert disposed of sixty-four trunks filled with dresses, jewelry, and garments that had never been worn.

Is ambitious and determined; can seem strong

The borderline Queen can seem invincible, strong, and courageous to those who do not know her well. Mrs. Lincoln's sister described her as "the most ambitious woman I ever saw" (Simmons 1970, p. 53). My patient, Lindsey, dominated relationships with others and was the leader of groups to which she belonged. Lindsey chose relationships only with those who could be controlled.

Baker (1987) states that "When Mary Lincoln failed to get her way, she intercepted cabinet officers and pressed state officials at her receptions" (p. 203). The Queen is determined, driven, almost possessed by the need to acquire what she desires. But she would gladly rid herself of the inner emptiness that leads to destructive behavior if it were possible to do so.

Lindsey's children accused her of caring more about her possessions than about them. When her son phoned to tell her that he had been in a car accident, Lindsey's first question concerned the condition of the car. Her son told her, "All you care about is yourself and your things!" Lindsey feared that he was right.

THE QUEEN'S MOTTO: IT'S ALL ABOUT ME

The tenacity of the Queen contrasts sharply with the hopelessness of the Waif and the reclusiveness of the Hermit. The Queen never gives up. Adversity merely renews her commitment to obtain compensation. Of the four types of borderline mothers, the Queen may be the least likely to commit suicide. Although she may threaten to kill herself, she is most likely seeking attention rather than expressing a wish to die. No suicide threat should be ignored, however. Attention-seeking suicidal attempts can result in accidental death.

Lindsey's children had no sympathy for their mother. Her son told her that he was sick of her unreasonable demands and disturbing mood swings. Her children saw her as completely self-absorbed and grew more estranged from her each year. Although Lindsey occasionally complained about not feeling loved by her children, she seemed relieved that they had no expectations of her.

Unlike the Waif who resigns herself to deprivation, the Queen will fight for what she wants and she is determined to win. Mary Todd Lincoln suffered numerous losses throughout her lifetime. The childhood death of her mother, the deaths of three of her own children, and the assassination of her beloved husband destroyed her emotionally. Although Mrs. Lincoln's life was filled with sadness, she never lost her will to fight for financial compensation. When Lindsey's attorney implied that her expectations regarding her divorce settlement were unreasonable, she professed, "He owes me everything he has! If you're not willing to fight for me I'll get another attorney!" Lindsey's husband complied with the majority of her demands, agreeing to pay for higher education not only for the children, but for Lindsey as well.

Messages from the Queen Mother

- "You deserve the best, but I deserve better."
- "What's mine is mine and what's yours is mine."
- "It's never enough."
- "I love you when I need you."
- "I resent you needing me."
- "I am a special exception."
- "The rules don't apply to me."
- "I deserve more."
- "It's never good enough."

Adult children may have a distant or conflicted relationship with their Queen mother. The Queen's "me first" message inevitably breeds resentment in her children, who feel deprived themselves. Young children may display regressive behavior such as thumb sucking, baby talk, whining, and temper tantrums in order to win attention. As children grow older and gain more power, conflict increases as they compete with the Queen for the spotlight.

No one can fill the Queen's inner emptiness. Her children may resent her expectations and give up trying to please her. She is particular about everything, rejecting gifts that do not measure up or thinly concealing her disappointment. Adult children may dread her birthday, shopping for gifts, or providing a meal for her. Consequently, these children long for approval, recognition, and validation, and are at risk for giving in to feelings of hopelessness. They may strive to secure her attachment by constantly striving for perfection, only to discover that her love is conditional. Love is withdrawn when the Queen's child fails.

Lindsey's children seemed destined for self-destruction. Her daughter's drug use provided an escape from their no-win relationship and her son dropped out of school. Lindsey's daughter exhibited characteristics of a borderline Waif and her son displayed the angry yearning, feelings of entitlement, and exploitation of others that Lindsey recognized in herself. The future of the Queen's children may be marred by an ominous darkness.

Some children learn too late that it is better to let the Queen rule her own life than to ever try to control her. Robert Todd Lincoln paid a high price for trying to control his mother's self-destructive behavior. After being released from the asylum, she turned her paranoia into revenge. During this period she reportedly threatened to kidnap Robert's daughter and once threatened to have him killed. During his lifetime, Robert Lincoln protected his mother's privacy as much as possible. Following his death, his grandson discovered a bundle of papers labeled "MTL Insanity File," with instructions that it not be released until at least twenty years following Robert Lincoln's death. Although Robert was accused by Baker (1987) of committing "an unforgivable breach" of trust against his mother, (p. 350), the "Insanity File" stands as a haunting testimony to the truth. Although Queen mothers emotionally sacrifice their children, their children may go to their graves protecting her.

6

The Witch Mother

"Husband, listen to me. Tomorrow at daybreak we'll take the children out to the thickest part of the forest . . . They'll never find the way home again and that way we'll be rid of them."

—*Hansel and Gretel*

"Telling my fears to my mother is like feeding flies to a spider. She savors digesting them. Nothing satisfies her more than knowing how to scare me."

Therapists hear horrifying stories of child abuse that never make the headlines. The media seem drawn to stories about children who die, as if the suffering of those who survive is any less terrifying. Children of Witch mothers never outgrow their fear. Although Amy, a 50-year-old patient, survived being raised by a borderline Witch, she described the mind-numbing terror:

"After all these years I still tense up when my 80-year-old mother sits too close to me. My breathing becomes shallow as I focus intently on her breathing. I can't make it obvious that I'm waiting to be attacked. My muscles ache from the tension of holding myself still. When I finally have a chance to move away from her, I relax. Being trapped in a car with her is the worst. I have to be able to get away."

Some children may not survive simply because they are too young to get away. On a warm fall night in 1994, Susan Smith, a separated mother of two, strapped her toddlers in their car seats and took them for a ride (see Rekers 1996). Moments later, her 3-year-old son Michael started to cry. His mother was driving erratically, sobbing, and biting her nails. Michael's 14-month-old brother, Alex, must have realized that something was wrong. By the time a baby is 7 months old,[1] he is capable of sensing his mother's mood. Children of borderlines know when the good mother has turned into the Witch.

Susan Smith drove to a lake near Union, South Carolina, and parked her car at the top of a boat ramp. She stepped out of the car, released the parking brake, and let the car roll into the water with her babies strapped inside. Covering her ears with her hands so she could not hear their screams, she ran up the ramp as the car rolled toward the lake. It took six minutes for the car to sink, drifting away from the ramp, bobbing nose first into the water. David Smith, the father of Alex and Michael, recollected:

> there were some troubling things that I learned in the aftermath of the killings . . . There was only one conclusion I could make. Susan had watched the car as it sank. This was too awful, too terrible to imagine. Susan waiting, seeing Michael and Alex die. If that were true, there was no doubt of something truly evil in Susan's character, something unspeakable. [Smith 1995, p. 229]

The nation believed her initial claim that the children had been victims of a carjacking. She pleaded with the kidnapper on national television to return her children to safety. Nine days later, when she

---

1. Stern (1985) explains that between 7 and 9 months of age, infants develop a subjective self that reflects their need for affect attunement. They are capable of evoking and responding to changes in their caregiver's mood.

confessed to drowning the children, public sympathy turned to outrage.

Susan Smith sacrificed her children in order not to be abandoned by her boyfriend, the wealthy heir to the town's largest industry.[2] He wrote a letter to Susan explaining that he was not interested in dating a woman with children, and so she disposed of them. Television viewers, confused by home videos of this young mother playing with her two small children, were dumbfounded. She seemed so normal. How was it possible?

Two lessons can be learned from the Susan Smith case. The first is that a borderline's fear of abandonment can lead to tragically desperate acts. The second is that failing to recognize the borderline Witch can have deadly consequences. Family, friends, and health-care professionals must learn to recognize the symptoms of BPD, insist on treatment, or continue to pay the high price of ignorance.

Obviously, most borderline mothers do not kill their children. *Most borderline mothers do not physically abuse their children.* But the Witch's children live in terror of her power. The look in her eyes strikes fear in their hearts. Words alone can shatter their souls.

The mother's heartbeat is the first sound a child hears. Devices that imitate the steady beat of a mother's heart are marketed to calm newborn babies. Infants are intimately familiar with the sound of their mother's voice and the rhythm of her breathing. When her heart turns cold and her breathing becomes shallow, the Witch's children freeze with fear. Anything is possible when the Witch emerges.

On May 19, 1983, Diane Downs drove her three children to a

---

2. Susan and her husband David had filed for divorce and were separated at the time of the drownings. Susan's boyfriend sent her a letter on October 17, 1994, explaining his reasons for terminating their relationship, ". . . like I have told you before, there are some things about you that aren't suited for me, and yes, I am speaking about your children" (Rekers 1996, p. 131).

secluded road, took a rifle out of the trunk, and shot them as they sat helplessly in the car. Seven-year-old Cheryl died instantly, but 9-year-old Christie and her 3-year-old brother miraculously survived. Months of physical therapy, speech therapy, and psychotherapy enabled Christie to testify that her mother had shot her and her siblings. Nine-year-old Christie Downs speaks for all children of borderline Witches when she asked, " 'Why didn't anybody hear us screaming? We were screaming and screaming' " (in Rule 1987, p. 463).

Across most species, the cries of the young are physiologically designed to trigger a mother's protective response. Their screams are designed to pierce the mother's heart and bring her running. A human mother can recognize the distinctive sound of her child's cry by its third day of life. Yet Diane Downs aimed the gun at her screaming children and pulled the trigger anyway.

Children are the first to recognize and the last to admit that something is wrong with their mother. Yet, the public's response to Christina Crawford's autobiography illustrates how readily others disbelieve even adult children. In her subsequent book *Survivor* (1988) Christina wrote: "It never dawned on me that instead . . . [of being believed], a nightmare would be in store for me . . . for my sense of self was rocked once again with the publication of my book *Mommie Dearest* . . . never did I imagine it would ignite years of soul-shattering controversy that would threaten my life and my sanity" (p. 13). Christina believed that her near fatal stroke resulted from personal vilification following the publication of *Mommie Dearest*.

The voices of children are easily silenced by the fear of not being believed. If 3-year-old Michael Smith had somehow miraculously survived, would he have told anyone that his mother tried to drown him? Would anyone have believed him? No one wants to believe that a mother would sacrifice her own child, especially the child.

Louise Kaplan (1978) writes that, normally, "the mother's presence is like a fixed light that gives the child the security to move out safely to explore the world and then return safely to harbor" (p. 42). The Witch's children have no safe harbor. Because the Witch emerges when the mother and child are alone, no witnesses can verify the child's experience. The Witch's children feel like prisoners of a secret war. By the time they grow up they often unconsciously repress their memories, and their terror may be transformed into hatred. The Witch's grown son may become a sadistic serial killer, able to have intercourse only with dead women who cannot reject or humiliate him.[3]

Children of borderline Witches know that their mother can make people vanish. They have seen her cut people to shreds with words, shatter the reputations of those who betray her, and stab them in the heart with false accusations. They know the feeling of sinking into nothingness by soul-wrenching verbal attacks. Alex and Michael Smith sank into the darkness knowing what all children of borderline Witches know—that their own mother sacrificed them to save herself.

Recognizing the borderline Witch requires more than a superficial glance at her external character. In 1994 Susan Smith duped an entire nation. The search for her children cost taxpayers more than two million dollars and broke the hearts of millions of people. In his book, *Beyond All Reason*, her appalled husband claimed that she did not seem genuinely sorry. David Smith (1995) wrote:

> When I thought back over the visit, what struck me most was that she didn't seem really sorry, despite saying she was again and again.

---

3. Readers who are interested in learning more about the early childhood experiences of serial killers of females should review research by Dorothy Otnow Lewis. Her findings suggest that some of these men accept the death sentence adamantly protecting their mothers, and repress memories of maternal sexual abuse. See Lewis et al. 1986.

If the roles were reversed, I would have been stretched out on the floor, wrapped around her ankles, bawling my head off that I was sorry, wailing for forgiveness.

It was like her written confession. If you read it, you see she doesn't talk that much about the boys. She says she's sorry a few times and that's it. Mostly it's about *Susan*, how *Susan* feels. [p. 246]

Understanding the feelings of the borderline Witch is critical to determining the risk to her children. Those closest to the Witch often minimize, deny, and ignore signs of her desperation until tragedy strikes. Although denial may be useful in avoiding unpleasant emotion, it also prevents intervention and thus can have deadly consequences.

After her arrest, Susan Smith wrote to her husband complaining that "'*Nobody gives a damn about me*'" (Smith 1995, p. 214). David Smith stated, "I couldn't believe it. The letter shocked me. It made me think that Susan didn't have a firm grasp of reality. I thought to myself, 'What kind of person would write a letter like this after she killed her kids?'" (p. 214).

MEDEAN MOTHERS

The Medean Mother is the most pathological type of borderline Witch. Although she can emerge from any one of the other three types of borderline mothers, most Witches are not Medean Mothers. Medean Mothers are extremely rare.

In 431 B.C., Euripides, the Greek playwright, wrote a compelling drama about a mother who murdered her two sons to punish her unfaithful husband.[4] Centuries later, when the play was performed on Broadway in 1947, one critic (in Young 1953) claimed

---

4. For lines quoted from Euripides' drama *Medea*, see *Euripides: Medea and Other Plays*, translated by Philip Vellacott (New York: Penguin Books, 1963).

that while it was believable that a "discarded wife might dispose of her blond successor by any means in her power . . . the ensuing infanticide is too much" (p. 89). Yet the play *Medea* survives as the epic story of the murderous mother because of its inherent truth— the disturbing reality that rejection, in Medea's case by "he who was all the world to me," can drive some women to infanticide.

Like Medea, Susan Smith justified murdering her children because she felt that life had been unfair to her. Medea convinces herself, "For one short day forget your children, afterwards weep; though you kill them, they were your beloved sons. Life has been cruel to me." Susan Smith wrote, "Why was everything so bad in my life? I dropped to the lowest when I allowed my children to go down that ramp into the water" (Rekers 1996, p. 117).

Adler (1985) explains that borderlines continually fight to manage separation anxiety and are "forced to rely on . . . [others] . . . for enough sense of holding-soothing to keep separation anxiety in check—to avoid annihilation panic" (p. 82). Rejection triggers the desperate fear of sinking into the cold, dark abyss of abandonment, a fate the Witch feels is worse than death. Murder, therefore, becomes an option. Her terrified children sense her desperate determination and horrifying reversal of the protective instinct of maternal love.

Convicted murderer Diane Downs obtained copies of photos taken at her daughter's autopsy. She insisted on showing the gruesome images to fellow inmates as if to say, "Look what I can do!" A televised interview captured her sinister expression when the nauseated reporter interrupted Downs's all-too-graphic description of the bloody car. "It was a smile—but such a strange smile—her eyes narrowed, her lips in a smirk" (in Rule 1987, p. 287).

The need for power and control over others, the need to elicit a response of fear and shock is a source of pride for borderline Witches. Terrified and powerless as children, Witch mothers project repressed rage and terror onto others. Their sense of self-importance may be primarily derived from their ability to elicit fear, and their pride may be thinly concealed.

Most Witch mothers do not physically sacrifice their children. Emotional sacrifice is much more common. For example, a Witch mother who discovers that her husband has sexually molested her daughter may punish the daughter by sending *her* away. Indirectly, these mothers punish the husband by taking away the object of his desire. They view the experience in terms of how *they* were hurt, rather than recognizing the child's trauma. A pseudo—self-righteousness or a justification based on religious dogma may conceal their lack of true remorse. They may cling to the belief that they are forgiven and believe that they have spared their children from further suffering. Susan Smith's chilling words reveal the twisted perspective: " 'My children, Michael and Alex, are with our Heavenly Father now and I know that they will never be hurt again. As a mom, that means more than words could ever say' " (in Rekers 1996, p. 117).

A Witch mother can be insanely jealous of her daughter, may not be able to tolerate displays of affection between her daughter and husband, and may accuse the father of incest. A patient explained that whenever her mother witnessed her father playing with her, her mother flew into a rage and accused the father of being "sick." The patient, confused by her mother's reaction, assumed that she had done something wrong. The patient felt guilty about loving her father, complicating the resolution of the oedipal complex.

The Witch mother may be unable to tolerate such displays of affection because she feels left out and abandoned. Such mothers may say to themselves, "He never plays with *me* like that, *we* never have that kind of fun together. He is my husband. I should come first. There's something wrong with *him*." Jealous rage can lead to murderous rage toward the *child*.

Guilt does not deter the Medean Mother because she feels

justified in her actions. Medea convinces herself, "Yes, I can endure guilt, however horrible; the laughter of my enemies I will not endure." When Diane Downs walked into the state penitentiary,

> She wore skintight Levi's, so tight that every mound, cleft and tuck was accentuated. Her jeans were tucked into the wildest pair of boots . . . shiny black leather with six-inch, spiked heels. Yes, the prisoners in the state penitentiary would remember Diane Downs's arrival. She looked mean, she looked bad, and she looked sexy. She did not look like . . . a grieving mother. [Rule 1987, p. 448]

The Medean Mother may sacrifice her children, but never, ever her pride.

THE WITCH'S EMOTIONAL STATE: ANNIHILATING RAGE

> But the old woman had only pretended to be so kind. Actually she was a wicked witch, who waylaid children and had built her house out of bread to entice them.
>
> —*Hansel and Gretel*

In his book *The Gift of Fear*, Gavin De Becker (1997) warns, "We must learn and then teach our children that niceness does not equal goodness . . . People seeking to control others almost always present the image of a nice person in the beginning" (p. 67). Clarnell Kemper was apparently a well-liked and competent administrative assistant at the University of Southern California. Her co-workers apparently never detected the Witch within. The Witch in the workplace can function effectively *unless* she is threatened or cornered.

Cheney (1976) described Mr. Kemper's experience living with

his ex-wife: "suicide missions in wartime and the later atomic bomb testings were nothing compared to living with his wife, Clarnell" (p. 8). Mr. Kemper recalled that, " '[she] affected me as a grown man more than three hundred and ninety-six days and nights of fighting on the front did. I became confused and was not certain of anything for quite a time' " (Cheney 1976, p. 8).

Clarnell Kemper was a large, loudspoken woman who bore a son and two daughters. When her son, Edmund, was 9 years old, she and her husband divorced. A year later Edmund's father discovered to his horror that Clarnell kept Edmund trapped in the cellar at night. Edmund was terrified because the only way out was a door that was blocked by the kitchen table.

The darkness within the borderline Witch is annihilating rage. All mothers lose their temper, but ordinary mothers do not turn on their children, set traps, ridicule, humiliate, or enjoy watching them suffer. Ordinary mothers would sacrifice their lives to save their children. In contrast, the borderline Witch sacrifices her child to save herself. Lachkar (1992) observes that "Borderlines will frequently sacrifice themselves, their family or their children. In court custody cases, children become the sacrificial objects, are placed in the middle of arguments, and are deprived, made to be go-betweens, and treated as little adults playing the role of mediators, therapists and saviors" (p. 78).

Few borderline mothers are always Witches, and some are *never* Witches. *The child's perception defines the borderline Witch.* The Witch who hides in the Waif, the Hermit, and the Queen appears only to those who trigger her rage. She represents an ego-state that can be triggered by criticism, betrayal, or abandonment. The Witch is therefore deceiving in appearance and manner. Like a cat with a mouse, she may lie in wait, pouncing when the child least expects it, deceiving the child into believing that she is no longer angry, and then unleashing her rage. Each Witch has her own unique pattern of behavior that reflects her early experience and the nature of her relationship with the particular child.

The borderline mother who *primarily* appears as a Witch is filled with self-hatred as the result of surviving a childhood that required complete submission to a hostile or sadistic caregiver. The Witch *may* exhibit antisocial behavior such as habitual lying, exploitativeness, sexual promiscuity, and physical, sexual, or verbal abuse—or she can be a cold, snobbish, self-righteous, withholding Witch. Either way, she sets up her children to be trapped and deceived in the same way that she was once deceived. She may trick her children to tell her what they want and then deliberately withhold those very things. She may force her children into embarrassing and humiliating situations and then ridicule them. She may betray their confidences, share their secrets, and exploit their fears. Her calculated cruelty can take many forms although she believes that her behavior is justified.

Children who dare to resist the Witch mother's control face further punishment. Yet Witch mothers may corner their children and provoke attack. Children may threaten the Witch physically, or attempt to ward her off with a knife or other weapon. Usually, however, they turn the weapon on themselves. The threat, "Don't come any closer or I'll kill myself" may be a desperate child's only recourse. Edmund Kemper recalled:

> My mother and I started right in on horrendous battles, just horrible battles, violent and vicious. I've never been in such a vicious verbal battle with anyone. It would go to fists with a man, but this was my mother and I couldn't stand the thought of my mother and I doing these things. She insisted on it, and just over stupid things. I remember one roof-raiser was over whether I should have my teeth cleaned. [Cheney 1976, pp. 37–38]

Female children are more likely to attack themselves than their mothers. Self-mutilation expresses rage at the self instead of the mother. Male children tend to externalize rage, cutting up small animals instead of their mother. In one case, an adolescent son pulled a knife on his borderline mother and threatened to stab her. At the last minute, however, he turned the knife toward his stomach and stabbed himself. Both male and female children of borderlines are more likely to hurt themselves than their mothers. Young children instinctually protect their mothers physically as well as emotionally.

The rage of the borderline Witch is as venomous as the bite of a viper. Her words can be difficult to remember because they are so unexpected and degrading. Her tone of voice conveys her sinister intent. As Daniel Goleman (1995) explains:

> Just as the mode of the rational mind is words, the mode of the emotions is nonverbal. Indeed, when a person's words disagree with what is conveyed via his tone of voice, gesture, or other nonverbal channel, the emotional truth is in *how* he says something rather than in *what* he says. One rule of thumb used in communication research is that 90% or more of an emotional message is nonverbal. [p. 291]

The Witch's tone of voice conveys a clear message of venomous hatred. But children of Witch mothers are like snake handlers who, frequently bitten, develop immunity. With time, a thick layer of scar tissue eventually covers the wounds. Author Susanna Kaysen (1993) eloquently describes the effect: "Scar tissue has no character. It's not like skin. It doesn't show age or illness or pallor or tan. It has no pores, no hair, no wrinkles. It's like a slipcover. It shields and disguises what's beneath. That's why we grow it; we have something to hide" (p. 16).

Managing the adrenaline triggered by an attack by one's mother is not easy. Children who fight back are punished. Children who hurt themselves may be labeled as crazy. Children who hurt someone else are referred to the justice system. The Witch's children must surrender themselves to her control and suffer the consequences of internalized rage.

Child analyst Elisabeth Geleerd (1958) treated a 7-year-old boy who demanded that she hit him. She recalled that the child would ask her to beat him, explaining that the only control he felt he possessed was deciding *when* he was to be beaten. All children need control over their environment in order to feel secure. Because attacks by the Witch mother are unexpected and unpredictable, the child experiences massive insecurity. Attacks by the Witch mother are like tornadoes: random, devastating, and unpredictable. Naturally, her children are on constant alert for changes in the atmosphere that might indicate when and where she will "Turn."

"THE TURN"

One of the most devastating experiences for children of borderlines is "the Turn." The Turn is a sudden attack, the abrupt withdrawal of love and affection, and razor-sharp words that can pierce the heart as painfully as an arrow. The messages aimed at children include: "I want you out of my life," "I'd be better off without you," and "I should never have had you kids." The child might inadvertently trigger the Turn by (1) showing affection for someone other than mother, (2) disobeying, or expressing an independent thought, (3) diminishing mother, (4) differentiating from mother, or (5) disagreeing with mother. The disturbing reality is that the Turn may be triggered by circumstances that have nothing to do with the child. Any situation that triggers feelings of betrayal, rejection, or abandonment might cause the good mother to turn into the Witch. When the borderline mother's partner is absent or frustrating, she may turn on her children.

Children have no way of knowing that the borderline's emotional state is primarily determined by the state of her relationship with her own primary attachment figure. They have no way of knowing that their mother sometimes views their existence as a threat to her existence. Thus, the Turn seems entirely random to the child.

De Becker (1997) explains that, "As with the shark attack, randomness and lack of warning are the attributes of human violence we fear most . . ." (p. 344). Although De Becker is referring to adults here, children have an even greater need for predictability because they possess so little power. Children who live with a predatory mother become unconsciously preoccupied with reading their mother's moods. A fleeting glance, a furtive gesture, deceleration, and a shift of direction are signals of an approaching Turn. Bracing, hiding, or merely holding on gives children a much-needed sense of control. Shutting down, avoiding eye contact, and getting away are other means of establishing control.

The Witch's children can feel blown away by her rage. Whichever child she chooses to target feels annihilated after the Turn. Although a few adult children had mothers who threatened to kill them, the majority recalled episodes of being emotionally discarded or disowned, and verbally dehumanized. The disposable child is depersonalized and referred to as *"that"* girl or *"the"* girl (or boy) rather than "my daughter" or "my son." Deliberately avoiding the use of a possessive pronoun or the child's name dehumanizes the child and symbolizes banishment. De Becker points out that for children, banishment equals death: "For all social animals, from ants to antelopes, identity is the pass card to inclusion, and inclusion is the key to survival. If a baby loses its identity as the child of its parents, a possible outcome is abandonment. For a human infant, that means death" (p. 342).

The Turn reverses the mother–child relationship from one of loving acceptance to life-threatening rejection. Masterson (1980) quotes a borderline's child as stating that his childhood was "like living in a permanent funeral, as if I might soon be buried" (p. 18).

The borderline's children are acutely aware of their disposability, and, like illegal immigrants, live in fear of sudden exile.

The Witch attacks her child one minute, later behaving as if nothing out of the ordinary occurred. Blinding rage seems to erase her memory. Kernberg (1985) provides one such example:

> A hospitalized borderline patient literally yelled at her hospital physician during their early half-hour interviews, and her voice carried to all the offices in the building. After approximately two weeks of such behavior, which the hospital physician felt unable to influence by any psychotherapeutic means, he saw her by chance shortly after leaving his office. He was still virtually trembling, and was struck by the fact that the patient seemed completely relaxed, and smiled in a friendly way while talking to some other patients with whom she was acquainted. [p. 86]

If mental-health professionals tremble in the wake of borderline rage, how do children survive? Children of borderlines may try everything in their power to hide. Like adults fighting for their lives, they may beg for mercy, try to cajole, cry, or plead, and promise to be good. When the Witch goes away, the child is indescribably relieved. But children of Witches are acutely attuned to the sound of their mother's voice, an early indicator of the Witch's return. When her tone is haughty and cold they are on full alert.

The human brain is designed to focus attention on the greatest threat to survival. Research (Schacter 1996) on individuals who have been victims of violent crimes discovered a phenomenon known as *weapon focusing* (p. 210). Witnesses of violent crimes tend to have accurate memories of the weapon but are unable to remember other details. Children of borderline Witches may not remember the details of previous attacks but are extremely sensitized to indications of imminent attacks. They remember changes in her tone of voice, her facial expression, and her body language.

Interactions with the borderline Witch are devastating and potentially dangerous to both mother and child. Borderline Witches have a sadomasochistic character structure and are extremely difficult, if not impossible, to help. The Witch, like a cyclone, skips over some children and destroys others, attacking those who are *perceived* as threatening. Although her attacks can provoke retaliation by the child, the Witch believes that retaliation justifies continued abuse. It is a vicious cycle that begins with the mother's projections.

Clarnell Kemper's death (see Cheney 1976) exemplifies the pathological dynamics that can develop between the Witch and the child who is the target of her rage. Edmund Kemper murdered his mother while she was sleeping. He slashed her throat, decapitated her, and performed intercourse with her dead body. He later cut out her larynx and threw it down the garbage disposal "in that way getting back at her for all the bitter things she had said to him over the years" (Cheney 1976, p. 187). The sadistic elements of Kemper's relationship with her son were replicated in the manner in which Edmund killed her—exploitation of her vulnerability, postmortem degradation, and annihilatory rage.

THE WITCH'S INNER EXPERIENCE:
SELF LOATHING AND
THE CONVICTION OF BEING EVIL

Witches have red eyes and can't see very far, but they have a keen sense of smell like animals, so they know when humans are coming.

—*Hansel and Gretel*

Witch mothers possess a laser-like ability to detect areas of vulnerability in others. Like the witch in *Hansel and Gretel*, the borderline

Witch has "a keen sense of smell" for human weakness. Witch mothers know what to say to hurt or scare their children, and use humiliation and degradation to punish them.

The Witch can be bitter, demanding, sarcastic, and cruel to the child who is the target of her rage. Other children may not perceive her as a Witch if they do not possess qualities that trigger her rage. Witches may make statements such as, "I'm going to kill you," "I'm going to make your life a living Hell," or "You are never going to hear the end of this." The sinister, sadistic message is a wish for total destruction of the child. When the child is an adult the roles may be reversed, placing the mother's life in danger.

Edmund Kemper was eventually convicted of eight counts of murder, including the death of his own mother. Murdering his mother, he explained, was something he *had* to do, "someone just standing off to the side . . . isn't really going to see any kind of sense, or rhyme or reason" (Cheney, p. 132).

Of the four profiles of BPD in women, the Witch is the least likely to seek treatment. Her conviction of being evil and her self-loathing prevent the Witch from being able to trust a therapist. She fears being trapped and is likely to become violent if hospitalized. The Witch may attack and provoke the therapist in order to evoke punishment or rejection. She is motivated by such powerful destructive urges that she seems unable to tolerate being helped. She lacks belief in her own basic goodness and the ability to perceive goodness in others, even her own children.

Masterson (1981) contends that some borderlines want "to get back—not to get better" (p. 188). The borderline Witch is not interested in being helped. She wants revenge. Witch mothers may seek treatment for their children, but never for themselves. They denigrate the mental health profession because they fear its power. The Witch's greatest fear is of having no control, of being locked up.

Borderline Witches are extremely threatened by mental health professionals and have been known to break objects, damage personal belongings, hit, bite, and become physically combative. They may try to destroy those who try to help them. A Witch mother who brought her son for treatment registered a complaint with the therapist's professional organization demanding that the therapist's license be revoked after the therapist recommended that the mother seek treatment. Although the complaint was dismissed, the mother's destructive intent was clear.

Witch mothers are more likely to bring their children for treatment than to seek help for themselves. They project their own pathology onto their child, and often expect the child to be institutionalized. Because the no-good child is the target of the Witch's projections of self-hatred, the mother may wish for the child to be sent away. She needs and wants to get rid of this hated part of herself. Working with children of Witch mothers requires careful consideration, as therapists need to take appropriate steps to protect themselves while acting in the best interests of the child. No one should underestimate the vindictiveness of the borderline Witch, but, most important, no one should leave her children unprotected.

CHARACTERISTICS OF THE WITCH MOTHER

Is sadistically controlling and punitive with her children

Ernest Wolf (1988) explains that "merger-hungry" personalities need to control others completely. The borderline Witch's merger-hungry personality leaves her children feeling devoured, suffo-cated, oppressed, and imprisoned. Even as adults, her children may dream about prison camps, holocausts, invasions, wars, and natural disasters. They fear for their survival.

The Witch needs complete control over her children and may be abusive with the child who is the target of her rage. Unlike the other three profiles of BPD in women, the Witch's behavior evokes submission and fear rather than compassion and concern from others. Her children are forced to submit to her control and may be victims of sadistic emotional, physical, or sexual abuse. Female children of Witch mothers may perpetuate the cycle and, as adults, become Witch mothers themselves.

When young children are deliberately hurt by their mothers, their first instinct is to repress recognition of their mothers as the source of their pain. A toddler whose mother slapped him across the face looked at his mother and exclaimed, "Somebody hit me!" The young child needs to preserve the image of mother as good in order to survive psychologically. The child concludes, therefore, that he deserved to be hurt. Physical, sexual, or verbal abuse delivers the message "you are bad" quite clearly and convincingly to a child.

Children who are victims of chronic abuse may eventually confuse love with hate. Edmund Kemper (Cheney 1976) described this confusion: "I had this love–hate complex with my mother that was very hard for me to handle and I was very withdrawn— withdrawn from reality because of it. I couldn't handle the hate, and the love was actually forced upon me" (pp. 29–30).

Such a child expects to be hurt by the person he loves. Kernberg suggests that the anxiety of expecting to be hurt is intolerable. Therefore, the child must have complete control of the one he loves in order to avoid being hurt. In Edmund Kemper's case (as with many serial killers of females), his fear of rejection was so overwhelming that it was impossible for him to have a relationship with a living woman. He fantasized about relationships with his dead victims, kept some of their personal belongings, and talked to their decapitated heads.

Male children of Witch mothers may grow up to become

criminals or sex offenders. One such example was Henry Lee Lucas. Those who knew Henry Lee's mother literally referred to her as a witch. Lucas murdered hundreds of women, including his mother and girlfriend. Viola Lucas (see Call 1985) beat Henry with broom handles, sticks, and pieces of timber, demanding that he not cry. After beatings she would explain that she had done it for his own good, that he was born evil. She often told him that he would die in prison. His teachers observed frequent bruises and injuries but felt powerless to intervene.

Possesses annihilatory rage

Adler (1985) states that "borderline rage can be annihilatory in intent and intensity" (p. 35). He explains that "recognition memory rage" is a level of rage so intense that the borderline is momentarily unable to recognize the person who is the target of her anger. The person is no longer recognized as human. Adler describes a patient who stated that she was so angry with him that she "stomped" him out of her mind. When children are stomped out of their mother's mind, they feel as though they have dropped off the edge of the earth, off the protective radar screen of the mother's mind, and into the abyss. Children can be physically abandoned without feeling annihilated if they trust in their mother's love. Trusting the consistency of their mother's love is unimaginable for the Witch's children.

Victims of annihilating rage describe feeling "blown away." The borderline Witch annihilates others *so that they no longer exist in her mind.* The child who is the target of the borderline's rage represents some hated aspect of the borderline that she wishes to destroy. Unfortunately, because the target child is abused, the child develops a self-concept grounded in hatred and behaves in a way that reinforces the mother's perception.

Organizes a campaign of denigration

The borderline Witch enlists others as allies against the person who is the target of her rage. She may seek out friends, family members (including siblings and children), and co-workers of her victim in whom to confide fabricated stories designed to discredit her enemy. She intentionally leaves out discussion of her own behavior, presenting the other person's behavior as entirely unjustified. A patient recalled that during her childhood her Witch mother frequently phoned her father to complain about the patient's misbehavior. Overhearing these conversations the patient was infuriated to hear her mother's distorted account. Her mother began haranguing her father with, "She's up to it again. She's out of control, yelling and screaming. You've got to do something about her when you get home." The patient was amazed and disgusted at her mother's deceptiveness.

Others may believe the Witch's allegations of mistreatment because of the intensity of her emotion. Misinformation is calculated and constructed in order to destroy the victim's reputation. Those who do not know the true situation may not notice inconsistencies in the Witch's story. It is difficult to verify the truth because the intensity of the Witch's emotion dissuades others from asking for details.

Kemper's sisters apparently joined their mother in denigrating Edmund. Cheney (1976) wrote that Kemper's older sister, Susan, "may have emulated her mother's sometimes punishing rejection of him" (p. 9). On one occasion, Susan apparently tried to push Edmund in front of a train, and yet another time, actually pushed him into the deep end of a swimming pool where he almost drowned.

The most common campaign of denigration is organized against ex-spouses and ex-partners of the borderline Witch. Divorces, separations, and endings of relationships can trigger a full-blown war; thus, custody battles may continue for years. The Witch is consumed with annihilatory rage and may seek financial, emotional, and physical revenge. After her husband asked for a divorce, a patient blurted out, "I want to hurt him as badly as he hurt me. I want him destroyed."

Stirs up conflict and controversy in groups

The divide-and-conquer strategy is an attempt by the borderline to control others by splitting groups into factions. Individuals may be unaware that they have heard different versions of the same story and may turn against one another rather than confront or question the Witch.

Christina Crawford (1978) explained that her mother attempted to deceive the nuns who ran the boarding school Christina attended. Letters she received from her mother were written to present their relationship as warm and loving because her mother knew that the nuns read mail. Christina's actual conversations with her mother, however, were laced with hostility. Later, Christina discovered that her mother called the boarding school weekly, hoping to be told that Christina had been misbehaving.

The borderline Witch's ability to enlist others as allies disrupts and divides groups. When hospitalized, borderlines frequently split and project different parts of themselves onto various staff members, causing conflict among the staff. Adler (1985) found:

Staff members who are the recipients of cruel, punishing parts of the patient will tend to react to the patient in a cruel, sadistic and punishing manner. Staff members who have received loving, idealized projected parts of the patient will tend to respond to him with a protective, parental love. Obviously a clash can occur between these two groups of staff members. These mechanisms also help to explain why different staff members may see the same patient in very different ways. [p. 204]

This destructive dynamic can have devastating consequences. Family members (including children) may be estranged or blacklisted for years, never knowing what went wrong. Robert Lincoln's mother refused to communicate with him for four years following her insanity trial.

Hostility masks her fear

The borderline Witch is terrified of vulnerability, of trusting, of not having control, of being helpless, of being hurt. Adler (1985) explains that the "diffuse primitive rage" of the borderline is an "unchanneled, generalized discharge of hate and aggression" (pp. 36–37). He believes that the borderline's separation anxiety becomes annihilation panic. In other words, when the Witch mother perceives her children as resisting her control (by expressing their own will) she perceives them as threatening her survival. Her mindset is "If you are not with me, you are against me."

The Witch mother's hostility is an attempt to discredit those with power. Portraying the enemy as weak, incompetent, or worthless reduces the threat to her. Thus, she is pleased when others feel diminished, vulnerable, and powerless. The Witch's children sense her pleasure (sadistic enjoyment) at their expense. In fact, degrading others *does* make the Witch mother feel better.

What must be understood, and what is so frequently overlooked by those who interact with the Witch, is the intensity of her fear that drives her hostile behavior. She is so effective in projecting fear onto others that even experienced clinicians may fail to recognize *her* fear.

Is intrusive, domineering, and violates the boundaries of others

The Witch mother may violate every aspect of her child. She may be sexually abusive or sexually degrade her children. She may subject them to unnecessary medical procedures and humiliate them in public. She does not recognize appropriate boundaries and exploits the child's trust. She may search through their personal belongings, ask intrusive questions, and deny them their right to privacy.

The Witch mother has an almost uncanny ability to perceive vulnerability in others. She watches for indications of fear, shame, or guilt, and intentionally elicits such feelings in order to control her children. Children with Witch mothers learn to hide their feelings and everything they love in order to survive. Christina Crawford described feeling as though her mother could read the secret vulnerabilities of her soul.

Edmund Kemper complained that his mother invaded every aspect of his life. She felt entitled to control every decision, from the smallest detail to the major decisions of his life. After he murdered his grandparents, Edmund was confused and disoriented, unable to think for himself. Predictably, he turned to his mother for advice. At the time, he was unaware of the connection between his hatred of her and the reason he murdered his grandparents.

Destroys valued objects or is intentionally withholding

Linehan (1993b) reports that borderlines in her clinic have broken clocks, torn bulletin boards apart, stolen mail, thrown objects, and written graffiti on walls. The Witch destroys what is loved or valued. Witch mothers may intentionally withhold what their children need or want, including medical treatment. When the child is physically injured, such a mother may fail to seek appropriate medical treatment, even if the child is near death.

Patients report having had favorite toys either broken or given away as punishment, and several had pets that suddenly disappeared. Henry Lee Lucas's mother shot and killed his pet mule after he told her that he loved it. One patient cried as she recalled that her mother set her pet rabbit loose following an argument. Joan Crawford cut up one of Christina's favorite dresses and made her wear it in shreds. Christina's mother believed in the convoluted philosophy that taking away what a child loves teaches the child how to give.

Other patients lamented that their Witch mothers intentionally withheld what they knew they loved or wanted. One patient explained that her mother gave her applesauce for dinner while she served the rest of the family spaghetti, the patient's favorite meal. Naturally, the Witch's children learn not to reveal what they love or want. The Witch mother honestly believes, however, that what she is doing is for her children's own good. She simply repeats what she learned as a child.

Possesses the conviction of being evil

Some borderlines feel as though they are possessed by the devil. The borderline Witch may feel, look, and act possessed. She survived her childhood by fighting and continues the battle as an adult. Children of borderline Witches are clearly at risk for becoming borderline themselves. For them, survival depends on their ability to become invisible or continue a never-ending battle. The Witch's children may suffer from acute anxiety or murderous rage for the rest of their lives.

Gunderson (1984) suggests that "latent convictions of innate badness may become overwhelming to some borderline patients"

(p. 89). Kroll (1988) observes that some borderlines feel "both deserving of special consideration and simultaneously so evil as scarcely to deserve being alive" (p. 65). This sense of evil contributes to the Witch's expectation of punishment from others. Some borderline Witches may adhere to rigid religious practices in the attempt to seek redemption. As Daniel Paul (1987) observes: "When a person negates his will and needs in the service of becoming invisible, the self is experienced as being claimed by a sinister aspect of the self or other. This sinister force becomes personified as an omnipresent demon: the Devil" (p. 151).

David Smith's (1995) statement that "there was no doubt of something truly evil in Susan's character, something unspeakable" (p. 229) is the terrible truth about how borderline Witches feel about themselves. Naturally, their children sense the presence of this evil force. The Witch's child knows the unbearable truth about what lies within the mother's heart.

Has a fear of entrapment

The Witch will not tolerate being controlled by others. If she is hospitalized or restrained she can unleash potentially destructive rage. She will lash out at others in order to escape or will find a way of controlling the situation by stirring up conflict. Kroll (1988) relates an experience with a borderline Witch:

> A 27-year-old divorced woman brought her three-year-old son to the hospital, where he was admitted with a diagnosis of pneumonia. Upon full examination there was a suspicion of child abuse and neglect. The next day, the woman's request that she take her son home was refused by the hospital staff. She became very upset and verbally abusive and was escorted from the pediatrics ward. Several hours later, in the evening, she returned and tried to remove her son

from the ward. She was discovered and a struggle ensued; hospital security was called. She ended up in four-point restraints . . . after she kicked a security officer in the groin . . . I arrived and . . . introduced myself and said that we might discuss her present predicament. She told me to have intercourse with myself. [pp. 47–48]

The patient successfully manipulated Kroll into releasing her from restraints and subsequently ran out of the hospital cursing him.

The tragic irony is that the Witch's combative resistance to being controlled invites the use of increasing control, restraint, and restriction. After Diane Downs escaped from the Oregon State Penitentiary in July of 1987 and was subsequently recaptured, she was transferred to a maximum security prison in New Jersey. The will of the Witch, however, may be stronger than any institution.

Has a poor prognosis for treatment

Kernberg (1985) believes that borderlines who were raised by sadistic caregivers have the least chance of being successfully treated. In fact, borderline Witches denigrate mental health professionals. The Witches' lack of trust in others and the tendency to misperceive interactions as aggressive make it nearly impossible to help them. They can be so effective in provoking others that a battle for survival can easily ensue. Often, borderline Witches will hurt themselves before allowing anyone else to help them.

As Joan Crawford lay dying, she refused to allow friends and family members to visit (Crawford 1997). Prior to her death she had been losing weight for a year and was no longer capable of bathing herself. Nevertheless, she refused medical treatment. Only a woman employed by Mrs. Crawford was present at her death bed. Christina later learned:

The woman, realizing there was nothing more she could do, began praying for mother. At first the prayers were silent but as she realized how close the end really was, her prayers became audible. She was praying aloud and mother heard the words. Mother raised her head. The last words from her mouth were: "Dammit . . . don't you *dare* ask God to help!" A few minutes later she was dead. [Crawford 1997, p. 387]

The borderline Witch may *never* relinquish control.

THE WITCH'S MOTTO: LIFE IS WAR

The Witch's childhood experiences taught her that life is a battle for survival. She prepares her children for life as she knows it, for life in a concentration camp, for hating, fighting, and killing. Her children may learn not to fear danger; in fact, they may learn to seek it. They may enjoy having control over others, sensing vulnerability and exploiting it. They grow up broken, unable to love, unable to trust, unable to feel. The Witch's children are victims of soul murder and may feel alive only when suffering or when inflicting suffering.

The Witch's Messages to Her Children

- "I could kill you."
- "You'll be sorry."
- "You won't get away with this."
- "You deserve to suffer."
- "I'd be better off without you."
- "You'll never escape my control."
- "It's my right as your parent to control you."
- "I'm going to make you pay."

The Witch's child is raised in a hopeless situation. The Witch's need for control and dominance leaves the child filled with rage, fear, and self-hatred. Her words can be vile, her heart cold as stone. One patient, Amy, survived the terror of her childhood by developing an unshakeable faith in God. Although she was left with permanent disabilities due to her mother's abuse, she was a loving wife and mother and a highly respected employee. Her faith in God, and her belief that she was loved, saved her soul from her mother's destructiveness. No one would believe what she endured as a child, or the strength of mind that saved her.

The Witch's children survive their childhood by learning not to feel, cry, laugh, smile, or frown in their mother's presence. Adult children raised by Witch mothers survived an emotional hell. Without intervention, young children may not survive.

7

Make-Believe Children

"O wicked child . . . what is this I hear! I thought I had hidden thee from all the world, and thou hast betrayed me!"

—*Rapunzel*

"Every entry in my childhood diary began with, 'I had fun today. I am happy.' I hid my true feelings completely, without realizing that I was pretending. I was faithful, obedient, easy-going, and quiet, hoping to win my mother's love. I became everything that she needed me to be, everything except happy."

Rachel was a brilliant scientist who worked for a major pharmaceutical company. Attractive, competent, and highly respected, she was dependable, faithful, obedient, and easygoing. She was everything but happy.

An only child of divorced parents, Rachel lived with her mother and grandparents. Rachel described her mother as a promiscuous Waif who paid little attention to her. Her mother resented Rachel and accused her of being selfish and evil. No matter how good she tried to be, Rachel could never win her mother's approval. Whenever her mother was affectionate, Rachel braced herself for the Turn. In the journals she kept as an adult Rachel recorded the painful truth: "*Her words can sear my soul like acid until it shrivels and turns black. All I can do is turn away, but then she accuses me of being too sensitive or misunderstanding. When she turns on me I am flung through space and time like a lifeless object. I am no longer her child and she is no longer my mother. I am a useless object she can throw away—a worthless piece of trash.*"

Rachel feared that others would discover the "truth" about her, that she was, indeed, worthless. She argued, "*I'm not 'one of them' . . . I have to work harder than everyone else.*" The I-beam of her soul was a fragile construction; thus, her sense of self easily crumbled. She felt driven to excel, set unrealistic expectations for herself, and was unable to relax. She saw herself through her mother's eyes, as an object that might be thrown away if she failed to make herself useful.

Rachel had a recurring nightmare throughout her childhood. One minute she is playing alone in the basement, dancing in ecstasy to her favorite music, when the sound of low growling draws her attention to the window. The piercing dark eyes of a wolf lock onto her gaze, while its fangs drip with saliva. Frozen with fear, she is unable to scream and gasps for breath. Finally, her mother appears and Rachel points frantically at the wolf. Her mother glances at the window just at the moment the wolf disappears. "What's the matter with you?" her mother scolds, "There's nothing there!"

Knowing that she had not imagined the wolf, Rachel follows her mother up the stairs in terror of being left behind, certain of the wolf's return if she is alone. As she reaches the top of the stairs, she glances back at the window. Crouching low to the ground, the wolf stares menacingly, stalking her every move. She, alone, sees the threat to her life. Her mother honestly did not see it.

Rachel's dream was eerily reminiscent of the song that 7-year-old Cheryl Downs heard just before her mother killed her, "Hungry Like the Wolf." Children cannot survive the terror of knowing that they are living with a mother who can emotionally devour them. They experience the terror unconsciously, in their dreams. Rachel saw the wolf outside. The real danger, of course, was inside. As long as children are trapped, dependent, and unable to survive without their mother, they deny the danger and protect their mother. Rachel's nightmares finally stopped during her freshman year in college, when she was five hundred miles away from home.

Several weeks after Rachel discussed her childhood dream, I asked her if she avoided eye contact with her mother. "Yes, I guess I do," she replied, "it's just a habit. I've never thought about it before . . . but I *am* afraid to look my mother in the eye." Eventually, Rachel connected her fear of her mother with the wolf at the window. Avoidance of eye contact is an instinctual response to possible attack.

Rachel referred to her mother as a fake, and felt manipulated when her mother was kind. Sometimes her mother treated her as if she was all-good and at other times, like "a worthless piece of trash." When her mother was kind, Rachel became suspicious.

*"All I can say is that sometimes the sound of her voice just gives me the willies . . . you know, like I'm being set up. She'll call me up crying and talking real sweet to me, saying, 'you know I love you' . . . blah, blah, blah. A shiver sets me on edge . . . this is it. It's no different than the abusive husband who's really, really sorry that he beat you up. If you fall for that line it's just a matter of time before you're dead. But my God, this is **my mother!**"*

Rachel accurately identified the parallel between abusive husbands (borderline personality disordered males) and her mother. Men who batter their wives typically express extreme remorse following beatings. Although borderline mothers are less likely than borderline males to become physically violent, emotional abuse and character assassination are equally devastating. The cycle of remorse, anger, and guilt pulls the borderline's children toward the edge of a deadly vortex.

Children of borderlines learn to sacrifice their true selves because survival requires that they meet their mother's emotional needs. Masterson (1980) defines the *true self* as: "a self that is whole, both good and bad, and based on reality; it is creative, spontaneous and functioning through the mode of self-assertion . . . in an autonomous fashion" (pp. 38–39). Autonomy, the freedom of self-direction and self-expression, is impossible for the borderline's child. Because the borderline mother views separation as betrayal and punishes self-assertion, the child develops a false self. The true self is buried alive.

Rachel expected harsh punishment to follow inconsequential mistakes. When she was a child, her mother berated her simply for forgetting her lunch money. Rachel was a perfectionist who felt worthless whenever she made the slightest mistake. She ruminated about decisions, interactions, and minor events. Everything had to be perfect. Naturally, she rarely relaxed.

Like Rachel, children of borderlines may never feel safe enough to let go, to be spontaneous, or to play. Winnicott (1971) wrote: "It is play that is the universal, that belongs to health: playing facilitates growth and therefore health; . . . the natural thing is playing" (p. 41). Children of borderlines may be diligent workers who have difficulty having fun. They don't know how to relax or how to feel consistently good about themselves.

Searching for Normal

Webster defines the act of mothering as "to care for or protect." Diane Goldberg (in Miller et al. 1999) describes her experience of being raised by an emotionally stable mother whose own childhood was marred by deprivation:

> When I turned six, my birthday cake was festooned with sunset-pink roses from Mama's garden. The sharecropper's scrawny kid

had become a lady in thick canvas gardening gloves. She cooked huge meals for us. She filled our plates and never chided us with tales about what it was like to be hungry. Our baths spewed scent and bubbles, and we never heard the story of how she and her sister stole soap from a filling station in order to get clean . . . She protected us from the real and imagined monsters of her own past. [p. 45]

Bowlby (1973) theorized that "what is believed to be essential for mental health is that the infant and young child should experience a warm, intimate, and continuous relationship with his mother" (p. xi). However, children of borderlines experience a qualitative difference in their experience of being mothered. Fortunately, most children do not get "the willies" when hearing their mother's voice.

The borderline's children become experts at deciphering emotional messages that often have hidden significance. As adults, these children may become preoccupied with discovering hidden motives behind the actions of others. An adult child explained, "Things weren't the way they were supposed to be when I was a child. Now, I'm suspicious whenever things are going well." Adult children may have difficulty expressing themselves and fear that others may take advantage of their honesty. They are never sure where they stand and question whether others mean what they say. As children, what they knew to be true one minute changed the next minute. They search for validation, for others who might confirm their reality.

Daniel Goleman (1995) describes the task of the emotional brain as focusing attention on threats to survival, "to make split-second decisions like 'Do I eat this or does it eat me?'" (p. 291). The borderline's children are preoccupied with what researchers call "risk assessment"—with determining the nature of their mother's state of mind from one moment to the next. *It is an unconscious and involuntary process*, like breathing. They do not realize they are doing it. A thick wall of denial protects children from seeing what is too terrifying to face.

Splitting

The borderline's all-or-nothing thinking results in split perceptions of her children. Because Rachel was an only child, her mother alternated between perceiving her as all-good and no-good. Brazelton (Brazelton and Cramer 1990) asserts that all parents unconsciously project either positive or negative attributes onto their children. From the moment of birth, characteristics in the newborn trigger unconscious associations of people from the parents' past. Brazelton explains: "Like the good fairy or the threatening witch of fairy tales, these ghosts can cast favorable or malevolent spells on the child" (p. 139). Brazelton claims that, normally, the child's real self draws the parent away from these projections and "the ghosts are banished to the background of the nursery" (p. 139). A borderline mother's projections, however, are intense and may fluctuate wildly from perceiving a child as all-good one minute to no-good the next minute. The daughter of a borderline mother described the emotional environment of her childhood in a poem she wrote when she was 11 years old:

WIND

Changing all the time,
Never knowing which way,
Some people guess,
But then it'll change.
So forceful and mean
But sometimes so softly and unseen
Sometimes holding back,

Then sometimes letting nothing lack
Cooling the hot summer days
Freezing the winter rains.[1]

Linehan (1993a) believes that borderlines should not be viewed as different:

> It is by making these individuals different in principle from our-
> selves that we can demean them. And perhaps, at times, we demean
> them to make them different. Once we see, however, that the
> principles of behavior influencing normal behavior (including our
> own) are the same principles influencing borderline behavior, we
> will more easily empathize and respond compassionately to the
> difficulties they present us with. [p. 26]

Children of borderlines should not be led to believe that their experience is normal. Borderlines *sense* that they are different and deserve validation of their suffering. The intensity of their fear, rage, jealousy, and resentment is *not normal*. To state otherwise discounts their experience as well as their children's. *Validation must be reality-based.*

A patient who was both a borderline mother and the daughter of a borderline mother asked her therapist how normal people organize their day. Her mother provided so little consistency that the patient never learned how to structure her time. She recalled that when she was a child, her friends' mothers called them in for dinner at the same time every night, whereas the patient never knew when or if she would have supper. Organizing and serving a meal overwhelmed her mother. For years, the patient never understood why people liked milk. Her mother had frequently served spoiled milk or milk that had been left out at room temperature. Discov-

---

1. Used with permission.

ering the difference between spoiled milk and a refreshing glass of ice-cold milk is an exciting experience. Life can be good, time can be structured, goals can be accomplished, but the borderline mother and her children need help in understanding what is normal and what is not.

Children know only what they experience. They may not realize that other mothers do not lash out unexpectedly over minor slights, are not chronically upset, depressed, fearful, or overwhelmed. Children have no experience other than their own by which to judge the world and themselves. Unfortunately, the tendency among borderline mothers to split their perceptions of their children leaves their children with distorted impressions about themselves. The way parents see their children is the way children see themselves.

Why one child becomes designated as all-good and another as no-good depends upon the nature of the mother's projections. Male children who are designated as no-good may have mothers who were sexually abused by a male. Mothers can unconsciously project their hatred of men onto their sons. Borderline mothers with more than one daughter may view the firstborn daughter as a rival for their husbands' love. In other cases, certain characteristics of the child may unconsciously remind the mother of a hated or loved part of herself. The origins of a projection vary with each individual mother. Without therapy, the source of the projection may never be understood. No parent deliberately chooses to love one child more than another.

THE ALL-GOOD CHILD

"I never understood why my mother was so mean to my sister. She used to tell my sister that she was born evil . . . their fights were so awful. I hid in the corner like a coward, and tried to comfort my sister later, in secret. I

felt so undeserving, guilty, and depressed because I'd been spared. My sister didn't do anything wrong. She didn't deserve the way my mother treated her. And I didn't deserve the way she treated me. I wasn't good! I was scared."

Three years into therapy, Joanna shed the shroud of secrecy and fear that protected her true feelings about her mother. Like a blossoming flower, she opened up in the safety of the therapeutic relationship. A recent milestone gave her a new perspective. She could see where she had been and where she needed to go.

"I was putting away the laundry when I noticed that my heart was beating faster than normal. I sat down on the bed and told myself that I should've eaten lunch. A few minutes later I felt dizzy, weak, and scared. I told myself, 'don't panic, this is nothing . . . it'll go away.' I kept folding the clothes but was concentrating on my heartbeat. My head felt light, disconnected from my body. My arms and fingers prickled. I was only 40 years old, too young for a heart attack."

Joanna called 911. Upon arrival, the paramedics found her on the couch and took her pulse. They checked her blood oxygen level and promptly diagnosed the problem as hyperventilation. Her short, shallow breaths had saturated her blood with oxygen, thus producing the rapid heartbeat, dizziness, and tingling sensation in her hands and arms. Through therapy, Joanna discovered what triggered this episode of survival anxiety.

The toy headstone on her birthday cake had been a joke but Joanna didn't feel like celebrating middle age. Why would her fortieth birthday trigger such anxiety? She discussed the possibility that she panicked when she realized that she had never really lived her own life. Time was running out. In subsequent sessions, her anger and resentment toward her mother began to surface.

Joanna was an all-good wife and mother. She never disobeyed, never argued, and never asserted her true self. In fact, at the time of her panic attack she was dutifully repressing her anxiety as she folded the laundry. Like an uncorked bottle that had been violently shaken, Joanna's true feelings exploded.

Characteristics of the All-Good Child

Does not develop borderline personality disorder

The all-good child does not develop borderline personality disorder because only the idealized parts of the mother are projected onto this child. Other serious psychological conflicts develop, however, because of the mother's need for merger with the all-good child. *Perhaps the most devastating psychic conflict the all-good child experiences is inauthenticity—feeling* as if *those who perceive her as good or competent are mistaken.*

The all-good child is the parentified child—trained to parent the parent. All-good children are typically obedient and loyal, and may function as little therapists in their families. The borderline mother attributes special power to the all-good child to rescue and protect her emotionally. Therefore, the all-good child is entrusted with secrets, enlisted as a surrogate partner, and develops an impostor syndrome that results from being treated as an adult while still a child. The impostor syndrome reflects the underlying belief that the adult child is undeserving, despite external indications of competence. Accomplishments bring no satisfaction because all-good children attribute success to good luck or good fortune, rather than to their own efforts.

The borderline mother unconsciously solicits the alliance of the all-good child. She lives vicariously through this child and seeks validation through the child's accomplishments. Without recognizing the child's need for separateness, the borderline mother emotionally merges with the all-good child, leaving the child feeling devoured. Nevertheless, all-good children fear betraying their mother and, therefore, betray themselves. The all-good child may be too uncomfortable and guilt-ridden to say no to her mother's demands for closeness.

De Becker (1997) calls "forced teaming" one of the most sophisticated manipulations used by con artists and criminals: "Forced teaming is an effective way to establish premature trust because a 'we're-in-the-same-boat' attitude is hard to rebuff without feeling rude" (p. 66). The mother unconsciously forces teaming by enticing the all-good child with comments such as, "You're just like me" or "No one else understands me like you do" or "You're the only one I can depend on" or "If it weren't for you, my life wouldn't be worth living."

The mother's need to merge with the all-good child can drive the guilt-ridden child away. The all-good child is treated as an idealized part of herself. Consequently, she cares for the all-good child according to her needs, rather than the child's needs. When mother is cold, she makes the child wear a sweater, regardless of how warm or cold the child feels. If the child rejects the sweater, the mother feels rejected and scolds the child.

De Becker points out, however, that anyone attempting to establish rapport should be seeking to put the other person at ease. A parentified child intuitively knows that her role is inappropriate and is terrified knowing that she is solely responsible for her parent's happiness. She should never be placed in the impossible position of being responsible for her parent's life.

Is anxious, depressed, and guilt-ridden

All-good children repress awareness of their true feelings and, consequently, are likely to suffer from depression and anxiety.

Because they are preoccupied with the emotional state of others, they have difficulty experiencing pleasure. Although they are acutely perceptive, they lack insight into their own psyche, and may be unaware of subtle depression.

All-good children may suffer from gratification guilt, a gnawing ache that accompanies experiences such as vacations, holidays, or parties. They do not feel entitled to their mother's idealized perception and may feel undeserving of a good life. They feel as though they have already been given too much, and do not feel entitled to having more. They may compulsively provide for others what they need for themselves.

Glickauf-Hughes and Mehlman (1998) report that non-borderline daughters of borderline mothers worried greatly about not being able to please their mothers. Consequently, the all-good child is susceptible to emotional depletion because of compulsive approval-seeking behavior. In addition, the tendency toward depression, anxiety, and guilt is common among all-good children. They can feel overwhelmed with responsibility for caring for others, yet not deserving of being cared for themselves. They have difficulty articulating their feelings and needs, and are extremely uncomfortable with recognition and attention.

Although all-good children need therapy as much as no-good children, they are not as likely to seek treatment. Glickauf-Hughes and Mehlman (1998) note that non-borderline daughters of borderline mothers have difficulty distinguishing normal feelings from more primitive feelings and tend to confuse feelings with actions. They fear becoming like their mothers and associate the expression of strong feelings with the behavior of a borderline. They may restrict emotional expression, appearing to be calm and easy-going. Internalized anxiety, guilt, and depression may therefore go unnoticed and untreated.

Tends to be successful professionally

All-good children become successful adults, but are not necessarily happy. A preoccupation with doing the right thing can suffocate the real and creative self. All-good children can tolerate unreasonable bosses, unpleasant work environments, and unhappy marriages because meeting the expectations of others is more important than their own happiness. They may have plenty of fame, wealth, or success, but rarely have fun.

All-good children continue to function in a parentified role in adult relationships and tend to be conscientious overachievers. They are often overcommitted and emotionally preoccupied because they fear disappointing others. They simply cannot say no. Minor mistakes can trigger a catastrophic plunge in self-esteem, and internalized anxiety prevents them from enjoying their accomplishments. The emotional energy of the all-good child is heavily invested in avoiding mistakes that could shatter the foundation of the self.

Although all-good children do not act on suicidal wishes, when the self is shattered following a minor mistake they may think to themselves, "I wish I were dead." *Success can trigger panic attacks in the all-good child.* The more successful they become, the more anxious they are. All-good children experience little contentment or peace of mind, especially if they believe that a no-good sibling was sacrificed.

Messages to the All-Good Child

- "You are the only one who can make me happy."
- "Without you, life isn't worth living."
- "Don't ever leave me."

- "You are special."
- "You are responsible for my happiness."
- "You are responsible for my life."

Whereas no-good children have a fear of rejection, all-good children have a fear of success. Because the all-good child was spared the abuse experienced by the no-good child, success triggers shame and guilt rather than pride and joy. All-good children who witnessed the abuse of the no-good sibling may struggle with survival guilt. One of Joanna's journal entries illustrates the depth of her pain:

> I read an article this month in *Time* magazine that made me sick to my stomach. The article was entitled, "War Wounds," and included a picture of a 13-year-old girl whose arms had been hacked off by a band of rebels in Sierra Leone. Her family wept for her and is helping her learn to eat with a make-shift prosthesis. She was quoted as saying, "I had no idea why they did that to me." I wanted to write to that little girl and tell her how lucky she is that she still has her soul, and a family who loves her.

> She reminded me of my sister. Except my sister wasn't so lucky. She, too, was maimed in a civil war that raged behind closed doors in suburban America. I had no idea why my mother kept hacking at her until there were only pieces left. My mother destroyed the one part of a child that can never be replaced. And forty years later my sister still struggles to survive. There is no prosthesis for a human soul.

> No one gets it because her arms aren't stumps. No one wants to read about that kind of war. Nobody seems to realize how many children are being maimed right now in wars that rage behind closed doors all across America. And nobody knows how to help people who have a stump of a soul.

Veterans of war know that survivor guilt can rob an individual of feeling entitled to living. All-good children can feel so guilty about having been spared the abuse experienced by the no-good sibling that they become compulsive caregivers, compelled to rescue victims of oppression, illness, injustice, or mistreatment. They do not realize how they were damaged by witnessing the destruction of a sibling. Although all-good children do not develop BPD, their hearts were pierced with tiny fragments of shrapnel. They feel sad and guilty without knowing why.

Slowly, over time, Joanna addressed her own victimization. She uncovered a great deal of buried anger about how much she had sacrificed for her mother, and deep sadness about not being able to save her sister. She had served her time enlisted in the service of her mother. The war was over.

If it were possible to x-ray the self of the all-good child, one might find a porcelain soul with tiny fractures. Although outwardly appearing uninjured, a child with a fractured soul lives with an inner sense of fragility. The internal self is at war with the external self. All-good children suffer silently, unable to articulate the source of their pain that is too deep and too old to identify. Although a fractured soul cannot fully mend, the all-good child learns to protect it from further injury. Defenses such as denial, repression, and sublimation keep awareness of their pain at bay. While all-good children need therapy as much as no-good children, they are unlikely to seek treatment. Analytically oriented therapy is the key that ends the inner war and opens the door to enjoying life.

THE NO-GOOD CHILD

"Sometimes I get really confused. I don't know what to blame. What do you do when it's 2:00 A.M. and you're sitting outside smoking a cigarette and you want nothing more than to poison the soft minds of America with

all the dirtiness and black that is you? To take away their television sets and replace them with thoughts of fratricide and self-doubt and apprehension. Sometimes I want to be a loathed and feared god . . . who sits on top of the ugliest mountain . . . in green clothes. I want to look at this farce . . . this capitalistic and jerky orgy from above and laugh and laugh. I never wanted to be down in it and so . . . so coated with it."

Katrina hated her life and herself. She wondered why, in the middle of the night, she felt blood rushing to her hands and fingers, the physiological reaction to anger needed to grasp a weapon, strike a blow, and take a life. She thought she had grown immune to her mother's vicious verbal attacks. Living with a mother who picked on her relentlessly filled her with anger that Katrina could only experience alone at night. The dreams she recorded alternated between suicide and homicide.

Chronic psychological degradation of a child, or an adult, can have deadly consequences. Katrina retreated to her room following arguments with her mother. There, she sliced herself with razor blades and wrote down her feelings. Katrina's journal was literally stained with her own blood.

Characteristics of the No-Good Child

Develops borderline personality disorder

It is only a matter of time before the borderline's no-good daughter becomes a borderline mother herself. The negative projections of the borderline mother grounded the no-good child's self-concept in self-hatred. Children who are perceived as evil by their mother have two choices: (1) to believe that they are evil, or (2) to die trying to be good. The mother's perception is immutable: *no-good children can never win no matter how hard they try.*

Without intervention, no-good children inevitably develop BPD. Typically, they become involved with drugs and alcohol at an early age. Their school performance reflects their negative self-view and their sense of hopelessness. Flagrant acting-out, such as antisocial behavior, stealing, drug abuse, promiscuity, and running away, reinforces the mother's belief that the child is no-good. Masterson (1980) explains that parents "will say that their adolescent has been enticed away by bad companions, not driven by conflicts at home" (p. 45). The borderline mother vehemently denies her role in the child's behavior. *She honestly does not see it.*

Suffers from pain agnosia

No-good children may develop *pain agnosia*, the lack of pain response. Seventy-five percent of abused children in one study (Money 1992) showed self-destructive tendencies such as trichotillomania (compulsive hair pulling), falling, nail biting, head banging, eating indigestible substances, swallowing hard objects, and ingesting pills and medicines. Children who were transferred to nonabusive environments, however, terminated these behaviors and a normal response to pain returned.

The no-good child, therefore, appears to be indifferent to punishment, increasing the mother's rage. Pain agnosia occurs as the result of the release of a brain opioid, called metencephalin, that induces euphoria and provides an anesthetizing effect (Money 1992). The effect is reminiscent of the dreamy look in the eyes of limp kittens being carried by the scruff of their necks. Much more research is needed to discern whether or not self-destructive behavior in abused children serves to release mind-numbing anesthesia that might, in fact, be an adaptive response to an abusive environment.

Feels doomed

Katrina referred to herself as a cancerous growth in her family. Masterson (1988) reports that some children of borderlines felt that "the only way they could please their own mothers was to kill themselves" (p. 82). No-good children feel marked, doomed for life, like a blight on the face of the earth. Their pervasive sense of hopelessness is conveyed in their artwork, their writing, and their behavior. Therapists (Lachkar 1992) theorize that the black holes that are commonly depicted in the artwork of borderline patients represent the emotional abyss of emptiness and loneliness. Several adult patients with BPD reported seeing the image of a black star whenever they felt hopeful, such as at the beginning of a new relationship. These patients explained that the black star represents the futility of hope.

No-good children see no good in themselves, in the world, or in their future. They feel certain that they will ruin good things, good people, and good times. When they wish upon a star they see only darkness. No-good children see no hope.

Messages to the No-Good Child

- "You ruin everything."
- "I'd be better off without you."
- "You are responsible for my unhappiness."
- "You make me sick."
- "You are sick."
- "I could kill you."
- "You are a disgrace to this family."

Of all the tragic aspects of no-good children, perhaps the most heartbreaking is their continued desire to please their mother.

Bowlby (1973) explains that even when the attachment figure elicits fear, children "are likely to cling to the threatening or hostile figure rather than run away" (p. 316). No-good children may stay attached to their mothers and give up on themselves. Unfortunately, by doing so they give up hope of feeling loved.

An x-ray of the no-good child's self might reveal a slow-growing tumor consuming the soul. No-good children are afraid of looking at themselves, especially of looking within. They sense an internal darkness, something withered and black, foul and rotten. Whatever it is, it feels beyond their control and is too terrifying to face. No-good children who come to therapy, therefore, must have a great deal of courage. They must be willing to look at their withered soul and let it be nourished in the warm light of acceptance and understanding.

THE LOST CHILD

"He would never have seen a therapist. He just didn't think his life was worth it. Bob was the kind of guy who was everyone's buddy. He'd give you the shirt off his back. That was his problem. I used to get really angry with him when we were teenagers. He was so smart but he never applied himself. All he wanted to do was to hang out with the guys and play basketball. He gave up on himself long before he died from the overdose."

Mary came to treatment shortly after her brother's death. Her sadness was tinged with anger about a life cut short, a life not lived. The lost child is like an empty shell that is tossed to shore or swept to sea—either way, it is lost forever.

Surviving the mixed messages of the borderline mother requires the ability to ride the waves of emotional upheaval. Lost children survive by floating, by resigning themselves to having no control. Lost children are confused about who they are and resist being controlled by authority figures. They have difficulty keeping a job, following through on commitments, or being responsible. They may numb themselves with drugs or alcohol and stay detached from their emotions. Like Peter Pan, they feel motherless and never grow up.

Lost children are strongly defended against attachment. Neither personal possessions nor relationships are perceived as necessary for survival. Although lost children can be friendly, fun, and affable, they have difficulty being reliable, consistent, or dependable. They avoid commitment of any kind.

Underneath the lost child's easygoing demeanor is cynicism about a life that feels meaningless and empty. Lost children may seem carefree but they are not happy. They live on the fringes of society and play by their own rules. They can easily end up on the streets, homeless. Family members may not see them for years and often state, "I don't know where he is. I've lost track of him." Lacking any sense of self-worth or meaning in their existence, lost children slip in and out of relationships, barely being noticed.

Children of borderlines cannot become healthy, autonomous adults unless they find a way of understanding their experience. Describing early experiences in words is difficult because memories "are stored in the amygdala as rough, *wordless* blueprints for emotional life" (Goleman 1995, p. 22, emphasis added). Like children who are born deaf and blind, children of borderlines have no way of organizing their emotional life. They do not realize that they are different, that other children are born into a world of sound and light. The lack of consistency in their emotional world creates a sense of meaninglessness, as if life itself is nonsense.

Therapy helps children of borderlines organize and express their feelings, and helps them find meaning in their own existence. The therapist may feel like Anne Sullivan Macy, the teacher who patiently taught Helen Keller how to communicate through sign language, but first had to teach Helen the meaning of words. Before she understood the meaning of the word "water," Helen Keller

(1902) had no words to describe her experience of the world. She explained, "I was without compass or sounding-line, and had no way of knowing how near the harbour was. 'Light! Give me light!' was the wordless cry of my soul" (p. 15). Children of borderlines search for light in their darkness. The Boston philanthropist, Dr. Samuel Gridley Howe (in Lash 1980), once pleaded for support for a deaf and blind woman stating:

> Can nothing be done to disinter this human soul? It is late, but perhaps not too late. The whole neighborhood would rush to save this woman if she were buried alive by the caving in of a pit . . . The chance is small indeed; but with a smaller chance they would have dug desperately for her in the pit; and is the life of the soul of less import than that of the body? [pp. 19–20]

Masterson's (1980) words regarding the treatment of borderline adolescents and their mothers echo Dr. Howe's: "Therapy is arduous, time-consuming, filled with . . . obstacles, but it is far from impossible. When it is pursued faithfully, it more than justifies the effort, providing, as it does, a life preserver to rescue and sustain the deprived and abandoned in their struggle and eventually a beacon [of light] to guide them" (pp. 265–266). Feeling buried alive is normal to the borderline mother and her children. Without help, they cannot be saved.

The father, however, can make a difference. As Freud (1929) once said, "I cannot think of any need in childhood as strong as the need for a father's protection" (p. 19). The father's character structure can either reinforce the pathological dynamics between mother and child, or provide a healthy counterbalance, depending on the degree to which he experienced healthy love in his own childhood.

8

Fairy-Tale Fathers

"No, wife," said the man. "I won't do it. How can I bring myself to leave my children alone in the woods?"

—*Hansel and Gretel*

In September 1999, a mother and father in Little Rock, Arkansas, left their two children alone in the wilderness to die. When the bones of their 18-month-old son were discovered, the father told police that the couple had abandoned the children near a pond, where police searched for the body of their other child, a 2½-year-old. Prosecutor Fletcher Long Jr. explained the parents' motive: "They wanted rid of two children" (Kissel 1999, p. A14).

Make-believe mothers and fairy-tale fathers are unbelievably real. Child abuse researcher John Money (1992) observes: "Collusional participation of one parent with the other in the abuse and neglect of a child represents a manifestation of shared irrationality known by its French psychiatric name, folie à deux. One person of the pair has a fixated irrational belief or a delusion which is assimilated by the partner" (p. 141).

Parents who were dehumanized as children often lack empathy for their own children. They reinforce each other's pathological behavior, displacing their repressed self-hatred onto their children. Obviously, most borderline mothers and their husbands do not murder their children. The degree to which they sacrifice their children depends on the unconscious conflicts of *both* parents.

Fathers, as well as mothers, reenact the unconscious dynamics rooted in their repressed childhood experiences. The father's role in the drama between the borderline mother and her child is crucial in determining the outcome for the child.

Joan Lachkar (1992), author of *The Narcissistic/Borderline Couple*, explains that borderlines frequently marry men with narcissistic personality disorder. Narcissistic men need to be perceived as special and therefore seek admiration from others. These men can be exploitative and self-absorbed, charming and charismatic, controlling yet indulgent. When they do not feel appreciated or desired they tend to withdraw. They cannot allow themselves to need others, and those who know them consequently feel devalued. Conflict then arises between borderline wives, who are easily demeaned, and narcissistic husbands, who frequently demean others.

However, it is neither fair nor accurate to assume that all borderline women marry narcissistic men. Although Mary Todd Lincoln referred to her husband as Shakespeare's King Richard II (in Baker 1987), Abraham Lincoln did not exhibit a narcissistic personality. Baker (1987) surmised, however, that Mary Todd's ambition to live in the White House attracted her to Lincoln "because he was a man of potential majesty" (p. 93). Obviously, not all men who marry borderlines are narcissists.

Generalizations must be understood for what they are: nonspecific, nonindividualized patterns by which to compare experience. In practice, the common denominator among the various types of men who marry borderlines is their tendency to reinforce the pathological dynamics between the mother and child. In his work with borderline mothers and their children, Masterson (1980) observes that "[these] fathers are, for the most part, passive men who are dominated by, but maintain great distance from, their wives. They relinquish their paternal prerogatives in exchange for complete freedom to immerse themselves in their work" (p. 47). Masterson believes that many borderline mothers marry men who will take care of them rather than men who will function as equal partners.

Understanding the father's relationship with the borderline mother is essential in understanding the child's experience. The borderline Waif tends to marry a Frog-Prince, someone she can rescue and who she hopes will rescue her. On her wedding day the tentative Waif may think, "Well, maybe he'll change." The Waif identifies with the Frog's helplessness and fantasizes about providing for him what she needs herself. Unfortunately, her dream rarely comes true because the Frog may enjoy being a Frog.

The Hermit seeks a Huntsman, a partner who will pity and protect her. The borderline Hermit envies the Huntsman's courage and desperately needs his soothing presence. The borderline Queen seeks a King, someone who attracts attention through his prominence, wealth, or power. The Queen, therefore, is more likely than the Waif, Hermit, or Witch to marry a narcissist—a King. The Witch seeks a Fisherman, someone she can dominate and control. She chooses a subservient partner who admires her courage and who relinquishes his will at her command.

The Frog-Prince, the Huntsman, the King, and the Fisherman represent generalizations that are useful only for identifying tendencies, not for understanding individuals. No two individuals share the same experience; thus, infinite possibilities exist regarding how their needs are met and expressed.

THE FROG-PRINCE

"But when he fell to the floor, he wasn't a frog any longer; he was a king's son with beautiful smiling eyes . . ."

— *The Frog King*

"My father was a disappointment in so many ways. His personality was bland, like milk toast. I have no idea what my mother saw in him. I remember asking her once why she stayed married to him. She said, 'He isn't what he seems . . . you don't know him like I know him . . .' She kept waiting for him to turn into something. That was before she found out about his gambling and the affair. When he left my mother for another woman, he left her in debt."

Danielle was the oldest of three children. She was the all-good child, a role that she both resented and cherished. Danielle was emotionally more mature than either of her parents and never had time to be a child. Her mother was 18 when Danielle was born and seemed more like a sister than a mother.

The Waif searches for a Frog-Prince, an underdog with whom she identifies and who she hopes will change into Prince Charming. She fantasizes about the Prince rescuing her from misery, but the Frog inevitably disappoints her. Because Frog-Prince fathers are unable to provide reliable emotional support, their children may be emotionally neglected.

A broad range of Frog-Prince fathers exists. They can range from being withdrawn and depressed to being violent and abusive. Underdogs or Frogs are defined primarily by characteristics that evoke sympathy from others, ranging from physical unattractiveness to unpopularity. The Waif feels sorry for the Frog and is drawn to his vulnerability. Because she hopes to provide him with what she herself needs, she may end up feeling used. When the Prince does not emerge, the Waif faces disappointment but can hold onto good feelings about herself. She accuses her partner of taking advantage of her, failing to appreciate everything she has done for him. Danielle's father was neither abusive nor violent. He was simply emotionally disengaged from the family. Danielle described him as a fixture, an object without sentience. Other Frog-Prince fathers may be alcoholics, drug abusers, wife batterers, or child abusers. Nevertheless, when Danielle's parents divorced, her mother became, once again, the victim.

Characteristics of the Frog-Prince

At her father's bidding, he became her dear companion and husband. He told her that a wicked witch had put a spell on him and that no one but she alone could have freed him from the spring, and that they would go to his kingdom together the next day.

— *The Frog King*

Is perceived as an underdog

The German folktale, *The Frog King*, begins, "In olden times, when wishing still helped, there lived a king . . ." The Frog-Prince and the Waif live a shared fantasy life, where wishing still helps. The Frog-Prince is drawn to the Waif by their shared wish to be rescued. In the real world, people know that "one partner cannot be the ultimate provider for the other, the rescuer, the reliever of persecutory anxiety, or the one to make up for all losses and deprivation" (Lachkar 1992, p. 170). In real life individuals must do more than wish: they must act.

Danielle's father created his own secret fantasy world by gambling. In this world he felt powerful, even invincible. Dreams of the big win kept him from facing reality, where unpaid bills and phone calls from collectors threatened his self-esteem. A bitter wife and ungrateful children exacerbated his depression and drove him further into fantasyland. Reality struck the day Danielle's mother discovered the truth about his gambling. Danielle's father left her mother shortly thereafter and found another woman who paid off his debt. The Frog never changed at all.

The Waif never marries the Frog-Prince for love. She confuses love with pity and, of course, cannot distinguish between his needs and hers. She identifies with his helplessness and overlooks negative aspects of his behavior. But the Frog-Prince's low self-esteem eventually takes a toll on his children. Young children need to be able to look up to their parents; unfortunately, children have little respect for Frogs. The Frog-Prince father may be so uninvolved in the family's emotional life that he may be barely noticed or missed if he leaves.

Is emotionally constricted; may numb feelings with drugs or alcohol

The Frog-Prince may feel as though he is under the spell of a witch who is trying to change him into something else. Many Frog-Princes were emotionally or physically abused as children. Low self-esteem, feelings of inadequacy, chronic depression, and addictive behavior are common among Frog-Princes. His tendency to numb painful feelings with drugs or alcohol can be a major obstacle to intimacy with his wife and children.

Danielle avoided depending on her father for anything. He was so unreliable in picking her up from school that she preferred walking home rather than waiting for him. She never had friends to her house because she was embarrassed by his drunken stupors. When her parents finally divorced, Danielle was relieved.

The Frog-Prince father often does not remember his early childhood. Painful circumstances are repressed, and the early use of drugs or alcohol covers feelings that could trigger memories. The only time Danielle recalled her father mentioning his childhood was a brief comment at the dinner table. When her brother announced that he didn't like the meal, her father muttered blandly, "I said that once, and my father almost killed me."

May suffer from borderline personality disorder

The Frog-Prince may share the Waif's belief that life is too hard. Such shared feelings of helplessness and victimization indicate a poor prognosis for the marriage, resulting in tragic outcomes for the family. One daughter of a Waif mother announced in group therapy that she was so tired of hearing her mother threaten to commit suicide that she wished her mother would just kill herself. Her Waif mother was married to a Frog-Prince who had committed suicide a year earlier. The parents had made a suicide pact before his death, but the Waif mother was ambivalent about following through on her promise. Their adolescent daughter felt that she would be better off with a dead mother than with a chronically suicidal one.

If the Frog-Prince suffers from BPD, he may be prone to abusing his wife or children or to acting on suicidal impulses. The broad range of symptom clusters among individuals with BPD makes it difficult to specify all the possible combinations of borderline women who marry borderline men. Their lives are full of turmoil, and the extent to which their children may be endangered depends upon the level of functioning of both parents.

Unfortunately, males with BPD tend to be unfaithful husbands. They may defend against their fear of abandonment by seeking serial relationships with females, avoiding the possibility of being completely abandoned or alone. Poor impulse control is primarily responsible for self-destructive behavior such as infidelity, drug or alcohol abuse, compulsive gambling, overeating, homicide, and suicide.

Steve Downs, the father of the three children shot by his ex-wife, Diane Downs, may have suffered from BPD. According to one source (Rule 1988), he abused alcohol, had affairs, and preferred drinking with his buddies to taking care of his small children. Apparently, he left his oldest daughter, Christie, alone in the house when she was an infant. Even after his ex-wife shot Christie, he allowed her against court order to spend time alone with Diane.

Children are unlikely to share the Waif mother's view of the Frog-Prince father; all they see is the Frog. The Frog-Prince, like the Waif, cannot possibly understand his children's emotional needs because his own emotional needs were so unmet as a child. Like a language they never learned to speak, Frog-Prince fathers have no idea of how to communicate emotionally with others. Their children cannot help feeling angry, afraid, and alone.

THE HUNTSMAN

"Oh, dear huntsman, let me live . . ." "Because of her beauty the huntsman took pity on her . . ."

—*Snow White and the Seven Dwarfs*

"My father was a gentle, moral man. He would never have divorced my mother, it was literally against his religion. In fact, he felt sorry for her. He tuned her out when she went on her rampages. He'd take her by the arm gently and say, 'Settle down, Jeanne.' Then he'd go out to the garage. She'd try to pick a fight with him, but he never raised his voice. He acted

like he didn't even hear her. Unfortunately, he seemed to think that if he could take it, we should too. But it's different for kids. There wasn't any place for us to go."

Emily was 28 when she entered therapy. Her mother had been hospitalized for depression several times during Emily's childhood, and Emily was left to care for her brother and sisters while her father worked. Vivacious and determined, Emily admitted that she did not know how to depend on others. Throughout her childhood, her Hermit mother depended on her.

The Hermit's underlying fear and anxiety draw her to a partner who can offer security and safety. The Hermit idealizes the Huntsman. Her ideal-hungry personality creates a longing for a principled partner who is steadfast and loyal. Wolf (1988) defines the ideal-hungry personality: "Ideal hungry personalities can experience themselves as worthwhile only by finding selfobjects to whom they can look up and by whom they can feel accepted" (p. 73). The Hermit is likely to marry a Huntsman, a man who protects her from danger and provides the stability she so desperately needs. The child of the Hermit and Huntsman, however, may feel betrayed by both parents, particularly if the Hermit is abusive and the Huntsman fails to intervene.

Emily's father worked two jobs in order to support his family. Like a martyr, he never complained. When she was little, Emily worshipped her father. She emulated his work ethic, his self-sacrificing behavior, and his compassion. As she grew older, however, she grew disillusioned and wondered why he failed to protect her and her siblings from her mother's abuse.

In the fairy tale, the Huntsman spared Snow White's life because his conscience would not allow him to kill her: "Not having to kill her was a great weight off his mind all the same" (Manheim 1977, p. 185). The Huntsman who marries the borderline Hermit is ruled by his conscience, which prevents him from violating principles of loyalty and fidelity. He represses and disavows his own emotions; thus, he does not perceive his own happiness to be important. The Huntsman fulfills his duty to his conscience, defining his self-worth in terms of the degree to which his behavior is congruent with his principles.

The Huntsman is humble, even if professionally successful. He does not seek adulation or fame. He gives credit to others, prefers to be anonymous, and thus feels at home with the Hermit's need to hide. At the root of his personality is guilt. The Huntsman felt guilty and undeserving as a child, and therefore is grateful for love. He fears being a burden to others because he felt like a burden as a child.

Characteristics of the Huntsman

Is good-hearted, loyal, principled, easygoing, and hard-working

The Huntsman is drawn to the Hermit's need for protection. His compassion for others may be derived from an early experience in which he himself was rescued by a compassionate caregiver. Emily's father was a tenderhearted man who felt sorry for her mother. At age 6 he had been rescued from an orphanage by an aunt and uncle, and he knew well the feeling of being frightened and alone. Just as swaddling calms a fussy baby, the Huntsman wraps the Hermit in an emotional blanket that protects her from the world.

The Huntsman compensates for feelings of inadequacy by hard work, outstanding performance, dedication, and dependability. His calmness balances the volatility of the Hermit. Although the Huntsman is rigidly defended against his own vulnerability, he identifies and empathizes with the Hermit's need for protection.

Uses denial and avoidance to regulate emotion

The Huntsman's passivity is a consequence of his defense mechanism of avoidance and denial. Rather than experience anger or rage, he distances himself from his wife and children when faced with conflict. Denial serves to keep self-esteem intact as the father's loyalty may be torn between his wife and children. Emily felt emotionally abandoned, however, whenever her father remarked, "There's nothing wrong with your mother."

The Huntsman protects himself from internalizing the Hermit's anxiety through emotional detachment and sometimes physical avoidance. Emily's father spent a great deal of time away from home, working and volunteering for various organizations. When home, he secluded himself in his workshop in a detached garage, where he worked until late at night. Emily understood his need for a place to escape her mother's tirades.

Derives self-esteem from duty, honor, and service

The Huntsman's sense of self is ruled by strict codes of behavior, such as a strong work ethic, honesty, loyalty, or religious doctrine. He feels most secure when expectations are clearly defined and when his role as husband does not conflict with his role as father. Others admire him for his outstanding performance, dedication, and integrity. The Hermit's paranoid fears of abandonment are unlikely to be realized because the Huntsman is unlikely to desert her.

Emily's father was an elder in his church and was highly respected. Although he was frequently nominated as president of various organizations, he never felt entitled to accept the power, recognition, or adulation that accompanied the role. The more praise he received, the harder he worked, and Emily rarely saw him relax. Because the Huntsman is highly regarded by others, his children may trust his judgment more than their own.

Huntsmen subtly encourage their children to tolerate the Hermit's abusive behavior. Doing one's duty, staying in one's place, and not causing trouble are messages from the Huntsman father that can endanger his children. He fails to validate his children's perceptions and in doing so minimizes their pain. Denial and avoidance, rigid adherence to rules of behavior, and invalidation of his children's feelings may allow the Huntsman to maintain attachment to the borderline Hermit at the expense of his children.

THE KING

The king laid his hand upon [the queen's] arm, and timidly said "Consider, my dear: she is only a child!"

—*Alice's Adventures in Wonderland*

"When I was little, I used to lie awake at night and cry for my father. The only time I felt safe was when I was with him, and that wasn't often. He was gone for weeks at a time. I can distinctly remember the first time I realized that other fathers came home every night."

Katie's father brought her lavish gifts when he returned from his frequent business trips. Although starved for his attention, Katie sensed her mother's jealousy. Her mother was easily enraged by displays of affection between Katie and her father. One day Katie came home from school and discovered that her favorite doll was broken. Although her mother insisted it was an accident, Katie did not believe her. She remembered the disturbing expression on her mother's face the day her father gave it to her.

Katie's father thrived on recognition and flattery. The paneled study in his luxurious home was lined with glass-enclosed cases displaying his various community awards. He seemed to rule over everyone except Katie's mother. His obsequious behavior toward his wife confused Katie, who hoped that he would protect her from her mother's abuse.

Masterson (1980) observes that: "It is instructive to note in these cases the amount of absence the father is permitted without any complaint from the mother. Beyond the fact of his frequent absence, the specific dynamics of his relationship with the mother and child when he is present again reinforce the mother–child exclusive relationship" (p. 23).

The borderline Queen, because of her inner emptiness and insatiable need for admiration, is most likely to marry a narcissistic King. Her mirror-hungry personality leads her on a quest for a high-profile partner whom others envy and admire. The King and Queen's child, however, may feel emotionally abandoned by both parents. The King is the prototypical narcissist.[1]

Lachkar (1992) proposes that "The borderline may be destructive in order to stir things up and to punish, while the narcissist may be destructive because of preoccupation with self" (p. 82). The King and Queen have a volatile relationship, and their children can lose themselves in drugs or alcohol to escape the conflict at home. If the couple divorces, battles over custody issues can continue for years. As Lachkar observes:

> In court custody cases, the narcissist may withhold because of exaggerated entitlement fantasies, but the borderline may be the one to withhold custody payments, and not participate fairly in property division and child visitation, out of a desire to get back at or to teach the other a lesson. Because of the false self, the borderline

---

1. For a more complete description of narcissistic personality disorder, see *The Diagnostic and Statistical Manual of Mental Disorders*, 4th edition (*DSM-IV*), published by the American Psychiatric Assocation.

(the one to promise the world) may fool others under the guise of being the perfect parent, the victim, or the hurt one. [p. 79]

Both the borderline Queen and the narcissistic King perceive themselves as innocent victims. The true victims, of course, are their children.

Fantasy plays an important role in the emotional life of the King father. Lachkar (1992) suggests that the narcissist creates a "delusional world of entitlement fantasies . . . and grandiose expectations" (p. 120). The narcissist also uses fantasy to create an idealized view of the Queen in the midst of disappointment or conflict. The borderline Queen's all-or-nothing thinking, however, leaves her completely disillusioned, devastated, and desperate when faced with disappointment. The guilt-ridden King, therefore, tries harder and harder to gratify the demands of the Queen.

Katie was astonished not only by her mother's unreasonable demands, but also by her father's compliance with them. One time, her father bought a second home and then sold it simply because Katie's mother had fallen in and out of love with it. He seemed to enjoy having the power to indulge his wife's various whims, but Katie perceived her parents' relationship as superficial and fake. Together, the King and Queen create a shared delusion of happiness. Although the King rules the kingdom while the Queen rules the family, their children may be lost in the shuffle.

Characteristics of the King

Feels entitled to special treatment

The King has a heightened sense of self-importance and feels entitled to special treatment. He embellishes his accomplishments and may blatantly lie in order to be perceived as superior to others. He is intensely envious of those he perceives as more successful or attractive. Katie had many embarrassing memories of her father's behavior in restaurants and airports when service did not meet his expectations. He could be ruthless, demanding, and intimidating. If service was slow, he expected a discount. He complained to managers, demanded refunds, and threatened lawsuits over the slightest inconvenience, announcing, "I run a $10 million industry and if I ran my company anything like this we'd go bankrupt!" In such situations, Katie's mother shared her husband's perception that they had been unfairly treated.

The King's grandiosity is an attempt to compensate for his fear of dependency. The King strives to be perceived as the ultimate provider and may overreact by giving too much, expecting too much, and blaming others when faced with failure. When others are unappreciative, he feels small and unimportant and either withdraws or explodes with rage. Giving too much protects him from feeling rejected but also leaves the other person feeling unneeded.

Requires constant attention and admiration

Despite the King's grandiosity, his self-esteem is fragile. Thus, he requires continuous attention and admiration in order to feel valued. He is preoccupied with how well he is doing and strives to achieve increasingly higher goals. Katie's father was preoccupied with his appearance, his possessions, and primarily with how well his company was doing on Wall Street. Although he grumbled about the business at home, he frequently spoke to others about his company's success.

Lachkar (1992) theorizes that the more validation the King receives, the more insecure he becomes. External validation provides only temporary relief from the lack of internal self-worth. Katie's father looked daily, sometimes hourly, at reports from Wall Street in order to assess his own self worth. Her father's self esteem depended primarily on his company's performance. Drops in the stock market drove him to despair. The Queen helps the King regain his grandiosity when external forces threaten their security. For example, when her father's business faltered, Katie's mother reassured him with, "We'll show them!"

Tends to withdraw when hurt

The King tends to withdraw when disappointed or wounded by criticism. Unlike the Queen, who reacts to criticism by attacking, the King is as likely to withdraw as to express rage. The King may calmly declare, "I don't deserve to be treated like this!" or "I don't need you *or* this relationship!" With an air of superiority, his defiant withdrawal leaves the Queen feeling abandoned, demeaned, and intent on revenge. The Queen's thought, "I'll show him," can lead to vicious displays of vindictiveness.

Predictably, when the King withdraws, conflict escalates. Katie recalled numerous arguments between her parents when her father secluded himself in his bedroom. Her mother chased after him screaming, "Don't you dare walk away from me!" The Queen cannot tolerate being ignored and may evoke a response from her husband by any means possible.

The King may also withdraw when conflict arises between the mother and the child, leaving the child emotionally abandoned. Lachkar explains that the narcissist's withdrawal, "can create profound feelings of inadequacy and confusion, especially in children" (p. 83). Katie was afraid to tell her father the truth about how she felt. He was gone so frequently that she simply could not risk the possible withdrawal of his love. Children intuitively recognize that acknowledging problems wounds the King and diminishes his self-esteem.

The narcissist King and the borderline Queen have insatiable needs to be mirrored and provide mutual, although inconsistent, idealization of one another. Children can be lost in the kingdom of mirrors their parents construct to inflate their own self-esteem. Unfortunately, as the kingdom grows larger, the children feel smaller.

THE FISHERMAN

"My wife, her name is Ilsebil,
Has sent me here against my will."
— *The Fisherman and His Wife*

"My father was completely controlled by my mother. We were all terrified of her, and he was the only one who could have done something about it. I have no respect for him. He left us alone with a crazy woman. I practically lived with my girlfriend down the street. One night after my mother had been drinking, she came storming over to my friend's house, demanding that I come home. I was standing at the top of the stairs when my friend's parents opened the front door. They told my mother that I wasn't there. They protected me . . . something my father never, ever did."

Becky's Witch mother married a Fisherman. In the Grimms' fairy tale, the Fisherman's wife is never satisfied with what she has, demanding that her husband return to the sea again and again to ask the magic flounder for more power. At first she asks for a little cottage. After the magic flounder provides the Fisherman and his wife with a little cottage, the wife asks for a castle, then a kingdom, and eventually asks to become God. Her reluctant husband feels powerless to disobey her and, under the threat of violence, gives in to her demands. The borderline Witch's insatiable need for power and control is captured in this classic fairy tale:

> She gave him a grisly look that sent the cold shivers down his spine and cried: "Get going now. I want to be like God."
>
> "Wife, wife!" he cried, falling down on his knees, "the flounder can't do that. He can make an emperor and a pope, but please, please think it over and just go on being pope." At that she grew angry, her hair flying wildly around her head. She tore her nightgown to shreds, and gave him a kick. "I won't stand for it!" she cried, "I won't stand for it another minute. *Will* you get a move on?" Then he pulled on his trousers and ran out like a madman. [Manheim 1977, p. 76].

Like the Fisherman and his wife, the borderline Witch and her husband quarrel constantly, relating to one another as enemies rather than lovers. Kaplan (1978) asserts that "Quarrelers test the extent of their hatred by raging as one. They come together in mutual acrimony. They look past each other and through each other. Their eyes rage, they shout simultaneously, the vilifications of one drowning out the denigrations of the other" (p. 111).

Becky's family life was one of abuse and turmoil. She survived her childhood by finding surrogate parents because neither parent provided affection, comfort, or safety. Had she not found sanctuary with another family, she, too, might have become a Witch. She never understood why her father stayed married to her mother.

Men who marry Witches typically were either motherless or had very sadistic and controlling mothers. They had no healthy mothering experience against which to compare their wife's egregious behavior. If they grew up with harsh discipline, they believed it was for their own good and did them no harm. These men fail to see how their children are hurt because they fail to recognize how they were hurt as children. The Fisherman believes mother knows best.

The Fisherman's fear of his wife prevents him from protecting his children from her vindictiveness and abuse. He relinquishes his will to the Witch, functioning as an extension of her. Men who are married to Witches participate in a folie à deux (literally a double madness), which reinforces the Witch's distorted perceptions of her children.

Becky, a bright and resourceful young woman, suffered from BPD. She did not want to have children because she was terrified of being like her mother. She viewed her father as totally emasculated and felt that he had sacrificed her as a child, offering her up for total destruction by her mother. After graduating from college, Becky never again contacted her parents.

No man who was raised by a loving mother would choose to marry a Witch. Men who marry a Witch may sometimes be trapped by circumstances such as physical disability, but are most likely trapped by their own psychological blindness. They have never known healthy love. What the Witch offers the Fisherman is a façade of strength and a sense of self that he lacks. He mistakes the Witch's aggression for courage, and not only fails to realize the danger to himself, but also the greater danger to his children.

Characteristics of the Fisherman

> Then the husband went, and he was very unhappy because of his wife wanting to be king. "It's not right, it's not right at all," he thought. And he didn't want to go, but he went.
>
> — *The Fisherman and His Wife*

Relinquishes his will to the Witch

The Witch seeks a mate she can control. She is drawn to passive, submissive, vulnerable, or feeble individuals. She denigrates those with power because of her fear of being controlled. Thus, she chooses a submissive husband who can be controlled by fear. The Fisherman who catches a Witch finds himself caught in a net of fear.

The Fisherman is too insecure to stand up for himself or his children. Becky's father was cynical and bitter, but never dared express his feelings directly. Instead, he muttered sarcastic comments under his breath in response to his wife's merciless ridicule. Becky's mother treated her father like a servant, shouting commands, dictating orders, and humiliating him in public. The Fisherman may express resentment by being passive-aggressive, like a reluctant child dawdling while responding to a parent's command.

Because the Fisherman colludes with the Witch's distorted perceptions of his children, he may unconsciously fuel her rage and rejection of the no-good child and reinforce her favoritism of the all-good child. He may join her in ridicule, punishment, and humiliation of the no-good child, but will remove himself quickly whenever conflict between mother and child escalates.

Has little or no self-esteem; sees himself as a loser

The Fisherman's low self-esteem contributes to his inability to assert himself and protect his children. He sees himself as powerless and worthless, perceiving the Witch as more important than himself. He may envy her ability to express rage and intimidate, and may derive vicarious satisfaction through her sadistic control of others.

Although the Fisherman lives in fear of his wife, he also fears living without her. The Witch meets the emotional needs of the Fisherman who, without her, would feel lost. He relinquishes responsibility to her, holding onto the view of himself as the innocent, suffering victim. A blind accomplice to his wife's malice, the Fisherman is bolstered in self-esteem by his role as the good guy, the obedient, subservient husband.

As a child, Becky admitted that she was often rude to her father. She viewed him as having no self-respect and, consequently, she had no respect for him. She saw nothing about him to admire and referred to him as a wimp and a loser. She and her father annoyed one another, demeaned one another, but shared one thing in common: they both feared the Witch.

Fails to protect his children from abuse

Masterson (1980) observes that a husband of a borderline wife "may have any one of the severe forms of character pathology, or even schizophrenia. The key feature is that he is not available to the child . . . to support the forces of individuation and mastery of reality" (p. 22). Becky's father called her "a pain in the ass" and blamed her for provoking her mother's rage. During one particularly violent argument, her mother slapped Becky across the face. When Becky raised her hand to protect herself, her mother assumed that Becky was going to strike her and grabbed Becky by the throat. As the violence escalated, her father phoned the police to have *Becky* arrested. Because the Fisherman himself lacks individuation, he is as unaware of his wife's pathology as he is of his own.

THEY KNOW NOT WHAT THEY DO

Once upon a time, the Frog-Prince, the Huntsman, the King, and the Fisherman were children who were left alone with their own pain. No one came to their rescue, eased their sadness, filled their emptiness, or quieted their fears. Alice Miller (1986), author of *Thou Shalt Not Be Aware: Society's Betrayal of the Child*, warns that

> Children cannot achieve integration by themselves. They have no choice but to repress the [traumatic] experience, because the pain caused by their fear, isolation, betrayed expectation of receiving love, helplessness, and feelings of shame and guilt is unbearable. Further, the puzzling silence on the part of the adult and the contradiction between his deeds and the moral principles and prohibitions he proclaims by light of day create an intolerable confusion in the child that must be done away with by means of repression. [p. 311]

A father who fails to intervene in the pathological dynamics between the borderline mother and his children does so because he repressed memories of how he was hurt as a child. The slippery Frog-Prince is concerned primarily with his own survival and emotionally abandons his children. The humble Huntsman denies and ignores the Hermit's irrational behavior in order to uphold his commitment to the marriage. The lofty King retreats behind the walls of his kingdom, leaving his children in the hands of the capricious Queen. The Fisherman is trapped in the Witch's net and is as helpless as a child. Without therapy, these fathers can never see how they were hurt, can never heal, and cannot protect their children. These fairy-tale fathers leave their children balanced precariously on the edge of reality. Only those fathers who validate their children's perceptions and feelings, and believe what their children tell them, can protect them from developing BPD.

9

Loving the Waif
Without Rescuing Her

At night, when she was tired out with work, she had no bed to sleep in but had to lie in the ashes by the hearth.

— Cinderella

"My mother spent days at a time in bed when she was depressed. I was afraid to leave her alone. Sometimes I stayed home from school just to make sure that she didn't kill herself. She was proud of telling other people that when I was a baby, I would stop crying whenever she cried. Apparently, I learned to repress my own feelings before I could talk. It didn't occur to me until recently how much I sacrificed for her."

Michelle was a 40-year-old marketing director who worked thirteen-hour days. Thoughts of depression and feelings of resentment brought her to therapy. Her mother lived in subsidized housing on a meager income from Social Security. Michelle stated bluntly, "I've taken care of my mother all of my life . . . but now I feel like I'm drowning."

Michelle realized that she needed help structuring a healthier relationship with her mother. As the all-good child, she felt enormous responsibility for her mother's well-being, yet felt suffocated by her mother's dependency. She wanted a recipe, specific guidelines for setting limits with her mother, in order to enjoy her own life.

Like many adult children of Waifs, Michelle feared becoming dependent on a therapist. She wanted an instruction manual to read on her own because self-reliance felt safer than accepting help. As a child, Michelle had found dependency costly; consequently, she frequently expressed concern about the cost of therapy. Patients such as Michelle make good progress in therapy but may not stay in long-term treatment. They learn not to need others and equate dependency with weakness. They appear to be strong and fiercely independent, a defense that protects them from vulnerability. Charlotte du Pont's eldest daughter, Anna, was apparently much like Michelle: strong, determined, and unbelievably self-reliant. The Waif's adult children typically believe that no one can meet their needs, and they may not allow anyone to try.

The Waif's children may feel and behave more like adults than children. Having functioned as a surrogate mother during her mother's chronic depression, Anna du Pont was determined that she and her siblings would stay together after the death of their parents. Shortly after her father's funeral, members of the extended family met to discuss the arrangements for the orphaned children; meanwhile, the children secretly held their own meeting to ensure that they would not be separated. Fifteen-year-old Marguerite and 13-year-old Alfred agreed with Anna to defend themselves physically if forced to leave each other. When an uncle arrived to announce that the children would be divided among four families, he was greeted by Alfred holding a shotgun, Anna carrying a hatchet, and Marguerite wielding a rolling pin. Two younger brothers brandished a bow and arrow and a flintlock pistol. The uncle needed no further convincing to allow Anna to raise her siblings alone in their home. The Waif's children become accustomed to feeling motherless and learn, too early, how to fend for themselves.

Linehan (1993a) laments that "the crisis oriented nature of the borderline individual's life makes it particularly difficult, indeed, almost impossible to follow a predetermined behavioral treatment plan" (p. 87). Understandably, the Waif's children are often disillusioned with mental-health professionals. If their mother sought psychiatric treatment during their childhood they often ask why it never helped. The Waif is extremely difficult to treat.

Managing the treatment of the borderline Waif challenges the most highly qualified experts in the field. Clearly, the borderline's children should not be expected to manage her behavior. Michelle constantly rescued her mother from one crisis after another, paying utility bills in order to prevent disconnection, taking her car for repairs, and driving to the emergency room for injuries her mother sustained when intoxicated. Michelle concluded that after everything she had done for her mother, nothing had helped. Although Michelle had grown up, her mother had not. Her mother continued to suffer from depression, bulimia, alcoholism, and migraines. Michelle came to treatment because she had reached her limit: *she had to change.*

The chaos of the Waif's life can drain her children financially and emotionally. Her adult children will never have control over their own lives unless they establish structure. *Loving the Waif mother does not require taking care of her. Loving the Waif means caring about her.* The Waif's children will never be capable of preventing the turmoil that characterizes their mother's life. Loving the Waif mother requires giving the responsibility for her life—and death—back to her. Only then can her children embrace the freedom of their own lives.

Young children have no choice but to repress their own feelings to protect the parents they depend on for survival. Adult children can function for years with repressed feelings of guilt, anxiety, and rage, despite the fact that they no longer need to repress their feelings. Until these feelings create conflict, physical illness, or enough psychic pain, they may never be consciously examined. Like those who live with chronic physical pain, people who live with psychic pain find that it feels natural, as if it has always been there. They do not remember feeling normal.

MANAGING THE UNMANAGEABLE

Only adult children have the power and freedom necessary to develop a reality-based relationship with their mother. Letting go of unconscious, conditioned reactions, however, requires awareness, practice, and patience. Children of Waifs who are competent, successful adults are often astounded by how easily their mother can shake their self-confidence. After her mother informed a patient that her chronic childhood illnesses "scared her to death," the patient explained, "My mother is the only person in the world who can make me feel guilty for being ill, and basically, for living."

Her adult child's power and success may unconsciously threaten the Waif mother. Although she may proudly discuss the child's accomplishments with others, she may be unable to directly praise the child. Instead, she may demean and devalue the successful adult child, leaving the child feeling that he or she has done something wrong. The child, therefore, is unable to enjoy success because it feels wrong and triggers anxiety.

The Waif unconsciously identifies with the no-good child who shares her perception that life is too hard. The no-good child internalizes her split-off negative projections and, together, the Waif and the no-good child may form an alliance against the all-good child. Perceptions of her children fluctuate, however, and the mother may demean one child to another, forming alliances that change with time and circumstance. Eventually, adult children may become emotionally depleted and may take turns distancing from the Waif or from each other.

"It's always something"

Chronic crises are not the child's responsibility

The Waif mother's repeated crises, anxious pleadings, medical emergencies, frequent accidents, and financial distresses create anxiety in her adult children. The all-good child feels compelled to rescue the Waif from her various predicaments, whereas the no-good child is more likely to be detached. Nonconstructive but common reactions to the Waif's unpredictability include withdrawal, abandonment, sarcasm, ridicule, or devaluation through negative comments. More helpful to both the mother and child are constructive, empowering, and supportive responses such as "I know you'll think of a solution," or "I'm sorry that I can't help you, I know you can handle this yourself." Adult children need to express their feelings and needs directly, as the Waif easily misinterprets indirect or vague communication. Rescuing behavior perpetuates the Waif's unhealthy emotional dependency because it reinforces her view of herself as helpless.

Adult children must accept responsibility for the way they communicate their needs and feelings. What works for one child may not work for another. Although the Waif behaves unpredictably, adult children can respond in a predictable, consistent manner. The Waif is *not* helpless. Regardless of the crisis, adult children must give the Waif mother the message that *she can and must help herself.*

Michelle's mother frequently complained about her finances, her health, and her loneliness. Michelle learned to ask what her mother actually needed, and responded to complaints by clarifying her mother's expectations of her. She would say, "Mother, are you asking *me* to lend you some money?" or "Are you wanting *me* to keep you company?" Depending on her mother's response, Michelle explained whether or not she felt capable of meeting her expectations.

The Waif does not realize that her children may sacrifice what they need for themselves in order to save her. The adult child can illuminate this dynamic by asking, "Is this really what you want me to do?" or "Mother, are you asking me to miss a day of work in order to take you to the doctor?" or "Are you wanting me to spend my free time with you instead of with my husband?" The Waif does not know how to respond appropriately to her children's needs. She has never experienced healthy mothering and must be told what her children need, even if she is unable to provide it. Being specific and direct is the best way of evoking the desired response. *Adult children need to be consistently direct with the Waif mother.*

"It's never as bad as she says"

Ask for details before reacting

The Waif may exaggerate, distort, and embellish stories in order to evoke sympathy from others. Before reacting out of sympathy or pity, adult children must consider the possibility of distortion. Rather than accusing the Waif of lying, adult children should ask for details, then evaluate the seriousness of the situation. The Waif's feelings should be taken seriously, but her perspective on the interactions should be questioned. *Inconsistencies or contradictions should always be pointed out.* For example, Michelle learned to say,

"You are really upset about this. But last week you told me that the car repairs cost \$250. Now you're telling me that they cost \$500." Because the Waif may not be able to express her needs directly, her adult children must be direct about clarifying expectations. Michelle's mother needed to borrow money, but felt that she needed to justify her request by embellishing a story about the cost of her car repairs. Michelle said simply, "Just ask me, Mother, when you need something. I don't like it when you aren't direct with me."

"Her memory is selective"

Trust your memory

The Waif, like all borderlines, may have difficulty remembering previous emotional states. She is not likely to remember emotionally traumatic experiences and may deny outbursts of rage or panic. Thus, adult children may question their own perceptions when the Waif mother invalidates their experiences.

Rather than arguing about the accuracy of each other's memories, adult children need to trust their own experience. Children of all ages find it extremely disturbing when their mother does not validate their emotional experiences. Only adult children, however, may feel safe enough to express their feelings. Michelle told her mother, "It really bothers me that you do not share my memory of the Christmas of 1975. It was one of the most painful memories of my childhood. I need to know that you believe me, even if you don't remember things the way I do." Adult children must find a safe way of expressing their feelings. All children, regardless of their age, need to trust their instincts of self-preservation.

"She makes me feel guilty"

Separate legitimate guilt from projected guilt; don't take advantage of her

The Waif mother is too permissive and may allow her children to take advantage of her. She may insist that her children take her last dollar, and then complain because they did not leave any money for her. She does not enforce rules and then complains that her children seem out of control. The Waif sets herself up to be exploited. Those who exploit her, however, may experience legitimate guilt.

No-good children may take advantage of her helplessness, becoming self-centered and exploitative. All-good children may experience projected guilt, and internalize the Waif's feelings of unworthiness. Although the all-good child does not exploit the Waif, guilt, anxiety, frustration, and worry rob the child of enjoying life. The Waif mother creates anxiety because her children never know whether they can rely on her.

Anger can generate guilt because destructive fantasies accompany anger. Michelle needed a great deal of support to work through her anger at her mother. When Michelle was in high school, her mother frequently forgot to pick her up, leaving her waiting alone in the abandoned building for hours. When her mother finally arrived, Michelle berated her by saying, "What kind of a mother *are* you?" No child should feel guilty about needing a reliable mother.

Adult children need to protect themselves from disappointment without feeling guilty. They have a right to expect their mother to be reliable. As an adult, Michelle rarely allowed herself to depend on her mother for anything. She wanted to distance herself completely, but occasionally found that her mother could be supportive. Michelle learned to ask her mother for help only when other options were not available.

"She forgets about me"

Explain the need for emotional validation

Adult children may resent the Waif's tendency to change plans at the last minute, to break engagements in order to attend more important social events, or to prefer the company of others to the company of her own children. One time, her mother canceled a planned vacation with Michelle because her mother discovered that a former boyfriend was coming to town the weekend of their trip. Michelle complained that she rarely had her mother's undivided attention and that her mother seemed preoccupied with her relationships with men.

Adult children often refer to the Waif as a fake because she does not follow through on commitments and is generally undependable. They may believe that the real mother is uncaring, unreliable, or deceitful. The truth is that the Waif mother does not feel real. Continually searching for validation from others, she is unaware that she fails to validate her own children.

After her mother canceled the trip with her, Michelle told her that she was hurt and explained that she felt discarded. Michelle avoided making drastic threats such as, "I'm never inviting you on a trip again," but informed her that she planned to invite a friend instead. Her mother was surprised to learn that Michelle felt hurt and accused her of being jealous of her boyfriend. Instead of reacting with hostility, Michelle repeated her hurt feelings and said, "I just need you to understand how I feel." Adult children can learn to explain their need for emotional validation, regardless of whether they eventually receive it. *The Waif is unaware that she forgets her own children.*

"She can be really fun, or really a drag"

Enjoy the good times and point out inappropriate behavior

The Waif mother has many appealing qualities. The good mother, the fun mother, the loving mother, and the interesting mother are all parts of the Waif that her adult children cherish and enjoy. The parts of her that are enjoyable make it difficult for her adult children to reconcile their anger and resentment. Adult children can hold onto the good parts of the Waif mother while detaching from the unpleasant, uncomfortable, or dangerous parts. To detach, how-ever, does not mean to ignore. Inappropriate or unpleasant behav-ior should never be ignored.

Pointing out unacceptable behavior is essential to maintain a healthy relationship with the borderline Waif. What annoys one child may be tolerated by another. What feels dangerous to one child may not threaten the other. Adult children must point out behaviors that cross the threshold of their individual tolerance levels, their own personal limits.

Michelle could not stand hearing her mother complain about her physical problems. She pointed out the offending behavior to her mother by declaring, "If you don't change the subject, Mother, I'm going to hang up. You know I can't stand to hear you complain about your health." Without Michelle's confronting her mother's intolerable behavior, her mother would have no opportunity to respond more appropriately to Michelle's needs.

"Nothing ever goes right for her"

Do not reinforce her negative self-view

Adult children have every right to expect and create more positive interactions with their mothers. The Waif's depressive view of herself and her life casts a shadow of negativity on her perceptions. Children can easily be led to believe that life is too hard, that things never work out, and that giving up is easier than going on. Adult children are not responsible for cheering up their mother, for building her self-esteem, or for preventing her from killing herself. For their own well-being, however, they must distance themselves from negative perceptions, and hold on to a more positive view of themselves, their mother, and life in general.

Michelle's mother habitually informed her of the latest bad news. Whenever Michelle phoned, the conversation focused on her mother's problems. When Michelle realized how much she dreaded these phone calls, she informed her mother of a new rule: for every piece of bad news, she wanted to hear a piece of good news. Occasionally, her mother simply laughed, lightening the conversation for both of them.

"It's safer not to need her"

Let your judgment be your guide

Adult children need to recognize ways in which the Waif's impulsive behavior can jeopardize their well-being. Their first responsibility is to take care of themselves. Safety always comes first. Ironically, attempts to help the Waif can trigger catastrophic reactions. In the midst of a psychotic reaction the Waif may become paranoid, perceiving her own children as threatening. The assistance of a trusted health-care professional is essential in obtaining appropriate medication and intervention. The Waif, though, may not be receptive to any kind of intervention.

The Waif is most likely to become psychotic when faced with rejection or abandonment. By the time her children are adults, they generally recognize the connection between abandonment and desperate, impulsive behavior. What they may not realize is that they cannot prevent these episodes from occurring.

Brazelton (Brazelton and Cramer 1990) explains that infants and children experience hopelessness when the mother withdraws due to her own depression. The Waif conveys her emotional message that life is too hard through her projections of helplessness. Adult children are only helpless in preventing crisis in the *Waif's* life.

Michelle discovered that the only thing that was too hard in her life was trying to help her mother. She could not live her own life until she separated from her mother. A recurrent dream captured the essence of her struggle. A ship carrying her family capsizes. She is thrown into the turbulent sea, struggling beneath the water to reach the surface. Breathless and desperate for air, Michelle panics when a hand grasps her foot and drags her beneath the surface. She suppresses the urge to kick the hand off her foot, recognizing her mother's grip.

Tired of feeling pulled under by her mother, Michelle was dangerously close to drowning. Many adult children of Waifs recount similar dreams and feelings. The Waif's children can benefit by heeding the American Red Cross (1968) advice on lifesaving:

> It is well known that the length of time that a person can stay in the water without succumbing to exhaustion and exposure . . . has limits . . . The tale of needless sacrifice in the history of

swimming is a long one wherein heroism displayed has availed nothing . . . Novice and even very good swimmers frequently find that their ability to make a rescue does not equal their good intent and *they either break away with great difficulty or drown with him.* [p. 24, emphasis added]

Reaching our limit is accompanied by the thought, "I can't stand it anymore. I have a right to live." Not being able to stand her mother's behavior was the turning point for Michelle to change *her* behavior.

"She drives me crazy"

Your peace of mind comes first

The conflicts Michelle experienced with her mother seriously jeopardized her mental health. She suffered from chronic depression, anxiety, and recurrent bouts of colitis. Although the Waif has the right to choose her fate, her children have a right to survive. This admonition from the Red Cross applies to emotional as well as physical survival: "The three major causes of drowning are, and always have been, failure to recognize hazardous conditions . . . , [the] inability to get out of dangerous situations, and lack of knowledge of safe ways in which to aid or rescue drowning persons" (p. iii).

The Waif and her children are engaged in a very real battle for survival. Children of borderlines will not survive emotionally unless they recognize the danger of *failing* to separate from their mother. Three steps are essential to loving the Waif mother without rescuing her: (1) confirm separateness, (2) create structure, and (3) clarify consequences.

Step 1: Confirm separateness: "I am . . ."

The Waif's internalized feelings of worthlessness and hopelessness can endanger her children. Adult children must recognize hazardous conditions that could threaten their well-being. The Waif's impulsivity and poor judgment may be evident in behaviors such as gambling, overspending, driving while intoxicated, neglecting her health, or mismanaging her finances. Her self-destructive behavior can also jeopardize her children's financial, emotional, and physical well-being. Although adult children are no longer dependent on their mother, their long-standing tendency to sacrifice their own needs for the sake of their mother's may continue for years.

The Waif becomes highly anxious when separated from her primary attachment figure, demonstrating clinging behavior, searching behavior, or rage. When children succumb to the fear that she might self-mutilate, attempt suicide, have an accident, or harm herself, it reinforces her destructive behavior. The Waif's adult children must protect themselves from being emotionally controlled by fear and guilt. They do not have to abandon her. In fact, the more successful they are at not being controlled, the more meaningful their relationship can become. *A healthy relationship is a choice, not a trap.*

Winnicott (1958) explains that the words, "I am . . ." represent a crucial stage in individual growth. "By these words the individual not only has shape but also life . . . The individual can only achieve the I am stage because *there exists an environment which is protective* (p. 33, emphasis added). Establishing separateness is easier for the adult child who has the support of a partner, spouse, friend, or therapist. No one should underestimate the intensity of the anxiety experienced by adult children who attempt to separate from the Waif mother.

Michelle suffered from gratification guilt and separation anxiety. As if she were leaving a newborn home alone, Michelle could not relax when away from her mother. Prior to taking vacations, Michelle experienced panic attacks, feeling guilty and worrying about her mother constantly. From the time she was a child, every positive event was marred by concern for her mother. After coming home from high school dates she often found her lying unconscious on the floor. It never felt safe to leave her alone.

As long as Michelle shared bad news with her mother their relationship seemed to go well. Telling her mother good news seemed to trigger resentment. As long as life was hard she maintained the connection with her mother. Michelle's success and ability to enjoy life threatened her mother and represented abandonment. Michelle explained, "I feel guilty when I go on vacations, to parties, or entertain friends. I feel like I'm doing something wrong whenever I do something fun." Eventually, she was able to tell her mother directly, "*I am* the child, Mother. I need you to be happy when things are going well for *me*."

Michelle developed a plan for her next vacation and explained what she expected of her mother:

"I'm afraid to leave you. Whenever I go on vacation it seems like something bad happens. The last time I left, you had a car accident and I felt guilty about being gone. If you have an accident or become ill while I'm gone, please call a friend or someone else instead of me. When I'm away, there's nothing I can do to help anyway. I am not going to leave my phone number with you anymore when I'm away on trips."

Michelle's mother was bewildered and offended by Michelle's suggestion. She denied recognizing a pattern of accidents and illnesses when Michelle left town. She said in a huff, "Well! I had no idea I am such a problem to you! You won't have to worry about me *ever again*! I won't be bothering you *anymore*!" Her mother did not call for the next three weeks and refused to return Michelle's phone calls. Although Michelle considered the possibility that her mother might harm herself and struggled with guilt, she knew she had done nothing wrong. Michelle understood why as a child, she never dared express her own needs. She stood her ground calmly, but firmly, and did not provide her mother with her telephone number while on vacation.

A healthy mother wants her child to be happy. The Waif mother does not understand the unhappiness she creates in her children. Her adult child must not expect her to be happy about the changes within the relationship. The Waif mother's worst fear, abandonment, is less likely to materialize if her adult children structure the relationship around *their* needs.

Pity Prevents Separation

Feeling sorry for the Waif is the worst possible reaction to her self-defeating behavior. Acknowledging pain, sympathizing or empathizing with another person's feelings is not pity. Pity legitimizes feelings of hopelessness. What the Waif needs most is to regain the ability to hope. Pity conveys subtle disrespect, a sense of superiority, and is therefore condescending. Rudolf Dreikurs (Dreikurs and Soltz 1964) observed, "Feeling sorry about the '*it*' which happened is sympathy. Feeling sorry for the '*you*' to whom it happened is pity" (p. 247).

Disappointment and adversity are a part of everyone's life. The ability to tolerate suffering and hold on to a positive view of life despite adversity is essential to mental health. Sympathy and encouragement are much healthier responses to the Waif's pleas of helplessness than pity and rescuing behavior. Sympathy can be expressed by stating, "This must really hurt. I am so sorry that this happened. What can I do to help you get through this particular time?" Sympathy conveys confidence in the person's ability to cope with the situation. Pity is expressed in statements such as, "I feel sorry for you, you poor thing." Pity is demeaning because it implies that the person is weak, as if one were saying, "I am so much better off than you are, I should step down from my pedestal and help you."

Michelle's unemployed, alcoholic, younger brother exploited her mother. He borrowed her car without paying for gas and borrowed money without paying her back. Michelle resented her mother's passive stance with her brother and suspected that he received half of the weekly allowance Michelle gave to her mother. Rather than feel sorry for her mother, Michelle stated:

"I am not willing to provide you with money to give to John. I expect you to give me the receipts from your purchases so that we can work out a budget. I need to know exactly how much you need. I won't be able to provide you with cash unless I have the receipts from the previous week."

Michelle's mother responded flippantly, "I never asked for your money in the first place!" Michelle answered gently, "I'm happy to help you, Mother, but if you don't want my help that's your decision." Michelle's mother refused to speak to her for two months following their discussion. Michelle knew in her heart that she had not been unfair and refused to feel guilty. She knew her mother would eventually speak to her, behaving as though nothing had happened. Nevertheless, she held her mother accountable for her decision not to accept her financial assistance. Slowly, over time, Michelle taught her mother that she meant what she said and that she could not be manipulated by pity or guilt.

Step 2: Create Structure: "I will . . ."

Structure determines the strength, resiliency, stability, and durability of relationships, as well as buildings. Because the borderline mother lacks internal structure, she is unable to maintain stable relationships, even with her own children. The Waif's loose, permissive parenting style fails to provide her children with stability, and adult children may need help setting limits, consequences, and boundaries. Relationships that lack structure eventually fall apart. Structure provides security and safety.

Michelle's mother often phoned her late at night while intoxicated, ruminating and rambling, and then having no memory of the conversation the following day. Late-night phone calls annoyed Michelle, left her exhausted the following day, and enabled her mother's self-destructive behavior. Michelle established structure with her mother by explaining:

"Mother, I am too tired at night to talk on the phone, and I do not want to talk to you when you've been drinking. If you call me after 10:00 P.M. *I will* not answer the phone. If you call me when you're drunk, *I will* simply hang up. There's no point in having conversations you don't remember."

The most important part of Michelle's plan was not what she told her mother but her ability to follow her plan consistently. The borderline mother responds well, as does anyone, to consistency, sameness of experience, and knowing what to expect. Michelle did not answer the telephone after 10:00 P.M. She purchased Caller ID service in order to screen her calls, and refused to speak with her mother when she was drunk. In less than six weeks, her mother stopped the late-night phone calls and stopped calling when intoxicated.

Michelle structured the relationship with her mother around her own needs, even though initially her mother responded with hostility. Michelle did not give in, and reassured her that she still loved and cared about her. The goal is not to deprive, frustrate, or punish but to *grow toward mutual understanding*.

"I will" statements express intention, self-direction, and autonomy, and reinforce "I am" statements that confirm separateness. These statements must be reality-based, or credibility and meaning will be lost. Saying one thing and doing another is contradictory and undermines trust. *"I will" statements must never be used as threats* but should convey logical, natural consequences for inappropriate behavior.

Draw a Line to Create Structure

The Waif's unmanageable life can engulf the adult child who does not create structure and set limits. Creating a healthier relationship with the borderline mother requires drawing a mental map that guides the mother and child toward the safe shores of autonomy. Structuring a healthy relationship with the Waif requires setting boundaries.

Adult children must define the line that separates them from their mother. Crossing the line of one's own limits leads to merger and re-creates the pathological dependency of the borderline Waif. The more the Waif depends on her children, the less likely she will learn to save herself. The adult child should not have to jump in the water to save her drowning mother. The Waif must learn to swim.

The American Red Cross (1968) describes the case of an elderly gentleman who saved the life of a drowning man. The elderly man walked with a cane and was standing on the shore when he saw a swimmer struggling in the water. The older man saved the swimmer's life not by jumping in the water, but by extending his cane from a nearby pier for the man to grasp. The drowning man then clung to the cane while his rescuer pulled him to shore.

If the Waif mother refuses to grab hold of the help that is extended to her, the adult child is not responsible. The Waif must be given the opportunity to experience her own strength, to gain confidence in her own abilities, and to be given only enough assistance to help herself. Lending a hand *at the crucial moment* is all that is needed to save a life.

Step 3: Clarify Consequences: "I won't . . ."

The Waif is extremely sensitive to rejection and to criticism, and expects to be punished. The principles of logical and natural consequences convey no moral judgment and are therefore useful when interacting with the Waif. Dreikurs (Dreikurs and Soltz 1964) developed an approach to child-rearing known as "logical and natural consequences." His novel concept introduced healthy, esteem-building techniques for parents who recognized the negative effects of punitive, shaming, and authoritarian parenting styles. His concepts have been widely accepted by contemporary parents and can be adopted for use in all relationships.

The Waif's adult children sense their mother's despair and may feel like giving up hope. Attempts to help her often fail, causing her children to become discouraged and depressed. Logical and natural consequences remind the Waif that she has control over her life and that helplessness can be unlearned.

Natural consequences are those that occur as a result of the natural order of the physical world; for example, standing in the rain and getting wet, not eating and getting hungry, not filling the car with gas and running out of gas. The Waif points to natural consequences as evidence of her personal bad luck, as if she had no role in their occurrence. "I ran out of gas, and had to walk three miles in the rain without an umbrella. Nothing ever goes right for me." The conditioned child says, "How terrible! I feel so sorry for you. You have the worst luck." The enlightened child states, "That's too bad. I'm sure you'll check your gas gauge before leaving home from now on. I never drive anywhere with less than a quarter tank of gas." Distinguishing natural consequences from bad luck helps the adult child break the cycle of responding with guilt or pity. Pointing out natural consequences conveys the message that "this happens to everybody, and you, too, can learn from experience."

Logical consequences are those that result from the reality of the social world, such as not showing up for work and being fired, not paying utility bills and having utilities disconnected, not studying and failing a course. Logical consequences convey the message that the Waif is capable of making more responsible decisions and encourage mature behavior without demanding compliance or using coercion. For example, Michelle's mother frequently arrived late for family meals. The family felt inconvenienced having to wait for her arrival, but Michelle, worried about insulting her mother, never said anything to her. Eventually, Michelle decided that the logical consequence was for her family to eat on time, regardless of when her mother arrived.

Logical and natural consequences do not guarantee reduction of conflict. No matter how carefully the adult child clarifies consequences, the Waif may feel rejected and punished. Adult children are not responsible for their mother's behavior. Logical and natural consequences simply provide a guideline for appropriate responses to inappropriate behavior.

Clarify Consequences for Suicidal Behavior

People who commit suicide generally do not tell their therapist, or anyone else, about their plans. Parents who tell their children that they feel like killing themselves usually want reassurance that they are cared about and would be missed. Paradoxically, the threat is often an attempt to *prevent abandonment*. Such statements evoke powerful feelings of anxiety in children, even adult children, and should never be ignored. Listed below are helpful versus nonhelpful responses:

Nonhelpful Responses

1. Rescuing behavior: "Oh, please don't say that, I will do anything for you."
2. Ignoring the threat or gesture: "Right, you've said that a million times."
3. Failing to take the feeling seriously: "I'm so sick of hearing you say that."

Helpful Responses

1. Calling the police when any suicidal gesture is acted upon.
2. Calling the parent's therapist when any suicidal thought is mentioned.
3. Responding honestly with concern and appropriate consequences such as the following:

    "Telling me that you feel like killing yourself upsets me. It scares me and makes me angry. I am going to tell your therapist. There is nothing else I can do to help. I am your child. I love you and care about you but I do not want to be responsible for whether or not you kill yourself. It is unfair to me."

Some adult children feel so frustrated or endangered in the presence of their Waif mothers that they choose not to have any contact at all. No one has the right to pass judgment on such situations. Every human being has the right to protect his or her own life. In some cases, it is in the best interest of both mother and child to disengage completely. *No one* can save a person who does not want to be saved.

BECOMING A PERSON

In 1961 Carl Rogers introduced a revolutionary concept to the field of psychology. His approach to psychotherapy was grounded in his belief in the ability of individuals to grow and mature. He did not use strategies, techniques, or tricks to create growth. He used his real self. He believed that only by being real could he help others. He observed, "Probably one of the reasons why most people respond to infants is that they are so completely genuine, integrated, or congruent. If an infant expresses affection or anger or contentment or fear there is no doubt in our minds that he is this experience, all the way through" (p. 339). But infants like Michelle learn to mask their inner experience, to respond to their mother's need, to be quiet when their mother cries, and to smile when their mother is sad.

Rogers emphasized that "congruence" is essential to being a genuine person. Congruence means that our internal emotional experience matches our behavior. We trust people who are real, even if they are sometimes offensive, because we know they are telling us the truth about how they feel.

Rogers warned that being oneself does not solve problems. Being oneself frees one to explore new solutions, consider new perspectives, experience greater intimacy, and appreciate life more deeply. Winnicott (1960) believed that "only the True Self can be creative and only the True Self can feel real . . . the existence of a False Self results in . . . a sense of futility" (p. 148). The Waif's children can develop a false self that is grounded in compulsive self-sufficiency or the opposite, overdependence.

Children of borderlines expect incongruent behavior from others. They learn to hide their real feelings, to express their needs indirectly, or not to need anything at all. Because this learning is unconscious, they are unaware of their own incongruence.

Children of borderlines keep the true self hidden, first from their parents and eventually from themselves. A spunky 7-year-old boy announced to his mother, "You don't know what I think! You don't know what my dreams are! I only tell you what I want you to know!" The real self will be hidden if it cannot be freely expressed. Rogers (1961) wrote: "only one person . . . can know whether what I am doing is honest, thorough, open, and sound, or false and defensive and unsound, and *I am that person*" (p. 23, emphasis added).

The Waif's adult children learn to doubt their own experience and can sink into needless despair. The Waif mother may believe that her children would be better off without her. The depth of her despair is truly frightening. Her pain feels unmanageable and thoughts of death mar her life. Naturally, her children internalize her feelings. They too, may wonder if they would be better off without her. They may also feel that her pain is unmanageable and wonder if death might provide the only serenity their mother will ever know. These forbidden thoughts terrify children, increase guilt and anxiety, and can lead to panic attacks.

Children want the freedom to enjoy life but not at the expense of their mother's life. The Waif wants freedom from her pain and may be unable to consider her children's feelings. A borderline Waif who had a history of suicide attempts and multiple hospitalizations told her friend, "I've decided that I just can't go on. I'm having lunch tomorrow with my 12-year-old son. If he is rude to me that will be the last straw. I'm going to kill myself." When the friend suggested that it was unfair not to consider the consequences for her son, the Waif stared at her blankly, unable to comprehend anyone else's pain but her own.

Excruciating physical pain can drive one to suicide. So, too, can emotional pain. The Waif's adult children must relinquish trying to save their mother's life and the anger that can destroy their own lives. The Waif's children cannot save her; they must swim to shore alone.

10

Loving the Hermit
Without Feeding Her Fear

Next morning Snow White woke up, and when she saw the
seven dwarfs she was frightened. But they were friendly . . .

—*Snow White and the Seven Dwarfs*

*"My mother lives in the safety of her shell, like a turtle hiding in the deep
end of a lake, avoiding the lures above. It's a depressing existence. She
doesn't trust anyone, not even members of her own family."*

From Sandy's earliest age, her mother undermined her self-
confidence and discouraged her curiosity about life. Because the
Hermit lacks internal calmness, she is unable to provide the
nonanxious presence needed to soothe and comfort her children
and may discourage them from exploring the world. She communicates anxiety through her fretfulness, tone of voice, and her
tendency to catastrophize. Although she believes that she is protecting her children, the Hermit's fear diminishes her ability to
solve problems, to think clearly, and to make decisions. During the
Great Depression President Franklin Delano Roosevelt warned,
"the only thing we have to fear is fear itself." The wisdom in his
admonition is evident in the Hermit's behavior. Her fear is the
greatest threat to her survival and to her children's self-confidence.

Sandy began treatment for depression when she was 45 years old. Everyone in her family had been treated for depression, except her mother. Too distrustful to confide in a therapist, Sandy's mother insisted that she did not need help. Although most Hermits may never come to the attention of mental health professionals, adult children such as Sandy verify their prevalence.

"My mother talked to her mother at least two or three times a day. She had no close friends and rarely socialized. Looking back on it, it's obvious that my mother never separated from her own mother."

When Sandy started therapy her mother warned her that "therapy will change your personality." She asked Sandy if she "talked about what a terrible mother you have." Sandy calmly replied, "Of course we talk about you, but not in the way you think."

Harold Blum (1986) explains:

> The paranoid personality tends to misperceive and distort reality in selected areas. Persistent fantasies of outer or inner danger coexist with unreasonable expectation and exaggeration of hostile threat and exquisite sensitivity to minor mishaps and injuries. Affection and commitment are unreliable, and disappointments in relationships are regarded as potentially menacing or malevolent. [p. 253]

When Sandy was a child, her mother smothered her with overprotection. Her mother controlled her television programs, her friendships, her clothes, and was jealous of Sandy's relationships with others. Blum states:

> The patient may imagine that thoughts and feelings are deviously communicated to or from others and secrets stolen and betrayed. Paranoid fears of invasion and engulfment are paired with paradoxical fears of desertion and disloyal rejection so that neither intimacy nor separation are acceptable. There is no comfortable distance or

position, and if the [child] is not being watched and controlled, then the [child] must be jealously guarded with monitoring of movement and direction. [p. 255]

Conversations with her mother increased Sandy's anxiety and undermined her tenuous self-confidence.

The Hermit may suffer from post-traumatic stress disorder, and uncontrollable fear rules her perceptions. Her children may find it difficult to understand why neither intimacy nor separation is comfortable. Sandy needed help managing the thoughts and feelings that result from living with a chronically anxious mother. The Hermit's children need guidance in structuring a relationship based on their own perceptions.

"The fear of the day club"

Reevaluate rather than react to fear

The nature and focus of the Hermit's anxiety can change from moment to moment. Because they expect something bad to happen they may avoid new experiences. They expect bad news, dwell on bad news, and report *unconfirmed* bad news. Sandy's mother telephoned one morning to tell her that a "terrible car accident" had occurred on one of two routes her husband took to work. Sandy's heart began racing as she considered the possibility that her husband might have been involved in the accident. When she pressed her mother for the exact location of the wreck, her mother breathlessly replied, "Oh, I didn't take time to listen; I don't know." At that point Sandy recognized a familiar pattern: *the distinctive mark of the false alarm—fear with no facts*. Sandy said gently,

"Mother, Pete left over two hours ago; I'm sure he made it safely to work."

Sandy's mother dreaded receiving the mail because she expected only bills or letters from collection agencies. Sandy joked that her mother belonged to "the fear of the day club" and tried to ignore her mother's obsessive, paranoid thoughts. She resented her ability to trigger adrenaline surges, exacerbate Sandy's own fears, and stir up anxiety.

The Hermit's adult children may resent the underlying message that life is too dangerous. Unlike the Witch, the Hermit does not *intend* to frighten her children. She controls her children in order to *protect* them. Anxiety, however, is contagious, and her children may feel more secure when they are away from her than when they are with her. Adult children of Hermits must protect themselves from internalizing their mother's fear by asking for details before they react. They should never react to incomplete, vague, or sketchy information provided by their mother and must learn to rely on their own perception, intuition, and judgment.

"She undermines my self-confidence"

She can't give you something she doesn't have

The Hermit teaches her children that the world is a dangerous place, because, for her, it was. Unfortunately, the Hermit's adult children need to be cautious about sharing their fears with their mother. Her response most likely will exacerbate their fear and undermine their self-confidence.

Sandy made the mistake of telling her mother about a conflict with her boss. Her mother catastrophized the situation, telephoning her several times a day, vilifying her boss, suggesting that he was "out to get Sandy," implying that Sandy would soon be fired. Sandy found herself having to reassure her mother that she would not be fired, and regretted having told her about the minor disagreement. The Hermit catastrophizes insignificant events and makes mountains out of molehills.

The Hermit cannot provide emotional support or bolster her child's self-confidence because she lacks self-confidence herself. The sad reality is that her children, and often her spouse, tune her out because she overreacts, leaving her increasingly isolated and paranoid. Unless someone helps her distinguish between legitimate anxiety and irrational fear, the Hermit's panic can escalate. Sandy said, "Mother, telling me that my boss is out to get me doesn't make me feel any better. In fact, it makes me feel worse. When I told you that my boss and I had an argument, I needed you to tell me that you understood my feelings. *I am not afraid* of being fired for disagreeing with my boss." The Hermit's adult children must separate their fears from their mother's fears.

"She denies what she said and acts like I'm crazy!"

Believe in yourself and your own basic goodness

The Hermit does not realize how panic prevents her from thinking clearly, from organizing her thoughts, planning activities, or participating in life. She lives from one fearful moment to the next. Nothing but the present matters to the Hermit, whose emotional energy is invested in scanning for danger. Therefore, she is not likely to remember previous paranoid accusations or inappropriate behavior. Asking the Hermit if she remembers saying that the store clerk tried to cheat her is like asking a soldier if he remembers dodging a specific bullet. The Hermit is in the midst of an ongoing battle for survival.

Sandy's mother denied inappropriate behavior and never apologized for her paranoid accusations. After her mother accused her brother of stealing her wallet and later found it in the closet, she denied the accusation. By the time she found her wallet, her mind was filled with worry about a credit card she had misplaced.

Sandy's mother projected her own confused thinking onto Sandy, making statements such as, "You twisted my words!" Sandy occasionally resorted to humor to respond to her mother's confused thinking. By holding on to her belief in her own basic goodness, Sandy was able to laugh and say, "Mother, you are the only person in the world who can leave me feeling so confused!"

"Sometimes we have fun together, but I always end up being disappointed"

Expect rejection to follow closeness

Sandy and her mother shared a love for reading. Their mutual interest in literature was one of the few warm connections between them, and nurturing this positive aspect of their relationship was important. However, an unexpected, hostile comment from her mother often ended enjoyable interactions.

Closeness makes the Hermit feel vulnerable. As if she suddenly realizes that her guard is down, warm interactions are often followed by abrupt attacks or paranoid accusations that push others away. Adult children are consistently disappointed in the brevity of positive interactions and may feel foolish for allowing themselves to trust her. Unaware of her role in these interactions, the Hermit may adamantly deny her hostility if confronted. Adult children can protect themselves by keeping interactions brief, and by ending conversations following positive interactions.

"She twists and distorts what really happened"

Calmly maintain your perspective

The Hermit often misperceives innocuous interactions as threatening or rejecting. For instance, Sandy's mother responded with hostility when a salesclerk asked for identification. Her mother perceived the clerk's request as intrusive and offensive, rather than a matter of policy established for the store's protection. When Sandy later asked why her mother was rude to the clerk, her mother blamed the clerk for being rude to her.

On another occasion, her mother reported that Sandy's husband had "bawled her out" and that she "could not repeat" what he had said to her. Sandy was surprised to hear that her husband had been rude to her mother and questioned him about the interaction. Her husband explained that her mother had been fretting about their 3-year-old son not wearing his hat. He said, "All I said to your mother was 'Betty, I don't want to hear any more about the hat.'" Her husband was shocked to hear her mother's distorted version of the interaction and resented the implication that he had been rude.

"She has no social life"

Being alone is her choice, not yours

Sandy invited her mother on several trips, encouraged her to volunteer for different organizations and to join clubs where she could meet other women her age. Her mother simply refused to participate in group activities and was too fearful to travel. Sandy felt sorry for her but eventually gave up trying to encourage her to participate in life. Her mother preferred being alone in her house with the doors and windows locked.

Adult children of Hermits must respect their mother's desire for isolation. They do not, however, have to join her. They are not responsible for entertaining her, for bringing her out of her shell, or for her decision to remain reclusive. The more they try to coax her out, the more fearful and resentful she may become. Efforts to change her environment are unlikely to succeed.

"Everything's a plot"

Respond to conspiracy theories with reason

Sandy's mother obsessed over daily news reports of crime, murders, robberies, and rapes. She followed international news with the eye of a CIA agent, proposing wild theories about possible attacks on the United States from various countries. Sandy's mother lived her life as though everyone was out to get her.

Adult children of Hermits should not ridicule, tease, or exacerbate their mother's fears. They must guard against succumbing to her anxiety in order to be able to evaluate situations rationally. In order to live their lives fully and meaningfully, they must free themselves from the Hermit's perspective of the world as a dangerous place. Although fear controls the Hermit, adult children must learn to control fear.

Adult children need to counter conspiracy theories with reason. For example, Sandy's mother became enraged when a neighbor built a fence near her property line. Her mother demanded that the neighbor remove the fence and accused him of intentionally intruding onto her property. Sandy pointed out that the fence surrounded the neighbor's yard on all sides, and therefore was certainly not meant as a personal attack against her mother. Although her mother calmed down, she stated, "Just wait and see, he's trying to provoke me."

"Her meals and eating habits are bizarre"

Plan meals in comfortable settings

Organizing a social event such as a dinner or a party may be overwhelming for the borderline Hermit. Anxiety can prevent her from being able to follow a recipe, decide what to do first, or set the table. Preparing food can feel like an overwhelming responsibility. One Sunday, Sandy's mother invited her family for dinner. When Sandy arrived with her husband and three children, she was amazed to find the table bare. She checked the refrigerator and found one small pan of Jell-O and bits of dried cheese and leftover meat. When she asked her mother what she intended to serve, her mother replied, "Oh, I just thought we'd fill in around Jell-O."

Because food is taken in and becomes part of the self, the Hermit may fear poisoning herself and others. Sandy's mother overcooked meat because she believed it was the only way to kill bacteria. As a result, Sandy learned to dislike meat and became a vegetarian after she left home.

Dinnertime in Sandy's childhood home was not a warm, pleasant experience. Sandy's mother frequently announced that they were "having scraps" for dinner. Her mother viewed meals as a time to use up food, rather than a time for emotional and physical nourishment. As an adult, Sandy avoided her mother's cooking.

Instead, she invited her mother to her home or suggested eating at a restaurant, relieving her mother from the dreaded responsibility of meal preparation.

Food serves to regulate anxiety for many Hermits. Their relationship with food reflects fluctuations in self-esteem. Food is used to self-soothe and may therefore be consumed in great quantities whenever the Hermit's anxiety is high. The Hermit may also project her feelings about food onto her family. One time when Sandy was cramming for a final exam, her mother brought her a bag of cookies and a piece of cake advising, "Just keep putting food in. You'll feel better." The Hermit may consume food unconsciously, particularly when alone, in a desperate attempt to fill herself up. Unfortunately, she is later filled with guilt and shame.

"She's afraid of the strangest things"

Point out the consequences of irrational fear

Hermit mothers have a variety of fears and may develop obsessive-compulsive rituals. Sandy's mother engaged in a number of rituals before leaving the house. She checked and rechecked the iron, the stove, the coffeemaker, and the locks on the doors. The Hermit may project her fear of losing control onto appliances, fearing that they may overheat and cause a fire.

Some Hermits fear being poisoned, robbed, attacked, or mugged. Afraid of answering the door, one mother refused to open it for a delivery man. Later, her adult daughter called her to see if the flowers she had sent for her mother's birthday had arrived. Many Hermits keep their blinds closed during the day, avoid going out at night, going out in public, or answering the door and the telephone. The Hermit misses out on the good things in life simply because of her fear.

Adult children of Hermit mothers should minimize, not ridicule, their mother's fear. Sandy's mother insisted that she call her after visiting, to ensure that Sandy had arrived home safely. Sandy refused to perpetuate her mother's fear by calling, and explained that if anything happened her mother would be notified anyway. No amount of reassurance will ease the Hermit's worry. When her mother fretted about leaving the house, Sandy reassured her, "Well, if the house burns down you can move to an apartment." "If I'm in an accident, the police will phone you." Pointing out the consequence of an actualized fear is the only necessary response.

"She drives me crazy"

Set limits to preserve your sanity

The anxiety of the Hermit mother is contagious. When riding in Sandy's car, her mother constantly shouted warnings such as, "Look out—that car is turning! Watch out! He's putting his brakes on!" Sandy would become so agitated and nervous that she could no longer concentrate on driving. She pulled the car over to the side of the road, saying, "Mother, you are *increasing* the chance of my having an accident by making me so nervous! If you say one more thing, I'm turning around and taking you back home."

Although the Hermit does not intend to undermine her children's self-confidence, the end result is that her adult children may not be able to tolerate closeness. When they feel they are losing their grip on reality, their ability to think clearly, or their ability to perform competently, they have every right to create distance.

The Hermit's adult children must trust their own intuition and their own feelings. They must separate their fears from their mother's and point out the consequences of irrational fear. Reacting to fear, instead of to the situation, can have deadly consequences.

THE DANGER OF FEAR

As children, we protect our mother because our survival is dependent upon hers. As adults, however, our survival depends upon our ability to protect *ourselves*. The Hermit's adult children must rely on their own judgment when determining the risks of a given situation. Rather than automatically reacting to their mother's fear, or completely discounting it, they must reevaluate the appropriateness of their mother's reaction. Some adult children react with hostility, resentment, or cynicism to the Hermit's obsessive worry. Negative reactions that demean the Hermit increase her hostility and feed her fear.

Reacting to fear complicates a problem. Reacting to the problem reduces fear. Numerous examples demonstrate how anxiety, fear, and panic can lead to death. Gavin De Becker (1997) recounts the story of a man who was attacked by a shark. Although the man was terrified as the shark dragged him under by his chest, he searched for a way to secure his release, and plunged his thumb into the shark's eye socket. The shark immediately released the man from its massive jaws. Perceiving the situation as a problem to be solved, rather than succumbing to fear, made the difference between life and death.

Adult children of Hermit mothers need to assess the source of their fear and anxiety. Answering three simple questions can help keep them calm:

1. Why am I anxious?
2. What is the problem?
3. How can I solve the problem?

Recognizing the source of anxiety and responding appropriately is essential to controlling it. A patient who worked as a nursing supervisor related the following incident. An elderly stroke patient who was unable to speak continually shrieked and moaned from her hospital bed until a nurse responded to her. The overworked and anxious nurse ran to the patient's room as frequently as possible, responding to every shriek. But as soon as the nurse left her room, the patient resumed her wailing. The second night, a different nurse was assigned to the woman's care. This nurse did not internalize the patient's anxiety and calmly responded to the shrieking patient by stating, "Mrs. X., I know you want my attention. But I have other patients who need me too. Wailing and crying will not bring me to you any sooner than I am able to come. Please stop wailing." When the nurse left the room, the patient stopped shrieking and patiently waited for the nurse's attention.

Responding to anxiety with anxiety feeds anxiety. Responding to anxiety with firm reassurance reduces anxiety. Adult children have a right to be angry, annoyed, and frustrated with the Hermit. They have a responsibility, however, to deal with their feelings as constructively as possible. Otherwise, their behavior replicates their mother's behavior and reinforces the negative cycle. Belittling, ridiculing, or teasing the Hermit is never constructive. Maintaining a sense of one's own basic goodness depends on the ability to confirm the self without disparaging others.

Step 1: Confirm separateness: "I am . . ."

"My mother lives vicariously through me. She actually depends on me to tell her what to do. I took care of her, protected her, and tried to make her happy. I just can't do it anymore."

When Sandy was a child, her mother told her, "You are my life, if anything happens to you I'll kill myself." The Hermit mother often relies on the all-good child to help her negotiate safely through life. Sandy's mother told her that she could not survive without her, a role-reversal that grew stronger as Sandy grew older. The Hermit may blame her unhappiness on the no-good child and attribute her happiness to the all-good child. Whether the projections are positive or negative, the Hermit's children struggle with separation.

Sandy's older brother was the designated no-good child. He minimized contact with his mother and kept conversations brief. No-good adult children must limit their interactions with their mother if she continues to undermine their self-esteem. Self-esteem can give way like an avalanche, burying the unsuspecting no-good adult child under cold, dark feelings of worthlessness. One negative comment from a borderline mother can trigger suicidal reactions in the already devastated no-good child. In cases of ongoing denigration, the no-good child may need to sever the relationship with the Hermit mother completely.

In order for the Hermit's children to individuate they must free themselves from their mother's perceptions and act in their own best interest. Kohut (1977) describes the "self" as "an independent center of initiative and perception" (p. 177). Expressing the self, therefore, requires the ability to act in one's own interest. Although Sandy understood her brother's need to distance himself, her separation anxiety emerged in the following dream. Sandy was crossing a rickety bridge with two young children, holding the hand of an older woman. A rotten plank broke under the weight of her foot, and she caught a glimpse of a cavernous pit below. As she neared the center of the bridge she recognized the danger of continuing further as well as the danger of turning back.

Sandy's dream symbolized the danger of holding onto her mother as well as the fear of letting go. Margaret Little (1993) commented that "the idea of losing one's identity, of being merged in some undefined homogeneous mass, or lost forever in a bottomless pit is very frightening and disturbing, an idea which we all tend to avoid" (p. 159). Sandy could no longer hold her mother's hand. Letting go, however, felt dangerous, as if Sandy or her mother might plunge into the abyss below.

Sandy had never taken a vacation without including her mother. When she decided to take her first vacation alone with her children she announced to her mother, "I need some time away, alone with the kids. I'm taking a trip." Making this step toward individuation was extremely difficult. Sandy's mother felt abandoned and begged her to phone her each night when she was away. Sandy said gently, "Mother, you worry too much about things that never happen. Your fear is contagious and it's hard for me to deal with. I don't want to call you every night." Her mother became defensive and hostile, retorting, "I'm not afraid of anything. You don't know anything about fear. Why don't you grow up!"

Sandy triggered a defensive reaction in her mother because she spoke the truth too directly. Her mother then projected her own failure to grow up onto Sandy, which insulted Sandy and left her feeling just as her mother felt—attacked. Winnicott (1963) explained, "Adults must be expected to be continuing the process of growing and growing up. . ." (p. 92). Growing up requires separating from mother, whether she likes it or not.

Although no approach is guaranteed to succeed, the most constructive method of separating from the Hermit is simply to make "I am" statements and to avoid "you" statements. Although empathy does not always work, the outcome for Sandy might have been more positive if Sandy had said, "Mother, I know this will be very hard on you. But I'm worn out and need to get away. I need some time alone. Please try to understand."

Although Sandy's mother expected her to phone daily, Sandy responded according to her own needs. She needed distance from her mother, and did not telephone her until she returned from vacation. When she returned home, she took more control of interactions with her mother.

Conversations with her mother felt tedious. Sandy mumbled an occasional "uh-huh," or "oh, really," without following her mother's rambling train of thought. She felt drained by the end of their conversations. Eventually, Sandy reduced the length of the phone conversations by interjecting simple "I am" statements. When her mother phoned she calmly but firmly stated, "I am in the middle of something. What did you want to tell me?" Sandy directed the conversation, kept her mother on track, and ended the conversation when her mother's train of thought derailed.

Sandy needed to repeat "I am" statements two or three times when speaking to her mother. Her mother had a habit of telling Sandy what she should wear, how to comb her hair, and even how to raise her children. Sandy responded calmly but insistently, "I am capable of deciding what is best for me." Although Sandy could not change her mother's point of view, she refused to allow her mother to change *her* point of view.

The Hermit's adult children do not have to relinquish their own beliefs in order to keep peace with their mother. *Confirming separateness requires holding on to differences in opinions and perceptions.* Sandy's mother denigrated successful, powerful people. She assumed that they were evil, self-centered, and greedy. When Sandy's mother made negative statements about such people, Sandy replied, "I am impressed with successful people. Some people might be corrupt, but many successful people are trustworthy and hardworking." Her mother grew silent and seemed to consider Sandy's perspective.

Several years after Sandy began therapy, she glanced at herself in the mirror as she dressed one morning. For the first time in her life, she felt beautiful. She saw a gentleness in her appearance that she had never noticed before, and a gleam in her eyes that reflected her heightened self-esteem. She had grown up seeing herself through her mother's eyes, afraid of success, of feeling good about herself, as if it were dangerous to enjoy herself and her life. She recalled her mother reproving her with, "Just who do you think you are?" whenever she had voiced pride in her accomplishments as a child. For the first time, she saw herself through her own eyes, and heard her own voice say, "I have something important to contribute. I am a good person, and I have right to feel good about myself."

The Hermit's adult children should not have to spend their lives ensconced within their mother's shell. They must allow their mother to make her own decisions about life without sacrificing the right to their own lives.

Step 2: Create structure: "I will . . ."

"When my husband and I bought our first home, my mother wanted to buy a home in the same neighborhood. My husband had a fit. He put his foot down and told me it was out of the question. It was easy for me to tell my mother that my husband wasn't comfortable with her living that close. But I didn't have the courage to say that I didn't want her living there either. I've always had the feeling that if I let her, she'd move in with us."

Sandy's courage to separate bloomed when she recognized that her mother's expectations were unreasonable and perhaps life-threatening. When she told her mother that she could not buy a house in the same neighborhood, her mother cried, "Nobody wants me around" and tried to hug Sandy. As if in the clutches of an octopus, Sandy felt both repulsion and pity and repressed the urge to peel her mother's arms off her and scream "yuck!"

The borderline mother's crying can become so wearisome that the Hermit's children lose the ability to empathize. Crying is the earliest and most primitive mechanism to assure attachment and evoke caretaking from others. Judith Nelson (1998) observes, "No matter what the precipitant, the purpose [of crying] is to bring the caretaker into physical proximity, first and foremost for protection, and secondarily for nurturing ministrations such as feeding or removing painful or noxious stimuli. Infant cries are a pre-verbal 'Come here, I need you' " (p. 11). The Hermit's adult children may ignore their mother's tears, feeling manipulated and resentful. The Hermit's pain, however, is quite real.

Eventually, Sandy learned to distinguish between what she needed for herself and what her mother needed. Sandy explained, "Mother, I'll always help you in an emergency. I won't abandon you but I'm not comfortable living so close. I need my own life." Sandy found it easier to comfort her mother when she focused first on her own needs.

Margaret Little (1993) explains that the child is trapped in the double-bind of love and hate and is in the impossible situation where he cannot *but* develop biologically, and yet must remain part of an entity that cannot be dissolved. Little wrote, "to stay dependent is to be destroyed" (p. 175). Sandy struggled with her fear that becoming her own person might destroy her mother. "To become a person means . . . literally to destroy the mother and to bear unlimited loss and guilt" (p. 175).

Because borderlines lack object constancy, they have no access to an internal, loving, approving, protective self that is constant regardless of external events. Therefore, they try to rely on their own children to hold them together. As adults, children of Hermits have a choice about how much they are willing to give, how much they can emotionally withstand, and how much of their own lives they are willing to sacrifice.

Step 3: Clarify Consequences: "I won't . . ."

"I guess I finally hit bottom five years ago . . . . The hole was too deep and I couldn't see my way out. That's when I decided to come to therapy.

Now my life finally feels like my own. I don't feel guilty about being happy, and I do what I can for my mother. I know I'm entitled to enjoying my life and when I think about my mother, I just feel sad. It's not my fault that she spent her life living in fear, and it's not my job to protect her."

Sandy gradually stopped parenting her mother. Surprisingly, her mother eventually formed a relationship with a widowed neighbor, and the two women looked after each other. Because the Hermit needs the approval of an idealized other, Sandy's mother was sufficiently motivated to meet Sandy's expectations. Sandy defined her limits, consistently enforced consequences, and encouraged her mother to become more independent. When her mother became critical, Sandy announced calmly, "I won't listen to negative comments. I don't think they're good for either one of us." Over time, Sandy established a more comfortable relationship with her mother.

Sandy wanted to hold onto the positive elements of the relationship with her mother without sacrificing her own life. She did not want her mother living too close. She did not want to have a conversation with her daily. She did not want to hear about her physical ailments, unless they were life threatening. She clarified these limits to her mother clearly, calmly, and firmly. She pointed out behaviors that irritated or annoyed her as soon as possible after they occurred.

Sandy used natural and logical consequences when dealing with her mother's inappropriate behavior. She shared brief stories about her life with her mother when time allowed. If her mother responded negatively, Sandy distanced herself and ended the conversation. She learned to conserve her emotional energy and paced herself like a marathon runner in order to prevent exhaustion. She gave what she could and kept her focus on her own self-preservation.

The Hermit mother leads a tragically lonely life. Adult children can neither please her nor protect her and should not try to control her. Adult children of borderline mothers should heed De Becker's (1997) advice:

> When a person requires something unattainable, such as total submission to an unreasonable demand, it is time to stop negotiating, because it's clear the person cannot be satisfied. Getting pulled into discussions about the original issue misses the point. It's as if one party has come to the table wanting a million dollars and the other party is prepared to give five dollars, or no dollars. In such situations there is nothing to negotiate. [p. 154]

Adult children cannot sacrifice their lives, their sanity, their health, or their well-being in the effort to protect the Hermit mother. They can give only as much as they feel is safe to give and must release themselves from guilt in order to enjoy life.

The average person cannot imagine the intensity of the anxiety experienced by children of borderlines who struggle with the process of separation. Adult children experience annihilation anxiety, the fear of ceasing to exist while still alive, when merged with their Hermit mothers. Because their mother fears living, the Hermit's children have no choice but to leave her alone.

11

Loving the Queen
Without Becoming Her Subject

The Queen's argument was that, if something wasn't done about it in less than no time, she'd have everybody executed, all round.

—*Alice's Adventures in Wonderland*

"When she doesn't get her way, heads roll. She is competitive, domineering, greedy, and jealous. She is rude to my husband and causes problems in my marriage. What am I supposed to do? I can't divorce my mother."

Like Robert Todd Lincoln, Ellen was torn between loyalty to her mother and loyalty to her spouse. Historians Neely and Mc-Murtry (1986) claim, "Mary Todd Lincoln all but destroyed Robert's marriage" (p. 36). In 1871, Robert and his wife separated for approximately a year and a half because of tensions between his wife and his mother.

Borderline Queens seem unaware of the loyalty conflicts they create between their adult children and their spouses. Kaplan (1978) explains that such children are used

ruthlessly as though they were mere extensions of the self; they use them to manipulate and destroy potential enemies; they use them in order to experience . . . pride . . . Such greed with regard to other people breeds the everlasting emptiness that is the silent dread of those without constancy. Inevitably they use up the all-perfect partner, who after all, is just an ordinary person who sometimes frustrates, who can't gratify magical wishes, a person whose comings and goings cannot be omnipotently controlled. [p. 43]

Ellen and her husband frequently argued about her mother's unreasonable demands. Her husband nicknamed her mother "Queen Anne" because no one dared to confront her. Although Ellen tried to comply with her mother's wishes, she resented the trouble she caused in her marriage. Separating from her husband seemed easier than separating from her mother.

The Queen's demands can exhaust her adult children, whom she may view as selfish and disloyal. Prior to the release of the Insanity File, Robert Todd Lincoln was described by various biographers as a bad son, perfidious, and disloyal. Like Ellen, Robert Todd Lincoln suffered from nervous exhaustion as a result of his mother's relentless interference in his adult life.

"It's never enough"

Let her rule her life, not yours

The Queen's adult children cannot fill their mother's insatiable need for attention or admiration. They cannot compensate for what she did not receive as a child. They cannot please her, control her, or change her. They can, however, change how they respond to her. When adult children place their mother's needs before their own needs, they not only sacrifice themselves but may be sacrificing their marriage.

Adult children must allow the Queen to rule *her* life, not theirs, and should never attempt to rule *her*. History demonstrates the disastrous consequences of attempting to rule the borderline Queen, lessons well worth remembering. After his mother was released from the asylum, Robert Todd Lincoln wrote, "As to interfering to control her in any way, I assure you and I hope you will so write to her, that under no possible circumstances would I do so . . . If I could have foreseen my own experience in the matter, no consideration would have induced me to go through it . . . the ordinary troubles and distresses of life are enough without such as that" (Neely and McMurtry 1986, p. 122). Robert learned, perhaps too late, to ignore his mother's irrational behavior, temper tantrums, retaliatory threats, and compulsive spending. The Queen's children must allow her the right to self-destruct while exerting their right to protect themselves.

The borderline Queen may be threatened by those with power, including her grown children who attempt to control her. Although not posing a threat to society, Mrs. Lincoln's compulsive spending was clearly irrational. The "border-line" nature of the Queen's irrational behavior poses the greatest threat to those closest to her. Had Robert been a young child when his mother informed her sister that she considered having him killed, the situation would clearly have required immediate intervention. But Mrs. Lincoln's threat to have her son murdered was triggered by Robert's attempt to control her. Robert's mistake was trying to control his mother instead of simply protecting himself.

The Queen's children need to tell their mother when her expectations are unreasonable or inappropriate. Ellen, too, learned not to control her mother. When her mother demanded more than she could give, Ellen said simply, "Mother, my husband comes first. I want you to be happy, but I can't give up my time with my husband for you." Although her mother responded with a sarcastic projection, "All you care about is yourself," Ellen knew in her heart that she truly did care about her mother's happiness. As if they were dealing with a child with unreasonable expectations, the Queen's adult children must explain the limits of what can be given.

Holding onto positive feelings about the self is essential in order to experience positive feelings toward others. When the Queen's adult children refuse to be provoked, they maintain their own self-esteem and dignity. Ellen shared Robert Todd Lincoln's feeling: "*I have not allowed her anger at me to have any other effect upon me than regret that she should so feel and express herself toward me*" (Neely and McMurtry 1986, p. 122, emphasis added).

"She won't take 'no' for an answer"

Say "no" with your actions, not just with words

The Queen learned that being demanding eventually evoked compliance from others. One Queen mother acknowledged her pride in her ability "to manipulate people." Emotional manipulation is the Queen's specialty and provides self-esteem and security. Saying "no" to the Queen, therefore, is essential for adult children who need to protect their own well-being, emotional energy, and possibly their financial resources.

Dreikurs (Dreikurs and Soltz 1964) advised parents of children who demand undue attention to learn to say "no." As he explained, "It may seem difficult at first glance to know how to distinguish between due and undue attention. The secret lies in the ability to recognize the demands of the situation as a whole. Participation and co-operation require that each individual within the family be situation-centered rather than self-centered" (p. 59).

Feeling obligated to satisfy an unreasonable demand from a parent is just as detrimental as feeling obligated to satisfy an unreasonable demand from a child. Although adult children may worry about being perceived as disloyal, they must worry first about their own needs. Dreikurs encouraged family members to be concerned with the demands of the situation and to be unconcerned with what other people think.

When the daughter of a borderline Queen announced she was getting married, her mother insisted on planning the wedding as if it were her own. The daughter wanted a simple, private ceremony as opposed to her mother's desire for a large, lavish wedding. Because her daughter insisted on a simple ceremony, the Queen mother refused to attend the wedding, complaining to extended family members that her daughter had "shut her out of her life."

In another case a Queen mother had a pattern of feigning illness to elicit guilt in her daughter in order to prevent abandonment. The mother suffered from diabetes and was hospitalized in a diabetic coma on the eve of her daughter's wedding. Although her daughter was filled with guilt and anxiety, she decided not to postpone the ceremony. She later learned that her mother had intentionally stopped taking her insulin the week before the wedding. In both cases the Queen's adult daughters were confronted by others who implied they had done something wrong with statements like, "How could you go through with your wedding without your own mother?" and "How can you go on your honeymoon when your mother is in the hospital?" The Queen's adult children must understand that those with healthy mothers cannot imagine the manipulativeness of the borderline Queen. Others therefore assume that the child, rather than the mother, is the selfish one.

Attempting to separate from the Queen mother can cause volcanic eruptions. Everyone reacts to seeing the smoke and red-hot lava once it is flowing, but few people understand the forces beneath the surface that created the disaster. The Queen mother and her children are like tectonic plates along a geological fault line. Once belonging to the same whole, they are separated by a fine line that is vulnerable to tremendous strain and pressure. What is witnessed on the surface as an earthquake or a volcanic eruption has been building for years. Although nothing can be done to prevent such disasters, adult children can learn to predict that their occurrence will coincide with attempts at separation. The ability to predict and prepare for disaster can mean the difference between life and death.

The Queen's adult children cannot hope to control their own lives if they cannot say no to their mother. They either must make decisions that protect their own interests, or accept responsibility for allowing themselves to be exploited. Although separation may cause splitting headaches for the adult child, to fail to separate is to be destroyed. The Queen may erupt with rage, but separation will not destroy her.

"Nothing is freely given"

Be wary of gifts with strings attached

Ellen's mother was a charming hostess whose guests raved over the elegant meals and lavish table settings. Her mother glowed with pride but grumbled as soon as the company left, complaining about how hard she had worked and how unappreciated she felt. Her mother gave resentfully to others, and her gifts often left Ellen feeling indebted.

The Queen's emptiness distorts her perceptions of interactions with others. Regardless of how much she is appreciated, loved, valued, or admired, she feels disappointed. Gifts from the Queen have strings attached because they are tied to her sense of self. She gives in order to receive what *she* needs or wants. She projects onto others her own desires and is surprised when gifts are not appreciated. The extravagant clothing Mrs. Lincoln purchased for her granddaughter appalled Robert's wife. An excerpt (in Neely and McMurtry 1986) from a letter Mary Todd Lincoln wrote to her daughter-in-law conveys Mrs. Lincoln's innocent blindness regarding the inappropriateness of her gifts:

My dear Mary:

> . . . Robert writes that you were quite frightened, about the baby clothes—Certainly they were made of the simplest materials & if they were a little trimmed there was certainly nothing out of the way . . . You have never mentioned to me if you had two parlors or how many windows you had. But I wish you the day, you receive this, to go & get silk biscatelle, *not worsted* curtains, to match the colour of your carpet, a piano cover—& lace curtains—cornices &&& charge to my account. Of course you will have to hurry about it—it would never do, for you to receive callers—New Year's day, with bare windows. [Appendix p. 174]

Mrs. Lincoln's letter illustrates the Queen's tendency to tell her grown children what to do, where to live, how to dress, and how to raise their children. The Queen can be extraordinarily intrusive, imposing her tastes, values, and preferences on her adult children and their spouses. An adult child reported that she came home from work one day to discover that her mother had let herself into her home and rearranged her furniture.

The strange combination of the Queen's extravagant gifts and her inability to give what is actually needed reflects her own longing to be indulged. Others see what the Queen cannot see: that her need for attention is so out of control and pathetic that it is frightening. Others are embarrassed *for* her. The Queen's behavior elicits embarrassment about her need for recognition, attention, and control, and her children may react by becoming intensely private individuals. Robert Todd Lincoln became what some biographers referred to as compulsively private (Neely and Mc-Murtry 1986).

When the Queen feels unappreciated, she may demand that gifts be returned, or she may cut off communication with those to whom they were given. Mary Todd Lincoln eventually demanded that her son and daughter-in-law return every gift she had given them. The deprived self within the Queen has nothing to give and eventually resents giving what she could not afford to give.

The Queen's adult children should accept only those gifts that do not leave them feeling indebted, uncomfortable, or guilty. When Ellen's mother offered to buy her a new car she was tempted to accept. Ellen's husband, however, was suspicious of her mother's motives, and discouraged her from accepting the offer. In order to avoid triggering a hostile response, Ellen said, "I appreciate your offer, Mother, but Tom and I aren't comfortable accepting such a generous gift. You may need that money for yourself someday." The Queen's adult children should avoid becoming enmeshed with their mother. They should encourage and *demonstrate financial as well as emotional independence.*

"I don't believe her"

Search for the kernel of truth

Queen mothers can manipulate their children by ploys for attention through reports of illness or accidents. Robert Todd Lincoln was so accustomed to his mother's reports of ill health that he discounted the seriousness of her condition just before her death. Ellen's mother sometimes lied in order to evoke attention. Although Ellen discounted most of what her mother said, she worried that she might not know when her mother was telling the truth. She was particularly suspicious of her mother's physical complaints, which ranged from migraines to what she described as strokes. She listened for inconsistencies, kept mental note of versions of the same story, and looked for evidence to corroborate her mother's stories. Unless they can verify the facts, children may not know how to respond appropriately. Adult children need to speak to the physician, ask for copies of medical reports and tests, and point out inconsistencies. No matter how offended their mother may be, adult children must have access to accurate information regarding matters of health and safety. Without verification through medical reports, the Queen's adult children are not likely to know the truth about their mother's health.

"I'm tired of being enlisted in her battles"

Choose your own battles

The Queen mother instigates chaos and conflict and then enlists her children to fight the ensuing battles. Divorces between Kings and Queens inevitably pull children in half, tearing their love and loyalty to their parents apart. Adult children must refuse to enlist in the Queen's army.

Claims of mistreatment, and threats of retaliation such as threatening lawsuits are common for borderline Queens. Ellen's mother organized factions and dominated groups either with her fury, or with deliberately embellished stories designed to win allegiance to her cause. She cannot rest until she wins. Although Ellen's parents had been divorced for many years, her mother remained bitter and jealous of Ellen's affection for her father. Ellen was furious when she learned that her mother had sometimes intentionally deprived her of seeing him. She felt set up and tricked, drafted into service in a war that was not her own. Ellen told her mother, "I have a right to love my father, regardless of how you feel about him." Adult children can and *must* discharge themselves from the Queen's battles, which may involve neighborhoods, schools, churches, and any group to which she belongs.

Dreikurs (Dreikurs and Soltz 1964) explained the motivation behind such attention-seeking behavior: "Her behavior is saying, 'Unless you pay attention to me, I am nothing. I have a place only when you are busy with me'" (p. 58). Even negative attention seems to fill the Queen's emptiness. Conflicts and controversy seem to follow her. Baker (1987) described Mary Todd Lincoln as "one of the most detested public women in American history" (p. xiii).

"I'm tired of being controlled"

Just say "no"

The Queen mother treats her children either like subjects or like objects to be used or admired. Loving the Queen mother requires that adult children embrace their power and use it only to protect themselves. The Queen's children can be exploited if they are not able to say no. Saying no to the Queen, however, is extremely difficult, even for those who are not her children.

It can take years for adult children to have the courage to tell a Queen mother the truth about how they feel. Like being run over by a semi-trailer truck, they feel flattened so quickly that it is difficult to think what to say. Margaret Little (1990) described how her analysis with Winnicott gave her the courage to confront her own domineering mother: "for the first time in my life, I *exploded* at my mother, at some piece of her jibing and 'clever' nonsense. I told her exactly what I felt: that she was being unkind and ridiculous, that she had had no business to marry or have children, and a great deal more in the same strain, quite regardless of any effect on her" (p. 55). Little added, "Although I did not see her again until she was dying, two years later, I have never regretted it" (p. 55). The Queen's behavior can be so outrageous that others think to themselves, "I don't believe you!!" At some point in their lives, her adult children must tell their mother the truth about how they feel.

When adult children finally find the courage to tell their mother the truth about their feelings, they no longer feel like children. Ellen's mother was a former dancer and coerced Ellen into taking ballet lessons when she was young. Ellen, however, had an athletic build and was more interested in sports than ballet. As a child, Ellen had no choice but to comply with her mother's demands and suffered through five years of dancing lessons. As an adult, Ellen struggled with telling her mother the truth about how she felt.

When her mother phoned to complain about how busy she was, Ellen replied, "I'm busy too, Mother. In fact, I could use *your* help." Although her mother was offended, Ellen felt confident in her right to fair treatment. She slowly dislodged the hook of guilt that her mother used to control her, and no longer swallowed the story that her mother's needs were more important than her own.

"It's always about her"

What about you?

The Queen regards inconvenience as an injustice and can seem oblivious to the needs of others. Her circumstance feels uniquely painful, singularly upsetting, and particularly unfair. Her adult children need to protect themselves from inappropriate pleas for sympathy or special treatment.

Ellen's mother unexpectedly offered to take care of her children over the summer. After weighing the advantages and disadvantages, Ellen questioned her mother's motives. It seemed odd for her mother to make such an offer. Her mother's words ran through her mind, "I'll just come to your house. That way, it'll be easier for you." Ellen did not believe her. She later discovered that a man her mother was dating had moved into Ellen's neighborhood. When she realized her mother's motive, she confronted her about her lack of candor, and suggested that she stay the following summer if she was still interested in babysitting.

Ellen handled the situation appropriately. She expressed her disappointment regarding her mother's lack of honesty and protected her own interests. Dreikurs (Dreikurs and Soltz 1964) explained:

> It is natural that we want to please our children [parents]. It gives intense satisfaction to satisfy their desires. However, if we reach the point where we try to please the child [parent] at the expense of order or give in to his demands unduly out of fear, then we need to be alert to the dangers in these actions . . . whenever the child's [parent's] desire or request is contrary to order or to the demands of the situation, then we must have the courage to stick to the "no" that expresses our own best judgment. [p. 180]

Adult children of borderline Queens struggle to manage their own feelings of entitlement. Quite naturally, they often wonder, "What about me?" Yet if they verbalize these feelings they are perceived as selfish. Baker's (1987) biography of Mary Todd Lincoln portrays Robert Lincoln in such a light. Baker accuses Robert of persecuting his mother and suggests that his view of her as mentally ill "was a peculiar and damaging defense, calculated more for the protection of his own respectability than his mother's well-being" (p. 278). The Queen's adult children cannot win. If they suggest their mother is mentally ill, they may be accused of attacking her, although treatment obviously cannot begin without acknowledging the need for it.

The borderline mother is not alone in her perception of individuation as aggression. Adult children, too, fear that separation will destroy their mother. The phrase "Excuse me for living" expresses the shame that the Queen's children may feel for having been born, for having needs, for having a self. How tragic that a child's efforts to assert the self, protect the self, or express the self are thwarted not only by the borderline mother, but also apparently by society at large. Robert Todd Lincoln has yet to be vindicated by historians who accuse him of betraying his mother.

MIRROR THE SELF INSTEAD OF THE QUEEN

The Queen conditions her children to respond to her needs. The behavior of young children universally reflects their feeling that they would do anything to win their mother's love. The Queen's young children willingly perform for her, defend her, admire her, and sacrifice what they need for themselves in order to win her love. Only adult children have the opportunity to separate their needs and desires from the Queen's. Submitting to the Queen's relentless demands requires relinquishing the self and jeopardizes the child's mental health. Masterson (1988) observes that

> In normal development, the mother introduces the child to increas-
> ingly difficult levels of frustration so the child will learn that she does
> not always get what she wants. At some point, the child's ego
> realizes, accepts, and internalizes this, understanding that it is a

normal, although disagreeable, fact of life. The child with an arrested ego, however, will have a poor ability to tolerate frustration . . . But when ego development is arrested, control will not be internalized and develop into a reliable ego strength. [p. 76]

Unfortunately, both the Queen mother and her children can suffer from arrested ego development. The Queen mother cannot supply her children with something she lacks in herself, and uses her children to mirror her self-worth. This aberration in parenting results in children with selves that either respond with angry defiance and feelings of worthlessness or with false compliance and feelings of emptiness.

Through therapy, the Queen's adult children can uncover the unexpressed real self hidden beneath the Queen's mirror. Without treatment adult children may continue to feel empty and inadequate, depressed and hopeless. Masterson (1988) asserts that "they will only feel good and actually 'loved' when they are passive, compliant, and submissive to the person to whom they cling for emotional supplies . . . their emotional lives are characterized by chronic anger, frustration, and feelings of being thwarted" (p. 80). Adult children must learn to mirror their true selves instead of the Queen's.

Ellen came to treatment submerged in feelings of emptiness, unable initially to see that fear kept her from separating from her mother. She misdirected her anger and frustration at her husband, who resented her mother's intrusiveness in the marriage. Ellen came very close to separating from her husband instead of her mother. Unconscious feelings govern relationships and are unlikely to change without therapy.

Adult children need help learning how to serve and mirror their own ego. Trying to satisfy the demands of the Queen prevents ego development and perpetuates feelings of emptiness. Winnicott (1962) observed, "We really do know today a great deal about the way adults grow out of children and children out of infants, and a first principle is that health is maturity . . . the drive to development comes from within the child" (p. 65).

The Queen's adult children need and want to mature, to rid themselves of frustration, subservience, resentment, and emptiness. The steps they must take include the following (Dreikurs and Soltz 1964):

1. Protect their own rights.
2. Minimize providing undue attention.
3. Say "no" with words *and* behavior.
4. Ask only for what is actually needed.

These behaviors can be difficult to follow. Change cannot happen by mere instruction. Instead, change occurs by resolving the underlying fear that individuation will destroy the self or the mother. Reading a self-help book can actually increase frustration if therapy does not accompany the knowledge gained. A self-help book can neither reveal what is hidden within the self, nor identify unconscious emotional needs. Therapy offers the crucial link between knowing what to do and being able to do it. The developmental steps listed below are unlikely to be accomplished without the help of a therapist.

Step 1: Confirm separateness: "I am . . ."

"My mother was disappointed when I was born because I had my father's features. It's been a battle ever since. I've spent so much of my life trying not to be like her that I have no idea of who I am . . ."

Ellen found herself hidden behind her mother's mirror. She learned to confirm her being by establishing boundaries between herself and her mother. The Queen's children are susceptible to developing BPD because they experience their own needs as shameful. Their self structure inevitably lacks cohesiveness, making them sensitive to rejection and failure. They tend to be self-critical and perfectionistic, and struggle to find their own identity. Confirming separateness from the Queen mother requires establishing boundaries between "me" and "not me."

Violations of boundaries should be pointed out as soon as they are noticed. It takes time to process feelings because emotional experiences are visceral. Ellen's stomach tightened into a ball the day she came home from work and discovered her mother planting flowers in her yard. She got out of the car and asked, "What are you doing??" Ellen recognized the slow burn of anger, a gut feeling of having been violated. The Queen's intrusiveness takes others by surprise and catches adult children off guard.

Borderline mothers need to be shown the border line between their children and themselves. Like drawing a line in the sand, "I am" statements confirm one's separateness. Ellen said, "You didn't ask me whether or not *I* wanted flowers planted in my yard! Maybe you're trying to be helpful, but *I am angry*." Pointing out "this is you, and this is me" establishes a protective boundary for both parties. Separating territory is essential in maintaining ownership of one's self.

The Queen assumes that her children share her interests, tastes, and values. Without boundaries, the Queen will rule. Adult children must identify their boundaries without attributing negative motivations to their mother's behavior. The Queen is most likely to respond to feedback when positive (or neutral) motivations are attributed to her behavior. Although Ellen's mother replied sarcastically, "You never appreciate anything I do!" Ellen stated simply, "That's not true." Regardless of the Queen's response, adult children must confirm their separateness.

Step 2: Create Structure: "I will . . ."

"There are so many ways that she can get to me. I never tell her what I'm thinking or feeling because I don't want her to see the real me. It's the only way I can have some control."

Gunderson (1984) warned that borderlines often manipulate others into compliance with their needs. Ellen felt caught in her mother's web of control. When she and her husband were first married, her mother offered to buy them a house. After Ellen discovered that her mother intended to move in with them, she declined the offer. The Queen can lure her children into traps that are built for two.

The Queen's intrusiveness must be confined, her greediness limited, and her anger endured. Adult children must be true to themselves. Ellen developed a mantra to help strengthen her conviction in her right to autonomy. When she felt herself slipping back into becoming her mother's subject she told herself, "I am the master of myself. *I will* do what is right and good for me. I won't allow others to control me." An unwavering commitment to the true self requires allegiance to the self, the only place where freedom reigns.

Step 3: Clarify Consequences: "I won't . . ."

"I won't lose my self ever again. I've worked too hard to get where I am and I finally feel entitled to my own life. My husband and children are entitled to my emotional energy—not my mother!"

For years Ellen submitted to her mother's demands for time and attention. She spent hours shopping with her mother, hours that she could have spent with her children, husband, or friends. She allowed her mother to borrow clothing, some of which was never returned. She took time off from work to take her mother to the doctor, instead of suggesting that she drive herself or ask a friend or neighbor. Ellen needed to acknowledge the validity of her feelings before change could occur. After discovering her own limitations, she clarified consequences for her mother.

Clarifying consequences for inappropriate behavior is the antidote for feelings of powerlessness and domination. Behavior becomes a choice instead of a reaction. Consequences give others a choice about how to behave: if they choose "A," then "B" will occur. Logical and natural consequences should be used to respond to inappropriate behavior and require awareness of personal limits. Thoughts such as "I'm losing my mind," or "I can't stand this," or "I've had it," or "I've hit my emotional wall" signify limits. Recognizing limits is crucial to survival and is not the same as giving up.

A fundamental difference exists between thinking "I can't go on," and "I can't go on *like this*." Ellen was sick and tired of being told that she was a terrible daughter. She said, "You're lucky to have me as a daughter. The next time you imply that I'm not a good daughter, I will hang up the phone." If Ellen had said, "I won't tolerate you treating me *that way*," her mother would not understand. The Queen does not know how her behavior affects others and does not know what is normal. Offending behavior, words, or tone of voice must be specified before they can be changed. The Queen is not aware that her expectations are unrealistic and will *never* know if no one tells her. Although Ellen learned to tell her mother how she felt, her mother responded by telling her that she expected too much. Regardless of how clearly and carefully a child expresses needs, the Queen may be unable to respond appropriately. The goal is not to change the Queen. The goal is to change how one responds to her.

The Queen mother may spend her life in front of her mirror. Her children, therefore, must find their own mirror. Ellen spent the first thirty years of her life in her mother's shadow. Margaret Little

(1993) once described the analyst as a living mirror. Through analytic treatment, the Queen's children can see themselves in the mirror of the analyst's eyes, where the true self is reflected and nurtured. Otherwise, as Masterson (1988) observes, "A life ruled by the false self's defense against inner emptiness ends up truly empty" (p. 72). Through therapy, one can discover the joy and freedom of being one's self.

12

Living with the Witch
Without Becoming Her Victim

"I have been wicked in my day, but I never thought a little girl like you would ever be able to melt me and end my wicked deeds."

L. Frank Baum
— *The Wizard of Oz*

"It's the desolate expanse of my homeland that leads the natives to drink. All along the highway hidden in the long grasses are filthy shells, the husks of our tools of self-destruction. A little farther from the highway, the shallow graves. But there is a sound that pulls us on. It is a dirge that accompanies our exodus, barely audible under the scream of the wind and the endless sound of cars. I know you sense it, even with a brain dulled from boredom, staticky Top 40 hits, and shiny, quickly prepared food. The sky is heavy, achingly beautiful; but I have no delusions of escape."

At age 13, Lynn expressed the feelings of the walking dead, the "goners" of the Communist gulags, victims of evil that requires relinquishment of "the personal core of one's being" (Des Pres 1976, p. 69). Lynn's homeland, however, was suburban America. Her dull, hollow eyes reflected her withered spirit.

The Witch's children may feel disconnected from life, internally dead, "trapped in a world of total domination, a world hostile to life and any sign of dignity or resistance" (Des Pres 1976, p. 13). The human spirit does not die as easily as the body. It shrivels slowly, like a plant deprived of water, and eventually succumbs from a "relentless assault on the survivor's sense of purity and worth" (p. 60). The body becomes a cumbersome shell, the mind a wasteland, the eyes a mirror reflecting the vanquished will. The human being becomes a human doing; the being no longer exists.

Therapists work desperately to rescue children held captive by Witch mothers. Although the Witch may appear for only a moment before the good mother returns, children glimpse their absolute helplessness and the futility of escape. The therapist becomes a lifeline for children to hold onto while the sand runs out of the hourglass. Time, eventually, will set them free. When they grow up, they can get away on their own.

Ernest Wolf (1988) explains that merger-hungry personalities must dominate others, "their need to control is often experienced . . . as a feeling of being oppressed" (p. 74). Merger-hungry personalities such as the borderline Witch desire complete control over their children. Dreikurs (Dreikurs and Soltz 1964) explained: "When parent and child become increasingly involved in a power struggle and each tries to subdue the other, a transaction of intense retaliation may develop. The child, in his discouragement, may proceed to seek revenge as his only means of feeling significant and important" (p. 62).

The no-good child is most susceptible to annihilation anxiety, functioning primarily as a receptacle for the Witch's self-hatred. Like an atrophied appendage of the Witch's body, the no-good child feels numb, useless, and despised. Some children fight for their lives and try to cut themselves free. They feel hated and learn to hate. Adult children of borderline Witches frequently dream of concentration camps, of escaping a holocaust, of human sacrifice and torture. They dream of killing their captors, their mother, or themselves. Lynn wrote, *"My mind is a dark, dirty cell in this prison. There's nowhere for me to go . . . just circles . . . there is no joy."*

No-good children dream of being sentenced to prison. They see themselves as sick, dangerous, bad, and guilty: *"I am sick, sick, sick in the head. The evidence lies in the dreams I've been having. I was in prison for mass murder, they kept me in a special part of the prison for those who were very angry and very dangerous . . ."*

Although the Witch seeks to destroy the spirit of the no-good child, she is unaware of her destructiveness. Like Nazi SS officers, she believes wholeheartedly that she is only doing her job. Lynn declared, "I don't have a mother. I have a parole officer." Having been raised by parents who demanded absolute loyalty and obedience, the Witch mother wields her power as blindly as she once relinquished her will to her own parents. Denial of her child's pain comes as easily to her as denial of her own pain. The Witch projects the war that rages within her onto the no-good child.

Witch mothers do not recognize their behavior as destructive; consequently, they are defensive when therapists confront or report their abusive behavior. Medean Mothers may believe the child is better off dead because the child is spared further suffering. The words of a concentration camp survivor (Klein 1957) reflect a child's blind faith in the parent: "Why did we not fight back? . . . I know why. Because we had faith in humanity. Because we did not really think that human beings were capable of committing such crimes" (p. 89). The Witch's children, too, fall victim to their own faith in humanity and therefore repress awareness of their mother's destructive power.

Children have faith in their parents and believe in their greater wisdom. No child wants to believe that her mother is capable of brutality. Alice Miller (1984) explains that both parent and child come to believe that such treatment is for the child's own good. In his book on moral life in concentration camps, Todorov (1996) observed, "In the totalitarian ethic, loyalty to the leader is a fundamental obligation" (p. 189). Young children need to believe that their mother knows what is right and good. Their trust and loyalty are truly blind, for they have no other experience by which to assess her judgment. They believe in her basic goodness, more so than they believe in their own goodness. It is safer to accept the view that *they* are evil than to consider the consequences if mother is evil.

Lynn was immersed in a hostile, dangerous environment, but her private world of psychological torture was the only world she had ever known. Guiltless but convicted, she was sentenced at birth. Unlike concentration camp survivors, the Witch's children never knew any other kind of life, and believe they deserved such treatment. They never knew love, freedom, or the joy of expressing their own thoughts prior to their imprisonment. Even as adults, they may have more faith in their mother's basic goodness than in their own.

Most adult children have no understanding of why they dream about concentration camps. The everyday experience of growing up in an emotionally hostile environment is normal to them and becomes repressed. As an adolescent, however, Lynn remained imprisoned and seriously considered suicide:

"If you only knew how much I hate you Mother. If anyone knew or understood how much I hate myself, and those who have made me that way. No. I am not human anymore and I don't care. I want to kill myself. There. I said it. I want to rip myself open and finally FINALLY be free. I've lost everything and I'm so, so sick of pretending."

Suicide represents the last act of free will, "to choose the moment and the means of one's death is to affirm one's freedom" (Todorov 1996, p. 63). Controlling feelings of rage, fear, and revenge can be a matter of life and death for the Witch's children.

The sheer number of books written about the effects of anger on one's health attests to the destructiveness of even low levels of chronic anger. Every child raised by a borderline Witch knows that anger kills, and feels the toll taken on the body when rage is repressed.

In their book, *Anger Kills*, Redford and Virginia Williams (1993) report that, "about 20 percent of the general population has levels of hostility high enough to be dangerous to health" (p. 3). But the level of rage experienced by children of Witches can be equally dangerous to society, resulting in homicide or suicide. Degradation by someone who claims to love you is qualitatively different than degradation by a stranger. Adult children of borderline Witches can learn a great deal about managing rage from studying how survivors of concentration camps managed their anger. The Witch's children cannot afford to live with hate.

Like members of totalitarian regimes, children of Witch mothers may exercise their will with angry defiance or continue to be controlled by fear. Provoking the ire of the Witch may be the only power the young child holds, and although he may be severely punished, the child feels more secure when in control of his environment. Adult children have other, healthier options because they have the power and freedom to get away. Yet, the Witch mother may remain steadfast in her desire for control, even when the child becomes an adult. Emotional set-ups, invisible traps, and vicious threats may intensify as the child matures.

Society cannot afford to ignore the level of rage experienced by children of borderline Witches. Demanding blind obedience or coercing others into compliance inevitably creates resentment or hatred. By the time the Witch's children are adults, they may suffer from uncontrollable rage or demonstrate passive compliance, cynicism, and unconscious hostility. Hatred must be dissipated before it destroys.

SURVIVING THE WITCH

"Remember that the Witch is Wicked—tremendously Wicked—and ought to be killed. Now go, and do not ask to see me again until you have done your task."

— *The Wizard of Oz*

Although the Witch is capable of evoking murderous rage, the key to survival lies in *disarming*, not attacking her. Physically attacking the Witch merely provokes her to further retaliation. Killing the witch did nothing to help Dorothy get back to Kansas. She won her freedom from the Land of Oz by using power she already possessed. Like Dorothy, the Witch's adult children must free themselves by using the power they already possess.

Survivors of prison camps document survival techniques that children of Witches develop unconsciously. Literature provides a cherished escape from a world filled with pain and suffering. Journal keeping and letter writing preserve verification of unspeakable experiences. Mind-numbing work keeps captives focused on the present and from despairing about the future. Hope is measured against time, and only a flicker is needed to keep the soul alive.

Prison camp survivors either flee for their lives or are eventually released from captivity. Children who run away from home enter the juvenile justice system and often face further punishment when they return home. The Witch's children unfortunately may face ongoing degradation, violent threats, humiliation, and depersonalization. The Witch's adult children are expected to be loyal, loving, forgiving, and obedient. They celebrate holidays, bring gifts, give hugs, prepare meals, and physically care for abusive mothers. They may tolerate mistreatment because it seems normal.

Like a snake, the Witch strikes when she is confronted or cornered. The Witch within the Queen may emerge when she feels controlled, or when others fail to admire her or treat her as special. The Witch within the Hermit may appear when she feels invaded, challenged, rejected, or cornered. The Witch within the Waif may appear when she feels blamed, criticized, rejected, or abandoned. Unfortunately, children have little control over when, where, or why the Witch appears. The key to survival lies in escaping her control.

Even in cases of self-defense, attacking one's mother *never* brings about a positive outcome. The child is at greater risk for continued abuse because aggression reinforces the Witch's perception of her child as a threat. When the Witch's children are young, they have no hope of escape unless they confide in someone they trust. Even then, however, they run the risk of not being rescued if they are not believed.

A social worker in a pediatric hospital was called to observe the mother of a newborn in intensive care. The baby experienced inexplicable episodes of apnea that occurred only during the mother's presence. After close observation, the social worker suspected that the mother was deliberately smothering the infant with her breasts while nursing. Although the case was reported to child abuse authorities, the child remained in the mother's custody. Five years later the mother was convicted of killing the child by injecting her antipsychotic medication into the child's intravenous line. This 5-year-old child had lived her entire life with a mother who was trying to kill her. Such children cannot be saved if others believe that Witches exist only in fairy tales.

Keep a safe distance

Surviving the Witch requires getting away. Only adult children have the power to decide how much contact they want with their mother. The all-good child may be more capable of tolerating closeness than the no-good child, who is the target of the Witch's hostility. The Witch's children must allow one another to make their own decisions regarding the amount of distance needed to feel safe. Some patients report being unable to tolerate having a conversation with their mother. They cannot tolerate the sound of her voice or the sight of her without feeling intense rage or disgust. The feelings that adult children have toward Witch mothers are intense and sometimes unmanageable. Personal limits must be respected, particularly in terms of safety.

Keeping a safe distance from one's mother may mean not being alone with her. The presence of another person can reduce the possibility of attack by the Witch *or* by the adult child. During his psychiatric treatment at Atascadero State Hospital, Edmund Kemper discovered "that I really killed my grandmother because I wanted to kill my mother" (Cheney 1976, p. 29). Kemper's psychiatrists emphatically recommended "*above all* that he [Edmund] never be returned to live with his mother" (p. 33). In spite of this recommendation, officials released Edmund to his mother's custody. Shortly thereafter, he murdered her while she slept. Failing to create distance can be disastrous. Some adult children are unable to tolerate closeness with their mothers because they fear hurting *her*.

Disengage from conflict

The Witch's hostility can trigger volatile arguments between her and her children. Adult children must disengage from conflict as soon as it erupts. Ending a discussion when her voice becomes haughty, her words become sharp, or her heart turns cold is essential. A verbal attack by the Witch evokes an instantaneous visceral response of feeling sick to the stomach, an indication of the power of her venom. Although she may state, "You make me sick," the Witch's words make others sick. Adult children have one option: not reacting to her attempts at provocation and leaving.

The Witch mother often uses threats to control adult children. De Becker (1997) warns that "How one responds to a threat determines whether it will be a valuable instrument or mere words. Thus, it is the listener and not the speaker who decides how powerful a threat will be" (p. 130). One patient reported that her mother threatened to hire a hit man to have her sister killed. Another patient recalled that her mother threatened to disown her. Although such threats may not be realized, adult children must trust their intuition. Adult children who believe they are in danger have every right and responsibility to protect themselves. Disengaging from conflict does not mean becoming submissive, complacent, or relinquishing one's will.

Never try to control her

Disaster is certain to follow any attempt to control the Witch. One patient recommended that her mother take medication to reduce her anxiety. The patient's mother felt controlled by the mere suggestion that she needed help and told the patient, "You're the one who needs medication!" If she chooses not to take medication properly, it is her decision. If she chooses to hide money in her mattress, it is her decision. Because the Witch is terrified of not being in control, adult children must respect her right to control her own life.

The Witch's adult children need to respond to her domination with firm resistance. Adults must not submit to the Witch's demands and should exert control only over their own behavior. Dreikurs (Dreikurs and Soltz 1964) recommended being firm without dominating. Domination is the imposition of one's will on another. Firmness expresses the conviction of one's own will. A

35-year-old patient was clearing the table after serving dinner for her parents when her mother commanded in a hostile tone of voice, "You put that dish down and listen to me!" Caught off guard, the patient realized that her mother expected her undivided attention. The patient replied firmly, "I don't want you to speak to me in that tone of voice. This is *my* house." Startled, her mother scuttled from the room like a frightened spider and retreated into a back room of the house. Firmness demonstrates strength of character, domination demonstrates underlying fear.

Cleanse the body and soul with love and goodness

The Witch's no-good children feel soiled, damaged, dirty, and defective. As adults, they carry remnants of feeling unclean and may have humiliating dreams of soiling themselves, of not being able to find bathroom facilities or privacy. Having contact with their mother increases the risk of possible humiliation. They fear having no place to retreat, no safe corner in which to hide from her denigration. Regardless of their age, they remain susceptible to the Witch's power to degrade and humiliate them.

Surviving degradation, as an adult in concentration camps or as a child in one's own home, requires maintaining a sense of dignity and purity. Des Pres (1976) explains that "washing, if only in a ritual sense—and quite apart from reasons of health—was something prisoners needed to do. They found it necessary to survival, odd as that may seem, and those who stopped soon died" (p. 63). Restoring a sense of purity and goodness is essential for anyone who has suffered from degradation.

The antidote for exposure to malignant denigration is to surround oneself with goodness, light, and love. Adult children must counteract the effects of the Witch's verbal venom by self-soothing, caressing the spirit, holding the self gently in the light, bathing the self in the friendship of those who love the real self, with the response of a loving dog or cat, by the warmth of one's own fireplace, a cup of tea, or a warm bath.

Do no harm

Power possessed by adult children threatens the Witch's control. An attractive young patient had plunged into despair following a conversation with her mother, who had called her a slut. During the session, a smile emerged through her tears as she discounted the ludicrous charge. Yet she could not shake off the feeling of being soiled. "I feel like I'm 4 years old again, when my mother said she'd be better off without me," she explained. This talented young woman, a caring mother with two young children, was an accountant. The more successful she became, however, the more her mother needed to degrade her. Rather than retaliate, the patient decided to take a short trip to visit a friend. She reminded herself how grateful she is to be grown up and to have the power to get away from denigration.

When it is clear that the Witch's hostility is escalating, it is time to disengage. If she is successful in provoking others to attack, she accomplishes her goal. If her hostility is ignored or tolerated, it will continue and possibly escalate. The Witch will throw every emotional stone she can find in the attempt to provoke others. One mother hissed, "You'll never hear the end of this," as her daughter calmly walked out the door. The Witch's words are alarming, designed to evoke fear, uncertainty, and apprehension. But she is powerless over adults who use their power to disappear.

The conviction to do no harm allows one to maintain a sense of basic goodness. Without this conviction, adult children can be provoked to respond to the Witch's hostile projections. Acts of vindictiveness, retaliation, and revenge fuel the Witch's control.

The single most powerful human is one who masters the talionic impulse: the need for revenge: "that deepest and most ancient of human impulses to exact revenge by taking pleasure in inflicting on others the hurt one has experienced" (Masterson 1981, p. 182). The Witch's children must demonstrate their greater power by mastering the need for revenge. Retaliation is unrestrained instinct and requires no strength of character. The Witch is trapped within her self-constructed cage of self-hatred. Inflicting pain on such a tortured soul is pointless. Her children must transcend their hatred by holding on to the belief in their own goodness. Children who seek revenge destroy their good selves.

Step 1: Confirm Separateness: Create Distance

"Oh gracious!" cried Dorothy. "Are you a real witch?"

"Yes, indeed . . . But I am a good witch, and the people love me."

— *The Wizard of Oz*

The Witch's adult children need to create distance in three separate realms of their being: spiritually, physically, and emotionally. Adult children can create spiritual distance by affirming their own goodness. Children of borderline Witches must think of their future, of the long-term consequences of acting on retaliatory impulses. They must, therefore, stand in the light of their own basic goodness, displaying strength and character by doing no harm.

Helene Deutsch (in Sayers 1991) struggled to manage her hatred toward her own mother: " 'She was a mean woman, and I did not want to be like her . . .' she felt her mother regarded her as 'poison' " (p. 25). In the effort to create spiritual distance from her mother, Helene named her country home in New Hampshire, "Babayaga," the Polish word for "Good Witch."

Creating physical distance sends the clear message "I am separate." Power lies in what the Witch's adult children do, not in what they say. "I am" statements are likely to be ridiculed by the Witch or used to provoke the child. Being different from the Witch, being separate, means not internalizing her rage, hatred, vindictiveness, and need for retaliation. Separateness requires the ability to walk away, or to ask the Witch to leave.

Picture the scene from *The Wizard of Oz* when the Good Witch of the North envelops Dorothy in her arms as the Wicked Witch of the West brandishes her broom, threatening to take the ruby slippers. The Good Witch laughs and says to the Wicked Witch, "Be gone . . . you have no power here!" The Good Witch has confidence in her goodness and power. She is not afraid, she believes in herself. Adult children have this power, but like Dorothy with the ruby slippers, they do not know how to use it.

The single greatest power adult children possess is their ability to get away. Talking about the source of the danger does not make it go away. Saying "I will not tolerate being treated this way," and failing to leave demonstrates ambivalence, which can be deadly. De Becker (1997) stresses: "'No' is a word that must never be negotiated, because the person who chooses not to hear it is trying to control you . . . Declining to hear 'no' is a signal that someone is either seeking control or refusing to relinquish it . . . If you let someone talk you out of the word 'no,' you might as well wear a sign that reads, 'You are in charge'" (p. 73). When one feels endangered, distancing is not negotiable.

Adult children can create emotional distance by not confiding in the Witch. No one should trust a Witch. The Witch uses the words of others in order to beguile and control. In 1890, psychologist William James wrote:

Neither threats nor pleadings can move a man unless they touch some one of his potential or actual selves. Only thus can we, as a

rule, get a "purchase" on another's will. The first care of diploma-
tists and monarchs and all who wish to rule or influence is,
accordingly, to find out their victim's strongest principle of self-
regard, so as to make that the fulcrum of all appeals. But if a man has
given up those things which are subject to foreign fate, and ceased
to regard them as parts of himself at all, we are well-nigh powerless
over him. [pp. 312–313]

Thus, the Witch's children instinctively know not to reveal their
true selves, their desires, feelings, or opinions to their mother.

Many adult female children create emotional distance by avoiding being like the Witch in any way. They despise those parts of
themselves that remind them of her. They may undergo cosmetic
surgery to change physical features that remind them of their
mother, and may avoid becoming a mother at all. The word
"mother" may mean "witch" to the Witch's children.

Step 2: Create Structure: Zero Tolerance

"You are a wicked creature!" cried Dorothy.
"You have no right to take my shoe from me."
"I shall keep it, just the same," said the Witch, laughing at
her, "and someday I shall get the other one from you, too."

— *The Wizard of Oz*

Structuring a relationship with the Witch requires one basic re-
quirement: *zero tolerance*. When the Witch appears, the adult child
must leave, hang up, terminate the interaction. No borderline
mother is always a Witch, and some borderline mothers are never
Witches. But when the Witch appears adult children must distance
themselves immediately and completely. They must have a plan so
that they are not caught off guard, trapped, or cornered with her.

Holidays can be especially difficult because family members often feel obligated to be together, to spend the day together, to share a meal or an afternoon. Regardless of the situation, adult children must leave when the Witch appears. This simple step is the single most effective way of disarming the Witch, but many adult children are afraid to take such a stand.

Adult children who cannot permit themselves to leave when they feel hurt or endangered must acknowledge that their behavior says "You can hurt me." The words "I will leave, I will protect myself, I will take care of myself" must be enacted, not spoken to the Witch. An individual can be made to feel subhuman merely by the tone of voice and the manner by which she is addressed. The right to protect one's spirit should be honored as highly as the right to protect one's body. Whether an attack is physical or verbal, adult children have the right to protect themselves.

Open-ended situations allow children of Witches to control interactions. When making plans with their mother adult children can protect themselves by saying, "I haven't decided how long I'm going to stay." They must have the ability to get away in case the Witch appears. They need to drive their own car and should never plan to ride with someone else. They must make it clear that they will come and go as they please. They should keep visits brief and avoid discussion of controversial topics. They should avoid being alone with their mother.

Structuring a relationship with the Witch requires being alert to signs of her emergence from the good mother. One Witch mother wistfully sighed, "I have so much fun talking to you, let's go shopping together next week." The adult daughter replied honestly, "We get along better when we keep our visits short. I'd rather not go shopping." Because the Witch often emerges following periods of closeness, her children are leery of offers of assistance and opportunities for closeness.

Emotional traps are not always obvious. Insinuation alone can trigger fear and guilt. De Becker (1997) explains that trusting intuition is the opposite of living in fear. One patient's mother casually mentioned to her daughter that she did not think she had long to live. Her mother said that she "felt it in her bones," and wondered if her daughter could spend more time with her. The daughter detected an edge to her mother's voice and felt like a fish on a lure. Uncomfortable, she realized that her mother was intentionally invoking guilt. The daughter replied that she had not been feeling well herself and needed to rest. The Witch's adult children need to trust their intuition, not their mother.

Step 3: Clarify Consequences: With Actions, not Words

> Then, being at last free to do as she chose, she ran out to the courtyard to tell the Lion that the Wicked Witch of the West had come to an end, and that they were no longer prisoners in a strange land.
>
> — *The Wizard of Oz*

Being an adult means being free to do as one chooses, accepting the consequences for one's behavior, and responding with consequences when one's personal limits are violated. Consequences teach others to respect personal limits. The first rule for interacting with the Witch concerns safety, hers as well as her child's. Adult children confirm separateness from the Witch by creating distance whenever they feel threatened, provoked, or unsafe. *The consequence for behavior that threatens the safety of others is to create distance.*

Secondly, the Witch can be disarmed by not responding to provocations, threats, emotional set-ups, or traps. The adult child can control what type of information is shared, how much time is spent together, and how much closeness will be tolerated. The relationship with the Witch should be structured on the need for safety, the need for privacy, the need for order, and the need for civility. The consequence of violations of personal limits should be consistent—leaving, escaping, and seeking freedom from the Witch.

An adult patient and his siblings dreaded celebrating holidays at their mother's home where they felt trapped, once again, with their Witch mother. When these middle-aged children suggested celebrating Thanksgiving at the patient's home, their mother snapped "You're full of shit!" and ended the conversation stating, "Fuck Thanksgiving and fuck you!" Although her children were well-respected professionals, they struggled with feelings of guilt and anxiety, expecting to be punished for expressing their feelings. Nevertheless, they celebrated Thanksgiving without their mother, recognizing that it was *her* choice not to attend.

In order for adult children to survive the Witch, they must fight hatred as well as fear. Etty Hillesum (in Todorov 1996) was 29 years old when she died in a concentration camp, but the journals she kept provide inspiration to those who suffer from oppression, maltreatment, or injustice. She spoke of the inner war against hatred, the only war that can be fought and won by oneself. The Witch's adult children must win this war in order to save themselves. Todorov writes of Hillesum's victory over hatred in *Facing the Extreme*:

> If we hate the enemy the way he hates us, all we are doing is adding to the world's evil. One of the worst consequences of the occupation and the war, Hillesum maintains, is that the victims of the Nazis begin to become like them. "If we allow our hatred to turn us into savage beasts like them," she writes, "then there is no hope for anyone." Someone who sees no resemblance between himself and his enemy, who believes that all the evil is in the other and none in himself, is tragically destined to resemble his enemy. But someone who, recognizing evil in himself, discovers that he is like his enemy is truly different. [p. 200]

How does someone stop hating? Primo Levi, after surviving the Nazi concentration camps, was unable to formulate and record his memoir until he met his wife. "The fact of being loved transformed him, freed him from the clutch of the past; recognized in the gaze and in the desire of another, Levi was confirmed in his humanity" (Todorov 1996, p. 261). The Witch's child can only stop hating through the experience of being loved. A therapeutic relationship, a surrogate parent, a relationship with an adult who believes in the child's goodness and worth, are the only experiences that can mitigate hatred. The tiniest stream of light, of love, can revive a weary spirit, because the Witch's children, like all captives, survive on hope.

There is no substitute for a loving relationship in the healing process. The adult child who turns inward, away from others and away from the world, will never heal from the wounds of the past. A loving relationship provides safety and freedom, and restores self-esteem. There is no short cut, no recipe, no twelve-step program that can heal self-hatred. There is only love. Not until one has entered the safety of a healthy, loving relationship is it possible to look back and acknowledge the pain of the past.

The personal limits of adult children may preclude them from taking care of their Witch mother. A 59-year-old patient shared her candid perspective:

"I've made it clear to my mother that she will never live with me. It would never work for me to try to take care of her. It wouldn't be safe for either one of us.

"No one understands . . . What everyone else sees is a sweet little old lady. I remember hearing a story about a female minister who was reported for abusing her mother. A neighbor saw the daughter slap her mother. My first thought was that the 'sweet' little old mother said vicious, degrading, terrible things to her daughter and her daughter finally snapped. A person can only take so much. It could have been me, but I won't let myself be in that position."

Adult children need to clarify consequences by doing rather than by saying, and by *not saying* what they are thinking or feeling. The Witch's children can assert personal power by listening to their own inner voices: "I won't tell her such and such . . ." or "I won't allow myself to get angry . . ." or "I won't allow her to live with me." The Witch's children learned what survivors of prison camps learned: that experiencing and revealing "emotion not only blurred judgment and undermined decisiveness, it jeopardized the life of everyone" (Des Pres 1976, p. 131).

Reflecting on their childhood, adult children of borderline Witches feel as though they passed through Dante's gates of hell, over which was written, "Abandon All Hope, Ye Who Enter Here." Cruelty endured from one's mother is unlike any other. The child may repress rage, direct it at the self, or direct it at those who represent the mother. Frequently, internalized rage takes a toll on the child's body, possibly contributing to autoimmune disorders and other physical ailments. In her book *Thou Shalt Not Be Aware*, Alice Miller (1986) observes:

> The truth about our childhood is stored up in our body, and although we can repress it, we can never alter it. Our intellect can be deceived, our feelings manipulated, our perceptions confused, and our body tricked with medication. But someday the body will present its bill, for it is as incorruptible as a child who, still whole in spirit, will accept no compromises or excuses, and it will not stop tormenting us until we stop evading the truth. [p. 316]

The body speaks for the soul if the soul does not find a voice.

Survivors cannot be silenced. A concentration camp survivor (Des Pres 1976) revealed in his journal, "I dare not hope that I shall live through this period, but I must work as though my *words* will come through" (p. 40). Auschwitz survivor Primo Levi (1989) recalled that

Those who experienced imprisonment . . . are divided into two distinct categories . . . those who remain silent and those who speak . . . those remain silent who feel more deeply that sense of malaise which I for simplicity's sake call "shame," . . . The others speak . . . because . . . they perceive . . . the center of their life, the event that for good or evil has marked their entire existence. [p. 149]

Pain that is expressed, heard, and believed is not experienced in vain. Pain that is heard can then be tolerated and healed.

The Witch's children grow up. They learn to speak; they remember the truth. Some may remain silent forever, protecting themselves from the unendurable horror of telling the truth that no one believes.[1] Those who speak find that very few people are prepared to hear what they have to say.

---

1. Primo Levi (1988) writes in *The Drowned and the Saved*: "Almost all the survivors, orally or in their written memoirs, remember a dream which frequently recurred during the nights of imprisonment, varied in its detail but uniform in its substance: they had returned home and with passion and relief were describing their past sufferings, addressing themselves to a loved one, and were not believed, indeed were not even listened to. In the most typical (and cruelest) form, the interlocutor turned and left in silence" (p. 12).

13

Living Backwards

"Living backwards!" Alice repeated in great astonishment. "I never heard of such a thing!"

—Lewis Carroll, *Through the Looking-Glass*

"The whole point of therapy is to talk about the things that you don't want to think about . . . the secret truth about your family, your feelings, and yourself. The most helpful, wonderful thing you said to me was that, whatever happened, whatever feelings I had to face, you wouldn't leave me alone with them . . . that we would work through it together. That is what I tell my children . . . and that's why I've been able to be a very different kind of mother than my mother."

Laura joked that she lived life backwards, creating the kind of childhood for her children that she needed for herself. She was unaware that in trying to please her mother, she had abandoned herself. Laura was determined not to repeat the dynamic with her own children. I recommended Alice Miller's (1984) book, *For Your Own Good*, because Laura needed validation and support for her feelings. She eagerly read the book and brought it to several sessions. Miller's words stirred up a great deal of anger and sadness for Laura, particularly the following passage:

> Loving parents . . . should want to find out what they are uncon-
> sciously doing to their children. If they simply avoid the subject and
> instead point to their parental love, then they are not really con-
> cerned about their children's well-being but rather are painstakingly
> trying to keep a clear conscience. This effort, which they have been
> making ever since they were little, prevents them from letting their
> love for their children unfold freely and from learning something
> from this love. [p. 271]

Miller encourages grown children to express their anger and pain to their parents, not in order to punish or change the parent, but because doing so is the only way of developing an authentic relationship. But children with borderline mothers must decide for themselves whether or not to risk such openness. The danger of being silenced, of being discounted, perpetually looms over the child. What matters most is that the cycle of BPD can be stopped through the way the borderline's children parent their own children. Adult children of borderlines must heed the advice of Margaret Little (1993):

> An important element in the integrity of the parents is their
> willingness to . . . take full responsibility for their child right from
> the time of conception (whether it was consciously intended or not)
> acknowledging that he did not ask to be conceived or born and
> therefore has a right to his existence and individuality without
> demands on him to pay emotionally or otherwise for his keep, or to
> be grateful. [pp. 171–172]

Like Alice in *Through the Looking-Glass*, the borderline's children sense the presence of another world where they can reverse the reality of their own childhood. Masterson (1988) observes that the borderline "remains perplexed and cannot see through the defensive structures of his life, his thinking, his ways of perceiving reality.

He senses, but cannot understand, the hollow core at the center of his life. He has lived too long on deception, fantasy, and the myths of the false self" (p. 81). Yet many borderlines enter therapy during middle age, when the hourglass is half-empty, time is slipping away, and the compromised life triggers existential depression. Children of borderlines are also likely to enter therapy at mid-life, anxious to free the real self.

Although therapy does not cure the borderline, gaining insight, understanding, and validation may prevent a borderline mother from passing the disorder to her children. Miller (1985) writes that "if a mother could feel how she is injuring her child, she would be able to discover how she was once injured herself and so could rid herself of her compulsion to repeat the past" (p. 32). Many borderline mothers seek treatment because they *know* their behavior is destructive to their children. Those who do not know, and those who do not *want* to know, are most at risk for passing the disorder to the next generation. But as Miller observes, "it is quite simply not true that human beings must continue compulsively to injure their children, to damage them for life and thus destroy our future" (p. 5).

FALSE BELIEFS

James Thurber's (1931) comical tale, "The Unicorn in the Garden," depicts the battle for sanity experienced all too frequently by children of borderlines. In Thurber's story, a man discovers a unicorn eating roses in his garden and rushes to the bedroom to wake his wife. "There's a unicorn in the garden eating roses!" he declares. His wife glares at him contemptuously and remarks that everyone knows that unicorns do not exist. The man rushes back out to the garden and feeds the unicorn a lily. Again, he tries to rouse his wife and tell her of the miraculous event. Growing annoyed, his wife calls him a "booby" and announces that she is going to put him in the "booby-hatch." After her discouraged and insulted husband leaves the house, the wife phones the police and a psychiatrist, demanding that they hurry to the house with a straitjacket. When the psychiatrist and police arrive, she tells them her husband's story about the unicorn. When her husband returns, the psychiatrist asks, "Did you tell your wife that you saw a unicorn in the garden?" "Of course not," the man answers, "everyone knows that there is no such thing as a unicorn." The psychiatrist informs the man that his wife is crazy and instructs the police to take her away to the "booby-hatch."

The borderline's grown children often feel like the characters in Thurber's tale. Sometimes they feel like the husband, hoping to share their excitement and wonder, but are discounted, discredited, and disbelieved. At other times they feel like the wife, fed up with wild stories, fabrication, and deceit. Regardless of which way they turn in the emotional labyrinth, they end up feeling crazy. Their lives are filled with false beliefs, mythology, fantasy, fabrication, distortion, and deceit.

"But you know she loves you"

When the good mother within the borderline holds and comforts her young child, the child's well-being is temporarily restored. Darkness within the mother, the self, and the universe becomes light. The chaos is organized. The void is no longer without form as day is separated from night, and the wind and the waters become calm. Why the storm has passed makes no difference to the young child, who is simply grateful to return to paradise in the good mother's arms. From there the small child sees, for the moment, that the world is good. Unfortunately, the good mother is a fleeting ego-state, and the storm inevitably returns. By the time her children grow up, they may fear the good mother because chaos always returns.

Concentration camp survivor Primo Levi (1989) wrote, "Compassion and brutality can coexist in the same individual and in the same moment, despite all logic" (p. 56). At a very early age, children of borderlines know that there is something wrong with their mother. Music theorists (Kramer 1998) use the term *counter-discourse* to describe the profoundly disturbing experience of receiving a message in which one parameter of a communication is at variance with another; for example, hearing a piece of music that was written to be played with soft elegance played harshly and loudly. Equivalent human experiences include a crushing embrace, an eerie smile, or an icy compliment. The visceral reaction is unbearable as the brain struggles to process two conflicting experiences.

When a preschool teacher observed a 3-year-old boy chewing gum in class, the teacher walked calmly over to the child and said sweetly, "Tommy, do you have chewing gum in your mouth?" Unabashed, the little boy looked up at her and answered honestly, "Yes, Mrs. Baker. My mommy gave it to me." Still smiling and talking softly to the child, the teacher said, "Tommy, I want you to take the gum out of your mouth and place it on the end of your nose. You get to wear the gum on your nose today!" Contentment fell from the child's face as he studied his teacher, trying to process the counterdiscoursive message. His faith deeply shaken, he dutifully obeyed his teacher's instruction while laughter broke out in the classroom. Young children have no choice but to tolerate mistreatment by adults. Someone else must notice. Someone else must help.

As a child, Laura hoped that her aunt might notice her mother's bizarre behavior. Her aunt, however, frequently told Laura how lucky she was to have a mother who loved her. She told Laura that she needed to "build her mother's self-esteem," reinforcing the pathological role-reversal. Adults who still idealize their own abusive parents are unable to acknowledge the absurdity of being asked to trust someone you fear. No one expects prisoners of concentration camps to trust their captors.

Children of borderlines are often told, "Your mother loves you," "That's just the way she is," "She didn't mean it," or "She can't help it," as if children should ignore their own intuition that tells them they have been hurt. These messages not only encourage repression of legitimate anger and pain, but also lead children to believe that their mother's behavior is acceptable. *Tolerating inappropriate or abusive behavior requires the betrayal of the self. Young children have no choice, but grown children do have a choice.* When grown children tolerate abuse, they reenact the sacrifice of the self. Hopefully, they would never expect their own children to tolerate cruelty, deception, or mistreatment. *Something is wrong if we fear the person who loves us. Anyone who encourages us to trust a person we fear does not have our best interests at heart.*

"Can she help it or not?"

Because children of borderlines feel both pity and fear for their mother, they do not know if they are entitled to express their feelings about her behavior. They may ask the therapist, "Can she help it or not?" The answer is both yes and no. Yes, she can learn to control her behavior when she realizes that negative consequences will follow. On the other hand, she is not able to change the way she feels. Although underlying feelings of desperation, fear, anger, emptiness, and rage do not change, her behavior can. The irony is that her fear of abandonment gives her adult children the power to structure the relationship. An aging mother needs her adult children more than they need her. *The borderline mother's fear of abandonment gives adult children the power to preserve the relationship by structuring it around their own needs.* They must live life backwards.

LIVING BACKWARDS

"Oh, Kitty, how nice it would be if we could only get through into Looking-glass House! I'm sure it's got, oh! such beautiful things in it! Let's pretend there's a way of getting through into it, somehow, Kitty."

— *Through the Looking-Glass*

Children of borderlines cannot understand themselves without first understanding their mothers. Although infant and mother mirror one another, the interaction is a matter of survival for the infant. Gopnik and colleagues (1999) explain that "understanding the people around you is . . . part of becoming a particular sort of person yourself. As children learn what other minds are like, they also learn what their own minds are like" (p. 24). Children of borderlines are not sure what their own minds are like and are frightened by what they see in their mother. Gopnik and colleagues also observe, "The wide eyes that sometimes seem to peer into your very soul actually do just that, deciphering your deepest feelings" (p. 1). Children of borderlines try to avoid seeing their mother's darkness. Although they sense their mother's helplessness, emptiness, fear, and anger, they develop defenses that prevent them from drowning in anxiety.

Attachment researchers (Shore 1997) report that when a "child has an anxious/avoidant attachment, she tends to behave as if the caregiver were not in the room" (p. 35). These studies indicate that children whose mothers are sometimes withholding but other times nurturing are most likely to become extremely dependent and anxious adults. By the time children of borderlines become adults, they behave as if their mother is "not in the room." They may ignore her, even when they are with her, in order to reduce anxiety; or they may spend their entire lives consumed by her neediness. With the help of a therapist, however, adult children can create a more comfortable relationship so that they no longer need to pretend that their mother is not in the room. Therapy helps adult children hold onto their true selves, even in their mother's presence.

Recreating the Self

Although everyone possesses some false self-beliefs, borderline mothers hold unique combinations of false beliefs derived from their childhood experience. Unfortunately, their view of the world, themselves, and their children is hard-wired into the brain and is difficult to change. An adult's false beliefs about the self are difficult to change partly because an adult's brain is less responsive to learning than a child's brain. Treating a borderline mother, therefore, is more difficult and time-consuming than treating her child. Developmental researchers (Gopnik et al. 1999) explain that young children create

> internalized working models that are systematic pictures of how people relate to one another—theories of love . . . Like scientific theories they can be changed with enough new evidence. As children get new information about how people work, especially how people work together in intimate ways, they modify their own views. Even abused children often seem to escape long-lasting damage if there is somebody around who doesn't turn away. [p. 49]

Although neuroscientists (Shore 1997) report that the lack of consistently warm, responsive care during childhood alters the brain's biochemistry, they have also discovered that the brain's plasticity allows new neural pathways to continue to develop in response to new situations and experiences.

Masterson (1988) refers to the therapist as the "guardian of the real self." Long-term difficulties with intimate relationships result because of the split in the perception of the mother as well as the self. The good-me is compliant, obedient, immature, and passive. The bad-me wants to grow, to separate, to explore the world, to be autonomous and adventuresome: "The 'good' mother approves of the 'good' child while the 'bad' mother disapproves of the 'bad' child. The 'good' mother supports and encourages the regressive behavior while the 'bad' mother grows hostile, critical, and angry when confronted with the child's assertive behavior" (p. 79). The child's belief that the "good-me" must not be assertive results in an unfulfilled life.

Changing false self-beliefs requires rerouting neural pathways. Although borderline mothers and their children can benefit from the use of antidepressants and antianxiety medication, long-term therapy is needed to rewire neural pathways in order to perceive the self and the world more positively. The safety of a therapeutic relationship allows the real self to surface without the fear of being judged, criticized, or misunderstood.

Laura no longer needed to repress her pain or her rage and therefore did not project it onto her own children. She learned the difference between fear and love, and was determined to raise her children with empathy and compassion for their true selves. She mourned with genuine sadness the losses she experienced in her own childhood, and felt a strong sense of entitlement to enjoying her children's childhood.

Children of borderlines may spend their entire lives trying to understand their mother and themselves. They are preoccupied with sorting out the meanings of interactions, studying their own perceptions, and questioning the intentions of others. Helene Deutsch, the first leading female member of Freud's Vienna Society of Psychoanalysts, was drawn to studying "the theme of phoney [sic] identity" and inauthenticity because of her resentment toward her own mother (in Sayers 1991, p. 35).

Children of borderlines must work through intense feelings of rage not only toward their mothers, but also toward their fathers. Masterson comments on the significance of the absent father in the stories of *Snow White* and *Cinderella*. The absence of a father in these stories replicates the real-life drama of children with borderline mothers. The father's failure to intervene in the pathological dynamics between mother and child can leave the child with fantasies of being rescued from the ongoing battle for emotional survival.

The father, however, is often torn between loyalty to his wife and loyalty to his children. The borderline wife's retaliatory rage and sensitivity to abandonment can leave both father and child fearful and torn between the objects of their love. The borderline's children often repress their anger at their fathers, and are not able to express these terrifying feelings until deep into therapy. Idealization of the father prevents depression and rage from surfacing and protects the child from feeling orphaned.

Without treatment, children of borderlines may never accomplish the crucial task upon which their survival depends: understanding their mother. Maternal depression is known to interfere with the part of the brain associated with the expression and regulation of emotions, and chronic stress can result in chronic illness (Shore 1997). Therapists note that no-good adult children of borderline mothers often suffer from autoimmune disorders such as lupus, scleroderma, chronic fatigue, or fibromyalgia. Unconscious muscle rigidity from living in a chronic state of fear may eventually take a physical toll. The nature of the attachment with one's mother has a decisive and pervasive impact on the self, both physically and emotionally.

Adult children of borderline mothers must return to the past for the sake of their future. The last half of their lives can become the best half if they disinter the real self and rediscover their lost exuberance, their own free will, and their uninhibited creative self. Many adult children who enter therapy report disturbing dreams of returning to high school, feeling ashamed to be middle-aged and having to catch up on something they missed learning. In these dreams, they report feeling angry, resentful, and embarrassed that no one had given them proper instructions or clearly explained the assignment. They unconsciously know that they missed a developmental step during adolescence, that they were not adequately prepared for separation and individuation. Their anxiety focuses on not knowing what to do, feeling lost, and left behind.

Therapy is the only course to take. No greater gift exists than a life of unrestrained love and joy. The relationship between therapist and patient provides the diploma needed to graduate to a brighter world.

FINDING THE LIGHT

Each new day brings us closer to untangling the complex web of BPD. As threads of various disciplines are woven together, researchers may soon discover more effective treatment for the cognitive and emotional dysfunction that characterizes BPD. Freud (1929) wrote, "The assumption that everything past is preserved holds good even in mental life only on condition that the organ of the mind has remained intact and that its tissues have not been damaged by trauma or inflammation" (p. 18). Neuroscientists now know that "people who suffer childhood trauma may suffer from persistent hyperactivity" in certain regions of the brain; and, that the brains of individuals who suffer from PTSD differ from those with depression (Heit et al. 1999, p. 5).

There is every reason to hope that BPD can be prevented, if not someday cured. Although childhood trauma and loss cannot be prevented, allowing children to express their grief fully and openly may prevent BPD. Children who are allowed to express overwhelming emotion will not drown in grief. Lewis Carroll conveyed the child's feelings in *Alice's Adventures in Wonderland*: " 'I wish I hadn't cried so much!' said Alice, as she swam about, trying to find her way out. 'I shall be punished for it now, I suppose, by being drowned in my own tears!' " (pp. 23–24). Children need to be held, to be mirrored, to be soothed, and to be given some control throughout their childhood, but especially following separation and loss. Unbearable pain that is expressed, heard, and believed becomes bearable.

The ideal mother lovingly accepts the child's true feelings, rage and all, because she faced her true feelings about her own upbringing. Although such a mother is rare, children of all ages know one when they see one. Every Sunday I watch groups of small children flock around an 81-year-old woman in our church. Harriet's radiant smile reflects the love she feels for all children, and her belief in their basic goodness. I once asked her to tell me about her own mother. Tears filled her eyes as she told me that her widowed mother raised five children during the Great Depression. The center of Harriet's universe was an unfailing source of warmth and light. After our brief conversation Harriet sent me a copy of a cherished poem written by her mother, appropriately entitled "Motherhood."

O! Youth! I would be mother to you all!
I know so well your deepest, direst needs,
Who have been mother to daughters and sons,
And learned to comprehend their thoughts and deeds.

I am so thankful that no bounds are set
On this estate so very near divine
But reaches world around and comes to fruit
Wherever needs of yours reach needs of mine.

In this there are no ties of blood or state
The blessed gift of motherhood can't bind.
O! Youth! I would be mother to you all
And make those needs of yours
meet needs of mine.

—Mrs. Katie Martin[1]

The blessed gift of motherhood knows no bounds. No ties of blood or state exist where the emotional needs of children are concerned. Healthy love is contagious. It is passed from one generation to the next, just as BPD is passed to future generations. One of Harriet's most precious memories is the day she was baptized by immersion in the stream on her family farm. She wrote:

After my immersion, on the most beautiful warm June day, and as the minister led me to the edge of the stream—there was my wonderful mother, holding a soft cotton blanket and she so lovingly enfolded me in her arms and held me so tightly that I felt great love, approval and safety in her arms. I do believe *that* part of the memory is even more significant and meaningful than the actual baptism.

Harriet had no fear of drowning as she was led to the edge and engulfed by water because she knew that her mother was watching. She trusted her mother completely, the opposite experience of children with borderline mothers.

Make-believe mothers are not hard to find in reality, although

---

1. Used with permission.

others may pretend not to see them. Although most people know someone who exhibits symptoms of BPD, few people have the courage to intervene. A patient who was raised by a borderline mother witnessed a mother belittling her child in a grocery store. The patient was filled with rage toward the mother and sadness for the child. After carefully weighing the consequences of intervening, she followed the mother to the checkout counter and said, "You are so lucky to have such a wonderful child. I can see how much he loves you, and how important your love is to him. I'm sure it isn't easy being a parent." Then she turned to the child and said, "You're a good little boy." The mother was momentarily speechless. Finally she muttered, "Thank you," and as she walked out of the store, the patient noticed that her tone of voice was softer and she saw a smile spread across the child's face. The patient had the courage to be honest, yet gentle, with a mother and child who needed help. She replaced the mother's negative projections with a positive perspective of her child, and gave the child a positive view of himself, at least momentarily. Such experiences provide light in the midst of darkness for both mother and child.

If we could remember our own childhood wish that some adult, somewhere, might notice our pain perhaps we could follow in this patient's footsteps. We must move beyond asking, "Why didn't somebody do something?" We must ask why *we* do nothing when children are abused in front of our own eyes in the grocery store, at the airport, or in the shopping mall.

For five years, an elementary school art teacher observed an obese fifth grader bullying and being bullied by his peers. Every day she had witnessed violent language exchanged by the student and his peers. "I'm going to get my gun and shoot you," the student threatened. "We'll shoot you back," his classmates taunted. Two weeks before the end of the school year, just before the student's graduation to middle school, the teacher sacrificed her lunch hour to speak to him. She called the young boy to her room and said,

"Damon, I don't give up my lunch hour for just anyone. But I want you to know that you have one person who believes in you. You are smart. You have a lot of potential. But if you don't learn to ignore people who pick on you, you'll be dead before you get to high school. I don't want to read your name in the obituaries."

Six years later the teacher received a phone call from the local school board, inviting her to attend a ceremony honoring Damon as the most at-risk student to graduate in the top 10 percent of his high school class. At the ceremony, Damon announced to the audience that the one person who had made a difference in his life and changed the way he saw himself was his elementary school art teacher. He described this pivotal moment, "Our lunch hour talk near the end of fifth grade was the first time in my life that anyone said they believed in me."

"I believe in you" are words that make-believe mothers and their children need to hear. Believing in the self is the key to healthy self-esteem and mental health. Borderline mothers cannot give their children this gift because they never received it themselves. Without intervention, their emptiness, hopelessness, rage, and fear will be passed to the next generation.

The British philosopher, Edmund Burke (letter to William Smith, 1795), claimed that "the only thing necessary for the triumph of evil is for good men to do nothing." Borderline mothers are not evil; evil lies in the darkness of unawareness. They cannot see what they are doing. Those of us who *can* see must shine the light of our understanding like a beacon guiding a ship to harbor, or share in the responsibility of allowing mothers to drown their own children in a sea of despair.

References

Adler, G. (1985). *Borderline Psychopathology and Its Treatment.* Northvale, NJ: Jason Aronson.

American Psychiatric Association. (1994). *Diagnostic and Statistical Manual of Mental Disorders, 4th ed.* Washington, DC: APA.

American Red Cross. (1908). *Life Saving and Water Safety*, 24th printing. New York: Doubleday.

Baker, J. (1987). *Mary Todd Lincoln: A Biography.* New York: Norton.

Balint, M. (1968). *The Basic Fault.* New York: Brunner/Mazel.

Baum, L. F. (1900). *The Wizard of Oz.* New York: Grosset and Dunlap, 1996.

Blum, H. (1986). Object inconstancy and paranoid conspiracy. In *Self and Object Constancy: Clinical and Theoretical Perspectives,* pp. 253–270. New York: Guilford.

Bowlby, J. (1973). *Separation: Anxiety and Anger.* London: Tavistock Institute, New York: Basic Books.

Brazelton, T. B., and Cramer, B. G. (1990). *The Earliest Relationship: Parents, Infants, and the Drama of Early Attachment.* New York: Addison-Wesley.

Call, M. (1985). *Hand of Death: The Henry Lee Lucas Story.* Lafayette, LA: Prescott.

Carroll, L. (1865). *Alice's Adventures in Wonderland and Through the Looking-Glass.* New York: Bantam Doubleday, 1992.

Cauwels, J. M. (1992). *Imbroglio: Rising to the Challenges of Borderline Personality Disorder.* New York: Norton.

Cheney, M. (1976). *The Co-ed Killer: A Study of the Murders, Mutilations, and Matricide of Edmund Kemper III*. New York: Walker.

Christianson, S. (1992). *The Handbook of Emotion and Memory: Research and Theory*. Hillsdale, NJ: Lawrence Erlbaum.

Crawford, C. (1978). *Mommie Dearest*. New York: William Morrow.

———— (1988). *Survivor*. New York: Donald Fine.

———— (1997). *Mommie Dearest: Twentieth Anniversary Edition*. Moscow, ID: Seven Springs Press.

Dean, M. (1995). *Borderline Personality Disorder: The Latest Assessment and Treatment Strategies*. Salt Lake City, UT: Compact Clinicals.

De Becker, G. (1997). *The Gift of Fear and Other Survival Signals that Protect Us from Violence*. New York: Dell.

Des Pres, T. (1976). *The Survivor: An Anatomy of Life in the Death Camps*. New York: Oxford University Press.

Deutsch, H. (1942). Some forms of emotional disturbance and their relationship to schizophrenia. *Psychoanalytic Quarterly* 11:301–321.

Dreikurs, R., and Soltz, V. (1964). *Children: The Challenge*. New York: Penguin.

Ellis, G., ed. (1999). *Blessings of a Mother's Love*. Grand Rapids, MI: Zondervan.

Erikson, E. (1950). *Childhood and Society*. New York: Norton, 1988.

Ferenczi, S. (1933). Confusion of tongues between adults and the child. In *Final Contributions to the Problems and Methods of Psychoanalysis*, ed. M. Balint, pp. 156–167. New York: Brunner/Mazel, 1980.

Freud, S. (1929). *Civilization and Its Discontents*. New York: Norton, 1961.

Geleerd, E. R. (1958). Borderline states in childhood and adolescence. *Psychoanalytic Study of the Child* 13:279–295. New York: International Universities Press.

Geller, J., and Harris, M. (1994). *Women of the Asylum.* New York: Anchor.

Giovacchini, P. (1993). *Borderline Patients, the Psychosomatic Focus, and the Therapeutic Process.* Northvale, NJ: Jason Aronson.

Glickauf-Hughes, C., and Mehlman, E. (1998). Non-borderline patients with mothers who manifest borderline pathology. *British Journal of Psychotherapy* 14(3): 294–302.

Goleman, D. (1995). *Emotional Intelligence: Why It Can Matter More Than I.Q.* New York: Bantam.

Gopnik, A., Meltzoff, A., and Kuhl, P. K. (1999). *The Scientist in the Crib: Minds, Brains, and How Children Learn.* New York: Morrow.

Grotstein, J., Solomon, M., and Lang, J., eds. (1987). *The Borderline Patient: Emerging Concepts in Diagnosis, Psychodynamics and Treatment, vol 2.* Hillsdale, NJ: Analytic Press.

Guiles, F. (1995). *Joan Crawford: The Last Word.* New York: Carol.

Gunderson, J. (1984). *Borderline Personality Disorder.* Washington DC: American Psychiatric Press.

Heit, S., Graham, Y., and Nemeroff, C. (1999). Neurobiological effects of early trauma. *The Harvard Mental Health Letter* 16(4):4–6.

Heller, N., and Northcut, T. (1996). Utilizing cognitive-behavioral techniques in psychodynamic practice with clients diagnosed as borderline. *Clinical Social Work Journal* 24:203–215.

Helm, K. (1928). *Mary, Wife of Lincoln.* New York: Harper.

Hughes, T. (1998). *Birthday Letters.* New York: Farrar, Straus and Giroux.

Hughes, T., and McCullough, F., eds. (1982). *The Journals of Sylvia Plath.* New York: Ballantine.

James, W. (1890). *The Principles of Psychology, vol. 1.* New York: Dover, 1950.

Kandel, J., and Sudderth, D. B. (2000). *Migraine: What Works.* Rocklin, CA: Prima.

Kaplan, L. (1978). *Oneness and Separateness.* New York: Touchstone.

Kaysen, S. (1993). *Girl, Interrupted.* New York: Random House.

Keller, H. (1902). *The Story of My Life.* New York: Bantam, 1980.

Kernberg, O. (1985). *Borderline Conditions and Pathological Narcissism.* Northvale, NJ: Jason Aronson.

Kissel, K. (1999). Parents left tot to die in wilderness, police say. Associated Press, *Indianapolis Star*, Sept. 9, A14.

Kleeman, J. (1967). The peek-a-boo game: its origins, meanings, and related phenomena in the first year. *Psychoanalytic Study of the Child* 22:239–273. New York: International Universities Press.

Klein, G. W. (1957). *All But My Life.* New York: Hill and Wang.

Kohut, H. (1977). *The Restoration of the Self.* New York: International Universities Press.

Krall, H., and Edelman, M. (1977). *Shielding the Flame.* New York: Henry Holt.

Kramer, L. (1998). *Franz Schubert: Sexuality, Subjectivity, Song.* New York: Cambridge University Press.

Kroll, J. (1988). *The Challenge of the Borderline Patient.* New York: Norton.

Lachkar, J. (1992). *The Narcissistic/Borderline Couple: A Psychodynamic Perspective on Marital Treatment.* New York: Brunner/Mazel.

Lash, J. P. (1980). *Helen and Teacher: The Story of Helen Keller and Anne Sullivan Macy.* Reading, MA: Addison-Wesley.

Lax, R., Bach. S., and Burland, J., eds. (1986). *Self and Object Constancy: Clinical and Theoretical Perspectives.* New York: Guilford.

Le Doux, J. (1996). *The Emotional Brain: The Mysterious Underpinnings of Emotional Life.* New York: Touchstone.

Lee, R., and Martin, J. (1991). *Psychotherapy after Kohut: A Textbook of Self Psychology*. Hillsdale, NJ: Analytic Press.

Levi, P. (1989). *The Drowned and the Saved*. New York: Random House.

Lewis, D., Pincus, J., Feldman, M., et al. (1986). Psychiatric, neurological, and psychoeducational characteristics of 15 death row inmates. *American Journal of Psychiatry* 143:838–845.

Linehan, M. (1993a). *Skills Training Manual for Borderline Personality Disorder*. New York: Guilford.

——— (1993b). *Cognitive-Behavioral Treatment of Borderline Personality Disorder*. New York: Guilford.

Little, M. (1990). *Psychotic Anxieties and Containment: A Personal Record of an Analysis with Winnicott*. Northvale, NJ: Jason Aronson.

——— (1993). *Transference Neurosis and Transference Psychosis*. Northvale, NJ: Jason Aronson.

Manheim, R. (1977). *Grimm's Tales for Young and Old*. New York: Anchor, 1983.

Mason, R., and Kreger, R. (1998). *Stop Walking on Eggshells: When Somebody You Love Has BPD*. Oakland, CA: New Harbinger.

Masterson, J. (1980). *From Borderline Adolescent to Functioning Adult: The Test of Time*. New York: Brunner/Mazel.

——— (1981). *The Narcissistic and Borderline Disorders: An Integrated Developmental Approach*. New York: Brunner/Mazel.

——— (1988). *The Search for the Real Self: Unmasking the Personality Disorders of Our Age*. New York: Free Press.

Miller, A. (1984). *For Your Own Good: Hidden Cruelty in Child-rearing and the Roots of Violence*. New York: Farrar, Straus and Giroux.

——— (1985). *Banished Knowledge: Facing Childhood Injuries*. New York: Anchor.

——— (1986). *Thou Shalt Not Be Aware: Society's Betrayal of the Child*. New York: Penguin.

Miller, J., Lewis, L., and Basye Sander, J. (1999). *Mothers' Miracles: Magical True Stories of Maternal Love and Courage*. New York: William Morrow.

Money, J. (1992). *The Kaspar Hauser Syndrome of "Psychosocial Dwarfism."* New York: Prometheus.

Moskovitz, R. (1996). *Lost in the Mirror: An Inside Look at Borderline Personality Disorder*. Dallas, TX: Taylor.

Mosley, L. (1980). *Blood Relations: The Rise and Fall of the du Ponts of Delaware*. New York: Atheneum.

Neely, M. E., and McMurtry, R. G. (1986). *The Insanity File: The Case of Mary Todd Lincoln*. Carbondale, IL: Southern Illinois University Press.

Nelson, J. (1998). The meaning of crying based on attachment theory. *Clinical Social Work Journal* 26(1): 9–22.

Paul, D. (1987). The analysis of autistic character structure in a borderline patient: a clinical case presentation. In *The Borderline Patient: Emerging Concepts in Diagnosis, Psychodynamics, and Treatment, vol. 2*, ed. J. S. Grotstein, M. Solomon, and J. Lang, pp. 149–171. Hillsdale, NJ: Analytic Press.

Putnam, S.W., Guroff, J. J., Silberman, E. K., et al. (1986). The clinical phenomenology of multiple personality disorder: review of 100 recent cases. *Journal of Clinical Psychiatry* 47: 285–293.

Rekers, G. (1996). *Susan Smith: Victim or Murderer*. Lakewood, CO: Glenbridge.

Rogers, C. (1961). *On Becoming a Person: A Therapist's View of Psychotherapy*. Boston: Houghton Mifflin.

Rule, A. (1987). *Small Sacrifices*. New York: Signet.

Santoro, J., and Cohen, R. (1997). *The Angry Heart: Overcoming Borderline and Addictive Behaviors*. Oakland, CA: New Harbinger.

Sayers, J. (1991). *Mothers of Psychoanalysis*. New York: Norton.

Schacter, D. (1996). *Searching for Memory: The Brain, the Mind, and the Past*. New York: Basic Books.

Shore, R. (1997). *Rethinking the Brain*. New York: Families and Work Institute.

Silverman, R., ed. (1994). *Helen Keller: Light in My Darkness*. West Chester, PA: Chrysalis.

Simmons, D. (1970). *A Rose for Mrs. Lincoln*. Boston: Beacon.

Smith, D. (1995). *Beyond All Reason: My Life with Susan Smith*. New York: Kensington.

Smith, S. B. (1999). *Diana in Search of Herself*. New York: Times Books.

Stein, M. (1995). *Jung on Evil*. Princeton, NJ: Princeton University Press.

Stern, D. (1985). *The Interpersonal World of the Infant*. New York: Basic Books.

Stevenson, A. (1989). *Bitter Fame: A Life of Sylvia Plath*. Boston: Houghton Mifflin.

Stone, M. H. (1977). The borderline syndrome: evolution of the term, genetic aspects, and prognosis. *American Journal of Psychotherapy* 31: 345–365.

Thomas, B. (1978). *Joan Crawford*. New York: Simon & Schuster.

Thornton, M. (1998). *Eclipses: Behind the Borderline Personality Disorder*. Madison, AL: Monte Sano.

Thurber, J. (1931). "The Unicorn in the Garden." In *The Thurber Carnival*, pp. 310–311. New York: Random House, 1999.

Todorov, T. (1996). *Facing the Extreme: Moral Life in the Concentration Camps*. New York: Henry Holt.

Turner, A. M., and Greenough, W. T. (1985). Differential rearing effects on rat visual cortex synapses: synapse and neural density and synapses per neuron. *Brain Research* 329: 195–203.

Turner, J., and Turner, L. L. (1972). *Mary Todd Lincoln: Her Life and Letters*. New York: Knopf.

Vaughan, S. (1997). *The Talking Cure: Why Traditional Talking Therapy Offers a Better Chance for Long-Term Relief Than Any Drug.* New York: Henry Holt.

Wallace, R. (1990). *The Agony of Lewis Carroll.* Melrose, MA: Gemini.

Werner, E. (1988). Resilient children. In *Contemporary Readings in Child Psychology,* ed. E. M. Hetherington and R. D. Parke, pp. 51–57. New York: McGraw-Hill.

West, M. L., and Sheldon-Keller, A. (1994). *Patterns of Relating: An Adult Attachment Perspective.* New York: Guilford.

Williams, R., and Williams, V. (1993). *Anger Kills: Seventeen Strategies for Controlling the Hostility That Can Harm Your Health.* New York: Harper.

Winnicott, D. W. (1958). The capacity to be alone. In *The Maturational Processes and the Facilitating Environment,* pp. 29–36. New York: International Universities Press, 1965.

———— (1960). Ego distortion in terms of the true and false self. In *The Maturational Processes and the Facilitating Environment,* pp. 140–152. New York: International Universities Press, 1965.

———— (1962). Providing for the child in health and in crisis. In *The Maturational Processes and the Facilitating Environment,* pp. 64–72. New York: International Universities Press, 1965.

———— (1963). From dependence towards independence in the development of the individual. In *The Maturational Processes and the Facilitating Environment,* pp. 83–92. New York: International Universities Press, 1965.

———— (1971). *Playing and Reality.* New York: Routledge.

Wolf, E. (1988). *Treating the Self: Elements of Clinical Self Psychology.* New York: Guilford.

Young, S. P. (1953). *The Women of Greek Drama.* New York: Exposition.

Index

322   INDEX

Food (*continued*)
 Hermit mother's children,
  235–236
Freud, S., 173, 302, 303
Frog-Prince, fairy-tale fathers,
 180–184. *See also* Fairy-
 tale fathers

Geleerd, E., 109, 132–133
Gifts, Queen mother's children,
 254–256
Glickauf-Hughes, C., 23, 164
Goldberg, D., 156
Goleman, D., 132, 157, 172
Goodness
 Waif mother, 71
 Waif mother's children, 210
 Witch mother's children,
  280–281
Gopnik, A., 299
Grant, U. S., 114
Greenough, W. T., 48
Guiles, F. L., 20, 40
Guilt
 all-good child, 163–164
 anxiety and, evocation of,
  Hermit mother, 94–95
 make-believe mothers,
  17–18
 Waif mother's children,
  208–209
Gunderson, J., 39, 50, 69, 94,
 114, 145, 165

Harm, Witch mother's
 children, 281–282
Heit, S., 13, 48, 304
Helm, K., 102, 105, 110, 113
Helplessness, Waif mother,
 58–60
Hermit mother, 79–97
 characteristics of, 86–95
  guilt and anxiety, evocation of, 94–95
  jealousy, 90–91
  pain and illness, over-
   reaction to, 93
  perceptiveness, 91–92
  possessiveness, 86–87
  reclusiveness, 87–88
  rejection fears, 88–89
  rumination, 89–90
  self-soothing behavior, 94
  superstitiousness, 92–93
 character profile, 37–38
 danger, 95–97
 fear, 81–84
 overview, 79–81
 persecution, 84–86
Hermit mother's children,
 227–246
 consequence clarification,
  244–246
 conspiracy theories, 234–235
 fear evaluation, 229–230
 fear management, 236–239

About the Author

Christine Ann Lawson, Ph.D., is a clinical social worker in private practice in Indianapolis, Indiana. She has previously served as adjunct faculty at Indiana University-Purdue University, Indianapolis, and Butler University.